SUSTAINABLE PUBLIC PROCUREMENT UNDER EU LAW

This book examines the effectiveness of the modernisation of EU public procurement law in light of the overarching treaty goals on sustainability. Contributors expertly cover core issues of public procurement, including life-cycle costing (LCC), eco- and fair-trade labels, the link to the subject matter (LtSM) requirement, the mandatory horizontal rule on environmental and social legal compliance and framework agreements. Also explored are the balancing of economic and non-economic objectives implied in sustainable public procurement. The volume proceeds to identify major unresolved issues in the use of sustainability considerations and highlights challenges and possibilities for the national implementation due to take place in 2016. The book contributes to the dismantling of the compartmentalisation that underpins unsustainable policy decisions by discussing the interface of company law and public procurement law and the implication of the new rules on sustainable public procurement for sustainable companies and specifically for small- and medium-sized enterprises (SMEs).

BEATE SJÅFJELL is Professor Dr Juris at the University of Oslo. She is the head of the research group 'Companies, Markets, Society and the Environment' as well as of the European Law Network at the Faculty of Law in Oslo. She also chairs the international Sustainable Market Actors Network and coordinates European and international research projects on sustainability and business law.

ANJA WIESBROCK is a senior advisor at the Research Council of Norway. She has previously worked as a postdoctoral researcher at the University of Oslo and as Assistant Professor in EU Law at the University of Maastricht. She has published numerous articles on the different aspects of EU law, including on state aid and on the role of the environmental integration principle in public procurement.

SUSTAINABLE PUBLIC PROCUREMENT UNDER EU LAW

New Perspectives on the State as Stakeholder

Edited by

BEATE SJÅFJELL AND ANJA WIESBROCK

CAMBRIDGE
UNIVERSITY PRESS

CAMBRIDGE
UNIVERSITY PRESS

University Printing House, Cambridge CB2 8BS, United Kingdom

Cambridge University Press is part of the University of Cambridge.

It furthers the University's mission by disseminating knowledge in the pursuit of education, learning and research at the highest international levels of excellence.

www.cambridge.org
Information on this title: www.cambridge.org/9781107129641

First published 2016

A catalogue record for this publication is available from the British Library

Library of Congress Cataloguing in Publication data

ISBN 978-1-107-12964-1 Hardback

To Katarina and Linnea, who hold the future in their hands

CONTENTS

CONTRIBUTORS

MARTA ANDRECKA is a postdoctoral fellow at Aarhus University, Denmark. She holds procurement courses in Public Procurement Law and Strategy LLM at Bangor University, United Kingdom. Her PhD completed at Aarhus University deals with public–private partnership (PPP) in the public procurement law context. She has an extensive international profile, which includes many research stays, conference contributions, publications and collaborations across Europe and Australia. She is also a procurement consultant and co-founder of the academic support for PPP Foundation in Poland.

ANNA BECKERS is Assistant Professor of Private Law and Legal Methodology at Maastricht University, the Netherlands. She is a fellow of the Maastricht European Private Law Institute and a Max Weber Fellow 2015–16 of the European University Institute Florence. She completed her law degree and bar exam in Germany and received her PhD degree from Maastricht University. Her research interests are related to private law and (socio-) legal theory and its links to public law.

ROBERTO CARANTA is Professor of Administrative Law at the University of Turin, Italy. He is Director of the Master on Public Procurement for Sustainable Development jointly managed by his University and ITC-ILO Turin. He is co-directing the European Procurement Law Series, DJØF, Copenhagen. He is a member of both the research networks Public Contracts in Legal Globalization/Contrats Publics dans la Globalisation Juridique and PLAN – Procurement Law Academic Network. He is a member of the dispute settlement board of the European Space Agency – ESA.

DACIAN C. DRAGOS is Jean Monnet Professor of Administrative and European Law and co-director of the Centre for Studies on Good Governance at Babes Bolyai University, Romania. He has previously been the Dean of the Faculty of Political, Administrative and Communication as well as a Marie Curie fellow at Michigan State University. He has published widely in public procurement law and general EU and administrative law.

SUZANNE KINGSTON is a senior lecturer at the University College Dublin. She has published widely in the field of European law and governance, especially in the environmental, competition and economic and human rights fields, including the monograph *Greening EU Competition Law and Policy* (Cambridge University Press, 2012). She has a special interest in how tensions between the EU's economic and non-economic aims play out in European law and governance.

BOGDANA NEAMTU is Associate Professor within the Public Administration Department at Babes Bolyai University, Romania. She holds an MA in urban planning from Michigan State University and obtained her PhD in sociology in 2008 with a topic on urban growth management in Romania. Her research interest is in sustainable development and how the concept applies to various fields including public procurement. She has published amongst others on secondary considerations in public procurement and on the Europeanisation of administrative law in Romania.

SARAH SCHOENMAEKERS is Assistant Professor of EU Law at Maastricht University and a practicing lawyer in Belgium. Her research focuses mainly on EU public procurement law and free movement and competition law. She has co-edited two books and written several articles on EU public procurement law and is a regular speaker at conferences on public procurement.

ABBY SEMPLE is an independent consultant with expertise on the legal, environmental and social aspects of public procurement. She has provided consultancy and training on public procurement law, practice and policy in various EU countries, and is the author of *A Practical Guide to Public Procurement* (Oxford University Press, 2015).

BEATE SJÅFJELL is Professor Dr Juris at the University of Oslo. She is the head of the research group 'Companies, Markets, Society and the Environment' as well as of the European Law Network at the Faculty of Law in Oslo. In addition to her monograph *Towards a Sustainable European Company Law* (2009), she has co-edited *The Greening of European Business under EU Law* (Routledge, 2015, with Anja Wiesbrock) and *Company Law and Sustainability* (Cambridge University Press, 2015, with Benjamin

Richardson). Her scholarship includes many papers on EU company and financial market law and the integration of sustainable development.

ANJA WIESBROCK is a senior advisor at the Research Council of Norway. She has previously worked as a postdoctoral researcher at the University of Oslo and as Assistant Professor in EU Law at the University of Maastricht. Dr Wiesbrock has published numerous articles, book chapters and a monograph on different aspects of EU law, including on state aid and on the role of the environmental integration principle in public procurement. She is also co-editor of *The Greening of European Business under EU Law*.

FOREWORD

'Sustainable procurement' has long been an expression primarily known to academics and practitioners dealing with public procurement. That might change, however: as environmental and social considerations become increasingly important components of the procurement process in Europe, the term may gain wider acquaintance.

The reader wishing to understand the most important issues and debates relating to sustainable procurement could hardly look for a better introduction than this volume. Prominent academics and practitioners (sometimes both in one person) map the terrain and discuss important questions from different perspectives.

This book is a very timely contribution to the debate. In 2014 a new set of European Union Directives on public procurement were adopted. The Member States are to transpose the new Union rules into their own legal systems by early 2016. Naturally, the debate involves more than an exchange of views: it is also the time to make policy choices and create national legislation. The book will also be an important contribution to the debate on sustainable public procurement in the years to come.

The complexity of sustainable public procurement (and public procurement in the European Union in general) stems from the fact that the regulatory landscape is formed by Union law, national law, as well as choices and practices of individual contracting authorities. Add to that obligations arising out of the Government Procurement Agreement and it becomes clear that neither the authors of the new directives – the Union legislator – nor authors of national laws are able to avoid some basic questions and dilemmas surrounding sustainable public procurement.

There are fundamental, conceptual issues – such as the relationship between environmental protection or social rights and market freedoms; the latitude Member States enjoy when formulating their own sustainability policies and the role public procurement should play in public policy. But it is not possible to solve these big questions in the abstract. Instead, they resurface time and again, under the guise of seemingly minor, practical issues: the rules of using environmental and fair-trade labels; methodologies to calculate lifetime costs; the limitations on imposing national minimum wage rules on subcontractors established in other Member States of the European Union.

Such questions are among those filling the annals of the European Court of Justice and national courts. Although the new Public Procurement Directives of the European Union are an important step, the debate will no doubt continue. The authors of this volume deserve thanks for an important and timely contribution to it.

Adrián Tokár[1]

[1] Member of the Legal Service of the European Commission. The views presented here are the author's alone and cannot be attributed to the European Commission.

PREFACE

> Future generations will neither excuse nor forgive us for ignoring the signals we see today. They will not accept that it is too difficult or too costly to keep our economic aspirations in balance with the impact on the environment and the effect our decisions will inevitably have on society.
>
> Sir Neville Simms (Chairman for the Sustainable Procurement Taskforce)

The rules on public procurement in the EU have often been approached and discussed on the basis of economic premises. With this book we seek to evaluate the new EU regime on public procurement from a sustainability perspective. The volume reflects our broader research interest in the balance between economic, environmental and social objectives under EU law within the context of the overarching objective of sustainability. It also bears witness to the immense interest in the subject that we have observed amongst scholars and practitioners. There is a great demand, not least amongst contracting authorities, for a clarification and interpretation of the EU rules on sustainable public procurement. This is in particular the case after the 2014 revision of the EU Directives, which contain many novelties and new opportunities for including environmental and social objectives in public purchasing decisions.

The book results from a conference on sustainable public procurement held in Oslo in December 2014. Most contributions in this book are based on papers presented in Oslo that have benefited from a vivid discussion during the conference as well as from several rounds of comments from the editors. After having received an offer for a contract from Cambridge University Press in the beginning of March 2015, we worked closely together with all authors in order to finalise all chapters within the agreed deadline of 20 April. Completing a manuscript in less than two months has been both a challenge and an opportunity, as it has required us to work effectively and to impose strict deadlines upon ourselves and our contributors, regardless of many other personal and professional commitments.

Our thanks go therefore first and foremost to our contributors. It has been a great pleasure to work together with such an excellent and responsive group of scholars, who have gone out of their way to address our numerous comments within the tight deadline. Special thanks go to Abby Semple and Anna Beckers, who have not only contributed a chapter each, but also helped to improve several other chapters with their insightful comments. We would furthermore like to express our gratitude to our research assistant Morten Emil Eriksrud Bergan for his meticulous assistance in preparing this book for publication.

Most important of all, we would like to thank our wonderful families, our partners and children, for being an invaluable source of inspiration and support and in particular for bearing with our absences at times of high productivity. We would like to dedicate this book to Katarina and Linnea, who hold the future in their hands.

Beate Sjåfjell and Anja Wiesbrock

1

Why should public procurement be about sustainability?

BEATE SJÅFJELL AND ANJA WIESBROCK

1. A new context for public procurement

Public procurement law, the rules regulating purchase of goods and service by public agencies, is an area of great economic interest. In the European Union, total public expenditure on goods, works and services amounted to over €2,400 billion in 2010.[1] While the main focus on the EU level has been on facilitating competition, transparency, non-discrimination and anti-corruption,[2] the last decade has seen a growing recognition of the importance of employing economic drivers to promote overarching societal goals. Next to the objective of increasing the simplicity and flexibility of EU public procurement law, a major aim of the 2014 Procurement Directives of the EU[3] is to enlarge the possibilities for using public procurement in support of broader social and environmental goals.[4] The EU

[1] Amounting to 19.7 per cent of EU GDP, see European Commission, *Public Procurement Indicators 2010*, 4 November 2011.

[2] Based on the assumption that 'Public purchasers cannot be assumed to have the same commercial pressure or organisational incentives in sound management of their expenditure as private-sector purchasers subject to strong competition', which has informed varieties of national legislation, to which the EU has sought to bring some common principles, facilitating cross-border competition, see EU Public Procurement Legislation: delivering results. Summary of evaluation report, p. 6, see https://ec.europa.eu/europeaid/communication-global-partnership-poverty-eradication-and-sustainable-development-after-2015_en.

[3] Directive 2014/24/EU of the European Parliament and of the Council of 26 February 2014 on public procurement and repealing Directive 2004/18/EC Text with EEA relevance; and Directive 2014/25/EU of the European Parliament and of the Council of 26 February 2014 on procurement by entities operating in the water, energy, transport and postal services sectors and repealing Directive 2004/17/EC Text with EEA relevance. We concentrate in this volume on Directive 2014/24/EU, leaving aside the special rules concerning utilities and concessions.

[4] European Commission, *Proposal for a directive on public procurement*, COM (2011) 896 final, 20 December 2011, p. 2.

Commission has defined public procurement as a policy strategic instrument to achieve sustainability, and as an essential contribution to the achievement of EU's goal of smart, sustainable and inclusive growth.[5] Public procurement is seen as a driver to stimulate innovation[6] and resource efficiency,[7] and as an integral part of an industrial policy for a global, low-carbon economy.[8] Public procurement is also repeatedly mentioned in the context of the UN Sustainable Development Goals.[9]

Sustainable public procurement has accordingly become an established term, without any authoritative definition of the concept. According to the United Nations Environment Programme, sustainable procurement seeks to 'achieve the appropriate balance between the three pillars of sustainable development, i.e. economic, social and environmental'.[10] The EU's definition is along these lines, albeit without the explicit mention of balancing: 'whereby contracting authorities take account of all three pillars of sustainable development (economic, social and environmental), when procuring goods, services or works'.[11] The EU Commission's policy strategic approach is evident from its statement that sustainable public procurement 'allows governments to leverage public spending to increase demand for sustainable products and services, based on social and environmental criteria, increasing their market share and providing business with tangible incentives'. This is seen in the context of policy coherence for development, with the EU Commission's emphasis that 'all policies at national and subnational level need to contribute coherently' to achieve the Sustainable Development Goals.[12] The UN's Sustainable

[5] Communication from the Commission, *Europe 2020: a strategy for smart, sustainable and inclusive growth*, COM (2010) 2010 final.

[6] Ibid., p. 12. [7] Ibid., p. 15. [8] Ibid., p. 16.

[9] For example, Commission Communication, *A global partnership for poverty eradication and sustainable development after 2015*, COM (2015) 44 final, see https://ec.europa.eu/europeaid/communication-global-partnership-poverty-eradication-and-sustainable-development-after-2015_en.

[10] United Nations Environment Programme (UNEP), Sustainable Consumption and Production Branch (2012), see www.unep.fr/scp/procurement/whatisspp/.

[11] European Commission, Sustainable public procurement, see http://ec.europa.eu/environment/gpp/glossary_en.htm, while the balancing is explicitly mentioned in the definition on the website of the EU Commission's Directorate General for the Environment: 'Sustainable Public Procurement (SPP) means that public authorities seek to achieve the appropriate balance between the three pillars of sustainable development – economic, social and environmental – when procuring goods, services or works at all stages of the project', see http://ec.europa.eu/environment/gpp/versus_en.htm.

[12] For example, Commission Communication, *A global partnership*, see https://ec.europa.eu/europeaid/communication-global-partnership-poverty-eradication-and-sustainable-development-after-2015_en.

Development Goals, building on the Millennium Development Goals,[13] are to be the international community's response to the Rio+20 promise 'to strive for a world that is just, equitable and inclusive', based on the commitment to 'promote sustained and inclusive economic growth, social development and environmental protection and thereby to benefit all, in particular the children of the world, youth and future generations of the world'.[14] In this process, the overarching objectives of and essential requirements for sustainable development are declared to be: 'Poverty eradication, changing unsustainable and promoting sustainable patterns of consumption and production and protecting and managing the natural resource base of economic and social development'.[15]

On this basis we can tentatively, as a starting point for the analysis in this volume, define sustainable public procurement as procurement rules and practices that contribute to global sustainability: a balancing of social and economic development, ensuring the fundamentals of quality of life for all people, within the ecological boundaries of the planet we live on.[16] We see this reflected also on Member State level, in for example the UK's definition of sustainable public procurement as 'a process whereby organisations meet their needs for goods, services, works and utilities in a way that achieves value for money on a whole life basis in terms of generating benefits not only to the organisation, but also to society and the economy, whilst minimising damage to the environment'.[17] Sustainable public procurement is thereby distinguishable from green public procurement, which aims solely at reducing the environmental impact,[18] and from social or socially responsible public procurement, which is

[13] One of the main outcomes of the Rio+20 Conference was the agreement to launch a process to develop a set of sustainable development goals (SDGs), which would build upon the Millennium Development Goals and converge with the post-2015 development agenda, see https://sustainabledevelopment.un.org/topics/sustainabledevelopmentgoals.

[14] Full report of the Open Working Group of the General Assembly on sustainable development goals, issued as document A/68/970, see http://undocs.org/A/68/970, p. 3, para 4.

[15] Ibid., para 3.

[16] This dovetails with the well-known definition of sustainable development in the Brundtland Report as a development that allows us to meet our needs today without compromising the ability of future generations to meet theirs; World Commission on Environment and Development, *Our common future* (Oxford University Press, 1987).

[17] DEFRA, *Procuring the future: sustainable procurement national action plan: recommendations from the Sustainable Procurement Task Force* (DEFRA, 2006), p. 10.

[18] Which may be formulated as procurement of 'goods, services and works with a reduced environmental impact throughout their life cycle compared to goods, services and works with the same primary function that would otherwise be procured', see http://ec.europa.eu/environment/gpp/versus_en.htm.

about promoting 'employment opportunities, decent work, social inclusion, accessibility, design for all, ethical trade' and seeks to 'achieve wider compliance with social standards'.[19] Sustainable public procurement thus encompasses both green and social procurement.

Reforming public procurement law to contribute to sustainability is not merely a matter of policy choice; it is arguably required as a matter of EU Treaty Law, as we will outline further below. This also gives direction and a framework for analysing whether the EU's public procurement law reform of 2014 is sufficient. Our approach in this book does not entail that public procurement from now on should have as its primary or only task to promote environmental protection, reduce greenhouse gas emissions and ensure that human rights including fundamental labour rights are respected, and ignore the economic aspects. Indeed, efficient use of public funds, also in the short term,[20] remains a core aspect of public procurement.[21] The issue is one of balancing and not of choosing either economic efficiency or environmental protection and social development. Indeed, ignoring environmental and social concerns is not economically efficient either, especially in the long term.[22] However, balancing environmental, social and economic interests will not lead to sustainability if it is not undertaken within the planetary boundaries (Section 2). This fundamental recognition is not apparent in the policy choices of the EU. As outlined in the contribution by Suzanne Kingston, the reality on political and policy level tends rather towards taking economic growth as the overarching objective and the framework within which environmental and social concerns may be taken into account.[23]

[19] European Commission, *Buying social: a guide to taking account of social considerations in public procurement*, p. 5, see http://ec.europa.eu/growth/single-market/public-procurement/other-aspects/index_en.htm.

[20] While internalising environmental and social concerns may be the best economic choice also in the short term, especially, in the long run ignoring these concerns does not make good economic sense.

[21] The Europe 2020 strategy stresses that public procurement policy must ensure the most efficient use of public funds and that procurement markets must be kept open Union-wide (all the more in times of financial crisis); European Commission Memo, *Revision of Public Procurement Directives – frequently asked questions* (14 January 2014), see http://europa.eu/rapid/press-release_MEMO-14-20_en.htm.

[22] A point that is touched upon in several contributions and which we return to in Chapter 11 of this volume by Anna Beckers.

[23] See Chapter 2 of this volume, where Suzanne Kingston discusses the important role of the Court of Justice of the European Union (CJEU) in this context.

Much public procurement law literature has likewise dealt with the intricacies of public procurement from an economic perspective.[24] This book therefore contributes to filling a void by evaluating the effectiveness of the modernisation of EU public procurement law from a sustainability perspective.[25] Through contributions covering core issues of public procurement, the new EU provisions on sustainable public procurement and the implied balancing of economic and non-economic objectives are analysed. This volume thereby identifies major unresolved issues in the use of sustainability considerations and highlights challenges and possibilities for national implementation to take place in 2016. It also contributes to the dismantling of the compartmentalisation that underpins unsustainable policy decisions by discussing the interface of company law and public procurement law and the implication of the new rules on sustainable public procurement for sustainable companies and specifically for small- and medium-sized enterprises (SMEs).

This chapter proceeds with a discussion of the legal status of sustainability in EU law, thereunder whether the EU 2020 goal of 'smart, sustainable and inclusive growth' is in line with EU law (Section 2). Thereafter, we outline the process leading towards the adoption of the 2014 Public Procurement Directives, give an overview of the main elements of the directives and the stages of a public procurement process where environmental and social concerns may be integrated, and present the other chapters in this volume (Section 3).

2. The legal status of sustainability in EU law

Sustainable development has a strong legal position among the overarching objectives of the European Union, underpinned by the growing recognition in the EU of the inextricable entity of humanity, our natural environment and our economic system. Debates on the significance of

[24] See, for example, F. Lichére, R. Caranta and S. Treumer (eds), *Modernising public procurement: the new directive* (DJØF Publishing, 2014), which, although having one chapter on sustainable public procurement (footnote immediately below), has as its main focus what it denotes as the primary objective of the revision of the EU public procurement regime: 'simplification and so-called flexibilisation' without any mention at all of sustainability or of environmental or social concerns (Foreword, p. 5, and first chapter 'Evolution of the EU public procurement regime: the new public procurement directive', p. 9).

[25] An overview is given in the chapter by D.C. Dragos and B. Neamtu, 'Sustainable public procurement in the EU: experiences and prospects', in F. Lichére, R. Caranta and S. Treumer (eds), *Modernising public procurement: the new directive* (DJØF Publishing, 2014), pp. 301–35.

the EU Treaties for economic areas of policy such as public procurement usually deal with free movement, freedom of establishment, enabling competition and facilitating the level playing field. EU law is, however, not just about free movement and market integration. On a Treaty level, the general objectives of the EU have a strong legal significance in the context of the teleological, dynamic EU legal method. The codification of the principle of sustainable development entails an all-encompassing legal duty to integrate environmental protection requirements in the policies and activities of the Union, and based on a broader selection of sources the same duty arguably applies to human rights and other fundamental social rights. This section outlines the legal nature of the overarching goal of sustainable development in EU law and the significance for the EU institutions and indirectly for the Member States, generally, and specifically for public procurement.

The European Union is founded on the following values: 'respect for human dignity, freedom, democracy, equality, the rule of law and respect for human rights, including the rights of persons belonging to minorities'.[26] The EU's aim is to 'promote peace, its values and the well-being of its peoples'.[27] This is an express formulation of the underlying motivation for the formation of that which originally was the European Economic Community: former wartime adversaries entered into mutual commitments to achieve peace – the end to all wars.[28] The European Union thus shares roots with the other post-war European project, the Council of Europe and its defence of human rights, democracy and the rule of law.[29]

To achieve this promotion of peace, the EU's values and the well-being of its peoples, sustainable development is a prerequisite: a balancing of

[26] Art. 2 TEU. See also the Preamble of the Treaty, where the Member States confirm their 'attachment to fundamental social rights as defined in the European Social Charter signed at Turin on 18 October 1961 and in the 1989 Community Charter of the Fundamental Social Rights of Workers'.

[27] Art. 3(1) TEU.

[28] See, *inter alia*, J. Steiner, L. Woods and C. Twigg-Flesner, *Textbook on EC law*, 8th edn (Oxford University Press, 2003), pp. 3–4, and E.D. Hansen, *European economic history: from mercantilism to Maastricht and beyond* (Copenhagen Business School Press, 2001), pp. 361–4.

[29] E.D. Hansen, *European economic history*, pp. 367–8, and M. Emberland, *The human rights of companies: exploring the structure of ECHR protection* (Oxford University Press, 2006), p. 50, on the European Movement as the forerunner both to the Council of Europe and the EEC, whose founders clearly saw business as a means to building links between countries and promoting peace.

economic, social and environmental interests. Sustainable development is the overarching objective and meant to be the guiding principle for the EU's policies and activities.[30] We see this expressed in the EU Treaty, which emphasises the position of sustainable development, in Europe and globally:

> The Union shall... work for the *sustainable development of Europe* based on balanced economic growth and price stability, a highly competitive social market economy, aiming at full employment and social progress, and a high level of protection and improvement of the quality of the environment.[31]

The global aspect is enhanced in an unprecedented manner on Treaty level, in the same article:

> In its relations with the wider world, the Union shall uphold and promote its values and interests and contribute to the protection of its citizens. *It shall contribute to peace, security, the sustainable development of the Earth, solidarity and mutual respect among peoples, free and fair trade, eradication of poverty and the protection of human rights,* in particular the rights of the child, as well as to the strict observance and the development of international law, including respect for the principles of the United Nations Charter.[32]

This is underlined further in the article dealing with the relationship between the EU and the international community, where the EU expresses its will to work to:

> foster the *sustainable economic, social and environmental development of developing countries,* with the primary aim of eradicating poverty;... help develop international measures to preserve and *improve the quality of the environment and the sustainable management of global natural resources,* in order to ensure *sustainable development.*[33]

[30] Concerning sustainable development as a pre-Lisbon objective of the EU, see B. Sjåfjell, *Towards a sustainable European company law: an analysis of the overarching objectives of EU law with the Takeover Directive as a test case* (Kluwer Law International, 2009).

[31] Art. 3(3) TEU (emphasis added). See also the Preamble of the Treaty, where the Member States express their determination to 'promote economic and social progress for their peoples, taking into account the principle of sustainable development and within the context of the accomplishment of the internal market and of reinforced cohesion and environmental protection, and to implement policies ensuring that advances in economic integration are accompanied by parallel progress in other fields'.

[32] Art. 3(5) TEU (emphasis added).

[33] Art. 21(2)(d) and (f) TEU (emphasis added).

The EU institutions have defined sustainable development as the overarching long-term goal of the EU in which economic growth, social cohesion and environmental protection go hand in hand and are mutually supporting.[34] The objective of sustainable development more broadly refers to the requirement to examine the economic, social and environmental effects of all policies in a coordinated way. In international law and politics, there is also growing recognition of sustainable development as an all-important objective and a general principle of international law.[35]

The integration of the environmental dimension is the basis of the EU strategy of sustainable development that was introduced to reconcile the diverse interests of promoting economic development, raising the standard of living, closer relations between Member States and the protection of the environment.[36] The environmental integration rule in Article 11 of the Treaty on the Functioning of the European Union (TFEU) constitutes a core tool to implement the sustainability concept and to promote the transition towards sustainable development. Article 11 TFEU states that

> Environmental protection requirements must be integrated into the definition and implementation of the Union policies and activities, in particular with a view to promoting sustainable development.

This rule encapsulates a legal principle that constitutes one of the most important elements of EU environmental law.[37] Indeed, Article 11 TFEU is arguably one of the fundamentally most important provisions in EU Treaty Law as a whole. Integrating environmental protection in all areas

[34] European Commission, *Mainstreaming sustainable development into EU policies: 2009 review of the European Union strategy for sustainable development*, COM (2009) 400 final, 24 July 2009, p. 2; Council of the European Union, Presidency conclusions Doc 16616/1/07/REV I, 14 December 2007; see also the 6th Environmental Action Programme, which defines sustainable development as a prudent use of natural resources and the protection of the global ecosystem together with economic prosperity and a balanced social development, Decision No. 1600/2002/EC, Recital 6.

[35] See C. Voigt, 'Article 11 TFEU in the light of the principle of sustainable development in international law', in B. Sjåfjell and A. Wiesbrock, *The greening of European business under EU law: taking Article 11 TFEU seriously* (Routledge, 2015).

[36] See the opinion of A.G. Leger in Case C-371/98, delivered on 7 March 2000, paras 55–7. The increasing importance of sustainable development considerations after the publication of the Brundtlandt Report 'Our Common Future' in 1987 was central to the establishment of the environmental integration principle and its increasingly prominent role in EU law and policy. See M. Herodes, C. Adelle and M. Pallemaerts, 'Environmental policy integration at the EU level – a literature review', *EPIGOV Paper* no. 5 (2007).

[37] See, for example, J.H. Jans and H.H.B. Vedder, *European environmental law* (Europa Law Publishing, 2008), pp. 16–23.

to the extent necessary to secure sustainable development is a prerequisite to securing the very basis of our existence. Economic development and social welfare, or as formulated as an objective of EU law: achieving 'a highly competitive social market economy, aiming at full employment and social progress', is in the long run fully dependent on the stability of our ecosystems. Likewise, societal stability is dependent on ensuring fundamental social rights. We see this illustrated in Europe in the aftermath of the financial crisis, when the economic basis of a society is under threat, with unemployment, cuts in welfare and a basic uncertainty for people, societal unrest threatens. In the global perspective, the harsh brutality of tens of thousands of people dying daily for poverty-related reasons[38] and refugees risking their lives for the hope of a better future,[39] underlines the necessity of striving for a global sustainable development, where the fundamental human and social rights of all people are protected. These rights are intrinsic to the objective of sustainable development; securing fundamental human and social rights is the minimum requirement of the social dimension of sustainable development.[40] While a European perspective on human rights may have tended to focus on civil and political rights, in a global perspective, we see clearly how fundamental human rights are inextricably connected to a viable environment: the right, not only to life, but to the basics needed to be able to live, water, food and health.[41]

[38] 'It is clear that improvements in the lives of the poor have been unacceptably slow, and some hard-won gains are being eroded by the climate, food and economic crises', UN Secretary-General Ban Ki-moon says in the foreword to the Millennium Development Goals Report 2010, issued on 23 June 2010, see www.un.org/millenniumgoals/.

[39] See 'EU ministers meet for crisis talks after hundreds of migrants drown in Mediterranean', *The Guardian* (20 April 2015), see www.theguardian.com/world/2015/apr/19/italian-prime-minister-matteo-renzi-emergency-summit-700-drown-mediterranean.

[40] We see this understanding reflected in a global context in high-level policy documents, such as, for example, the European Consensus; joint statement by the Council and the representatives of the governments of the Member States meeting within the Council, the European Parliament and the Commission on European Union Development Policy: *The European Consensus* (OJ 2006 (C 46/1–19)), paras 5–7, concerning the Millenium Development Goals, concluding with: 'We reaffirm that development is a central goal by itself; and that sustainable development includes good governance, human rights and political, economic, social and environmental aspects'.

[41] See, *inter alia*, A. Eide 'Realization of social and economic rights and the minimum threshold approach', *Human Rights Law Journal*, 10 (1989), pp. 35–51, and C. Warbrick 'Economic and social interests and the European convention on human rights', in M.A. Baderin and R. McCorquodale (eds), *Economic, social and cultural rights in action* (Oxford University Press, 2007).

Article 11 TFEU has contributed to and strengthened environmental protection as a general objective of EU law that is relevant in all areas of EU policy. The provision requires policymakers to promote environmental protection when defining and implementing EU policies,[42] both on the EU level and on the Member State level.[43] EU law can and must be interpreted in the light of the environmental objectives of the TFEU, even in areas outside the environmental field. Hence, the environmental integration obligation is not only one of the oldest integration clauses in EU law, it also holds enormous potential as a means of steering the interpretation and application of EU legal instruments that – in one way or the other – affect the environment. With its explicit aim of sustainable development, complying with the duty contained in Article 11 TFEU entails integrating environmental protection requirements and balancing environmental, social and economic interests with the aim achieving sustainable development.[44] The social dimension is thereby also included, while a number of other EU sources, including the values and aims expressed in Articles 2 and 3(5) TEU; the Charter of Fundamental Rights and the EU's own case law, provides further basis for the inclusion and promotion of fundamental human and social rights.[45] Indeed, in addition to the environmental integration principle in Article 11 TFEU and the principle of social policy integration in Article 9 TFEU,[46] we have a general principle of integration of policy objectives contained in Article 7 TFEU,

[42] About why it was perceived necessary to adopt, and through several Treaty reforms to strengthen, the environmental integration rule, see B. Sjåfjell, *Towards a sustainable European company law*, s. 10.5 and 10.7.

[43] See B. Sjåfjell, 'The legal significance of Article 11 TFEU for EU institutions and Member States', in B. Sjåfjell and A. Wiesbrock, *The greening of European business under EU law: taking Article 11 TFEU seriously* (Routledge, 2015).

[44] Arguably even clearer expressed in Art. 37 of the EU's Charter of Fundamental Rights (EUCFR): 'A high level of environmental protection and the improvement of the quality of the environment must be integrated into the policies of the Union and ensured in accordance with *the principle of sustainable development*' (emphasis added).

[45] For a discussion of the legal status of human rights protection after the Lisbon Treaty, which, *inter alia*, gives binding, primary law status to the Charter of Fundamental Rights, see S. Douglas-Scott, 'The Court of Justice of the European Union and the European Court of Human Rights after the Treaty of Lisbon', in S. Weatherill, S. de Vries and U. Bernitz (eds), *The protection of fundamental rights in the EU after Lisbon* (Hart Publishing, 2013).

[46] Art. 9 TFEU: 'In defining and implementing its policies and activities, the Union shall take into account requirements linked to the promotion of a high level of employment, the guarantee of adequate social protection, the fight against social exclusion, and a high level of education, training and protection of human health'.

requiring that the EU must ensure consistency between its policies and activities.[47]

However, while it is generally recognised that notably the sustainable development principle codified in Article 11 is a legally binding rule in EU law,[48] its precise legal effects are still uncertain.[49] In spite of its enhancement through various Treaty reforms, the principle of sustainable development codified in Article 11 has to a great extent been ignored by the legislator and the courts at EU and national level. And while the Court of Justice of the European Union (CJEU) has shown leadership in its application of Article 11 TFEU,[50] the references to the Article 11 TFEU have often been in general terms and the Court has abstained from spelling out the precise implications of such a requirement for the EU institutions and the Member States.

Public procurement is one of the few areas, especially in the economic field, closely linked to free movement and competition, where Article 11 TFEU, its duty to integrate environmental concerns and the overarching goal of sustainable development has had direct significance. The seminal case of *Concordia Bus Finland* illustrates the significant role played by the CJEU in this context. This public procurement case concerned environmental protection criteria in a process to determine, in economic terms, the most advantageous tender. The objective of the Public Procurement Directive then applicable was the elimination of 'barriers to the free movement of services and goods'.[51] Although the directive did not include any references to the protection of the environment or the objective of sustainable development, the Court found, by using the

[47] Art. 7 TFEU: 'The Union shall ensure consistency between its policies and activities, taking all of its objectives into account'.

[48] As opposed to just being a guiding principle in the environmental sphere, P.G.G. Davies, *European Union environmental law: an introduction to key selected issues* (Ashgate, 2004), p. 32.

[49] See D. Grimeau, 'The integration of environmental concerns into EC policies: a genuine policy development?', *European Environmental Law Review*, 9 (2000), 207–17.

[50] See, for example, Cases *Chernobyl I* (Case C-62/88 [1990] ECLI:EU:C:1990:153) and Case C-379/98 *PreussenElektra* ECLI:EU:C:2001:160, discussed in B. Sjåfjell, *Towards a sustainable European company law*. See also S. Kingston, *Greening EU competition law and policy* (Cambridge University Press, 2011), Chapter 3 and pp. 133–8, and Suzanne Kingston's overview of case law in Chapter 2 of this volume.

[51] Case C-513/99 *Concordia Bus Finland* ECLI:EU:C:2002:495, para 56; see also the Preamble to Directive 92/50/EEC relating to the coordination of procedures for the award of public service contracts (OJ L (209/1–24)) with reference to 'the need to complete the internal market'.

environmental integration principle, that environmental criteria could be included.[52]

This sparked a development that led to the adoption of the 2004 Public Procurement Directives, both referring in their preambles to the case law of the Court of Justice and the principle of integration with the aim of sustainable development in then Article 6 EC (now Article 11 TFEU):

> Under Article 6 of the Treaty, environmental protection requirements are to be integrated into the definition and implementation of the Community policies and activities referred to in Article 3 of the Treaty, in particular with a view to promoting sustainable development. *This Directive therefore clarifies how the contracting entities may contribute to the protection of the environment and the promotion of sustainable development*, whilst ensuring the possibility of obtaining the best value for money for their contracts.[53]

In its more recent case law, the CJEU has in *Max Havelaar* similarly emphasised that taking social concerns in a public procurement process is in line with EU law, which by then also followed directly from the 2004 Directives.[54] The concrete result, however, illustrates the potential challenges of reconciling clarity and transparency requirements with the inclusion of social and environmental concerns. The CJEU declared incompatible with the 2004 Directive the not sufficiently transparent and clear sustainability requirements as well as the reference to certain social and eco-labels in lieu of using detailed specifications.[55] Section 3 below outlines further the development from the 2004 Directives and to the topic of this volume: the 2014 Public Procurement Directives.

Viewing public procurement as an important instrument to achieve the overarching objective of sustainable development dovetails with the

52 With certain requirements as to transparency and legal certainty and compliance with fundamental principles such as that of non-discrimination, Case C-513/99 *Concordia Bus Finland* ECLI:EU:C:2002:495, paras 57 and 64.

53 Recital 12 and Recital 5, respectively, of Directive 2004/17/EC coordinating the procurement procedures of entities operating in the water, energy, transport and postal services sectors (OJ 2004 (L 134/1–113)) and Directive 2004/18/EC on the coordination of procedures for the award of public works contracts, public supply contracts and public service contracts (OJ 2004 (L 134/114–240)) (emphasis added); followed up by European Commission, *Buying green! A handbook on environmental public procurement* (Office for Official Publications of the European Communities, 2004).

54 Case 368/10 *Max Havelaar* ECLI:EU:C:2012:284.

55 *Max Havelaar*, paras 63ff. See further Roberto Caranta's discussion in Chapter 5 of this volume of the law regarding labels and the changes in the new 2014 Directives, which overturned the principle that contracting authorities could not refer to specific labels when choosing the most economically advantageous tender.

international perception. At the UN level, the Marrakech Process of 2003 set up a separate task force on sustainable public procurement, which was given the task to develop a practical methodology and to formulate recommendations for the design and implementation of sustainable public procurement policies.[56] And in the European Union, the concept of sustainable development in the EU Treaties has led to the adoption of numerous secondary legislative and policy instruments, many of which underline the potential of public procurement as a tool to implement and promote sustainable development policy objectives.[57]

We see a tentative recognition in the EU that sustainable development can only be reached when environmental requirements are integrated into other policies and economic, social and environmental interests are balanced. Indeed, the objective of sustainability establishes the direction to be followed when integrating environmental protection requirements into different sectors: incremental improvement of the environment is not sufficient. Environmental integration must serve to secure a safe operating space for humanity.[58] The global natural environment's non-negotiable limits set the boundaries within which the balancing must take place.[59] In

[56] At the World Summit on Sustainable Development in Johannesburg, 2002, delegations recognized that sustainable consumption and production is an overarching objective of and essential requirement for sustainable development. The Johannesburg Plan of Implementation (JPOI), in its Chapter III, calls for the development of a 10 Year Framework of Programmes (10YFP) 'to accelerate the shift towards sustainable consumption and production, promoting social and economic development within the carrying capacity of ecosystems, by de-linking economic growth from environmental degradation'. The Marrakech Process is a global and informal multi-stakeholder process, launched in 2003, in response to Chapter III of the JPOI. See www.unep.org/10yfp/.

[57] See the Renewed EU Sustainable Development Strategy as adopted by the European Council on 15/16 June 2006, document 10917/06; the Sixth Environmental Action Programme, Decision No. 1600/2002/EC; Commission Communication on the *Sustainable consumption and production and sustainable industrial policy action plan*, COM/2008/0397 final; Commission Communication on *Energy efficiency and its contribution to energy security and the 2030 framework for climate and energy policy*, COM (2014) 520 final; and the Strategy Communication from the Commission, *Europe 2020: a strategy for smart, sustainable and inclusive growth*, COM (2010) 2010 final.

[58] See J. Rockström, W. Steffen, K. Noone, Å. Persson, F.S. III Chapin, E. Lambin, T.M. Lenton, M. Scheffer, C. Folke, H.J. Schellnhuber, B. Nykvist, C.A. de Wit, T. Hughes, S. van der Leeuw, H. Rodhe, S. Sörlin, P.K. Snyder, R. Costanza, U. Svedin, M. Falkenmark, L. Karlberg, R.W. Corell, V.J. Fabry, J. Hansen, B. Walker, D. Liverman, K. Richardson, P. Crutzen and J. Foley, 'Planetary boundaries: exploring the safe operating space for humanity', *Ecology and Society*, 14(2) (2009), see www.ecologyandsociety.org/vol14/iss2/art32/.

[59] See C. Voigt, *Sustainable development as a principle of international law. Resolving conflicts between climate measures and WTO Law* (Martinus Nijhoff Publishers, 2009), pp. 40–1.

practice, this entails, with reference to the precautionary principle,[60] that environmental protection may have to be given the highest priority in a number of cases, also where it is not immediately obvious that the global natural environment's limits are being tested in the individual case.[61]

The essence of sustainability – what we strive for when we try to achieve a sustainable development – is balance, and the ultimate goal is a preservation of our ecosystems as the very basis of our existence and the achievement of the best possible world for all of humanity. The concept of planetary boundaries,[62] state-of-the-art natural science, embodies this fundamental recognition of non-negotiable ecological limits and should form the space within which all economic and social development is to take place. We see this recognition reflected in the EU's 7th Environment Action Programme 'Living well, within the limits of our planet', which sets out a vision of an 'innovative, circular economy'[63] where 'low-carbon growth has long been decoupled from resource use'.[64] And indeed, anything short of complete decoupling will mean a slowing down of the pace towards environmental collapse but not preventing it.[65]

Integrating natural science into the analysis of law is necessary to fully understand the implications of legally decisive goals of sustainability and the environmental integration rule. The EU policy goal of 'smart, sustainable and inclusive growth' is only compatible with the EU

[60] For example, J. Scott, 'The precautionary principle before the European courts', in R. Macrory (ed.), *Principles of European environmental law* (Europa Law Publishing, 2004), pp. 51–72.

[61] See B. Sjåfjell, *Towards a sustainable European company law*, s. 10.9.3.

[62] Introduced by Rockström et al., 'Planetary boundaries'; updated in W. Steffen, K. Richardson, J. Rockström, S.E. Cornell, I. Fetzer, E.M. Bennett, R. Biggs, S.R. Carpenter, W. de Vries, C.A. de Wit, C. Folke, D. Gerten, J. Heinke, G.M. Mace, L.M. Persson, V. Ramanathan, B. Reyers and S. Sörlin, 'Planetary boundaries: guiding human development on a changing planet', *Science* (January 2015), see www.sciencemag.org/content/347/6223/1259855.abstract.

[63] On the EU policy discussions concerning the circular economy, see A. Wijkman, 'Circular economy could bring 70 per cent cut in carbon emissions by 2030', *Guardian Sustainable Business* (15 April 2015), see www.theguardian.com/sustainable-business/2015/apr/15/circular-economy-jobs-climate-carbon-emissions-eu-taxation.

[64] Decision No. 1386/2013/EU *of the European Parliament and of the Council of 20 November 2013 on a General Union Environment Action Programme to 2020 'Living well, within the limits of our planet'*, OJ (L 354/171), 28 December 2013.

[65] The recognition that infinite economic and population growth in a physically finite world is impossible is not new, see, for example, D.H. Meadows, D.L. Meadows, J. Randers and W.W. Behrens III, *The limits to growth* (Universe Books, 1972); H. Daly, *Ecological economics and the ecology of economics* (Edward Elgar, 1999); P.A. Victor, *Managing without growth* (Edward Elgar, 2008).

Treaties if 'growth' is understood as 'development' within the planetary boundaries[66] – entailing that the EU sooner rather than later needs to discuss whether a full implementation of a circular economy[67] entails changes also to its fundamental economic system.[68] This question goes beyond the scope of this volume. However, it should form a backdrop for the analysis and lends urgency to the analysis of whether the public procurement reform is sufficient and how its scope of action should be used by the Member States.

The focus on planetary boundaries is not to say that there are not minimum requirements in terms of fundamental human and social rights that we should not transgress (or rather, that we need to continuously work to achieve compliance with);[69] indeed, the greatest global challenge lies in achieving the international Sustainable Development Goals within the non-negotiable ecological limits of our planet. Barriers to these goals include the externalisation of environmental and social impacts in the life cycles of products, typically made in developing countries and imported to the EU, as well as the lack of transparency and international regulation of the supply chains. These issues are crucial components of what sustainable public procurement law and practice may have an impact on.

However well formulated Treaty aims, values and objectives are, we see that in practice, on all levels, focus is often set on economic growth and efficiency in a narrow and short-term sense with the negative implications for the overarching global goal of a sustainable development. As legal scholars, we have a responsibility to society to shine a spotlight on the chasm between the overarching legislative and political goals of our societies, on the one hand, and the legislative and policy decisions that are taken, on the other hand.

[66] On the concept of sustainable development in light of the then EC Treaty's reference to sustainable growth, see B. Sjåfjell, *Towards a sustainable European company law*, s. 10.7.1.

[67] Which is meant to be centrepiece of the Dutch Presidency of the European Council in 2016, see 'Netherlands pulls ahead in circular economy race' (25 March 2015), see http://ec.europa.eu/environment/ecoap/about-eco-innovation/policies-matters/netherlands/netherlands-pulls-ahead-in-circular-economy-race_en.htm.

[68] This is not peculiar to the EU, we see the same formulation in the conclusions from Rio+20, and its commitment to 'promote sustained and inclusive economic growth', *Full report of the Open Working Group of the General Assembly on sustainable development goals*, document A/68/970, see http://undocs.org/A/68/970, p. 3, para 4.

[69] As Kate Raworth stated at the Earth Overshoot Day Seminar in Brussels, September 2013, we have a 'human undershoot day' every day; see also K. Raworth, *A safe and just space for humanity: can we live within the doughnut* (Oxfam International, 2012), see www.oxfam.org/sites/www.oxfam.org/files/dp-a-safe-and-just-space-for-humanity-130212-en.pdf.

In a previous volume, we have investigated what Article 11 TFEU and its duty to integrate environmental concerns should entail for important areas of business law: company law, state aid, product policy and insurance, touching also on public procurement.[70] Anja Wiesbrock has in an earlier article, before the 2014 reform, discussed public procurement in the perspective of Article 11 TFEU.[71] In this volume we analyse the 2014 reform of public procurement law, with its aim of using public procurement as a policy strategic instrument to contribute to sustainability in both the environmental and social dimension. The overarching EU Treaty obligation, to work towards a global sustainable development, securing fundamental social rights for existing and future generations, within the planetary boundaries and in recognition of the inextricable entity of humanity, our natural environment and our societies and their economic basis, forms the framework for this analysis.

3. The sustainable public procurement reform

Even though the practice of using government contracts to put social policies into effect has a long history,[72] the interest in using public procurement as a tool for promoting non-economic policies has increased enormously in recent years. The 2004 procurement package for the first time contained specific provisions allowing for the integration of social and environmental requirements into public procurement procedures.[73] Yet, the limited use of the Directive's social and environmental provisions by contracting authorities and the apparent gaps in the provisions revealed by the case law of the Court of Justice,[74] made it necessary to think about further reform only a few years after the 2004 Directives had been transposed into national law.[75]

70 B. Sjåfjell and A. Wiesbrock, *The greening of European business under EU law: taking Article 11 TFEU seriously* (Routledge, 2015).

71 A. Wiesbrock, 'An obligation for sustainable procurement? Gauging the potential impact of Article 11 TFEU on public contracting in the EU', *Legal Issues of Economic Integration*, 2 (2013), 105.

72 C. McCrudden, 'Using public procurement to achieve social outcomes', *Natural Resources Forum* 28 (2004), 257–67.

73 For a discussion of the relevant provisions in the 2004 Directives, see S. Arrowsmith and P. Kunzlik (eds), *Social and environmental policies in EC procurement law: new directives and new directions* (Cambridge University Press, 2009).

74 See, for example, Case C-532/06 *Lianakis and Others* EU:C:2008:40 and Case C-368/10 *Commission v. Netherlands* [2012] ECLI:EU:C:2012:284.

75 The implementation deadline was 31 January 2006.

The 2010 report for the European Commission on the re-launch of the internal market (the so-called 'Monti report') identified the question of a greater integration of horizontal policy objectives into public procurement procedures as a central element of scheduled reform initiatives. It envisaged the introduction of specific mandatory requirements relating to non-economic horizontal policy objectives so as to 'make public procurement work for innovation, green growth and social inclusion'.

The question of whether public procurement should be used to a greater extent in order to promote economic and social objectives was raised within the process of a public consultation (Green Paper) launched in January 2011 with a view to modernising EU public procurement law[76] and spurred significant responses and notable support from social partners, think tanks and non-governmental organizations (NGOs). It was followed by the adoption in December 2011 of three proposals revising the existing EU public procurement legislation: a proposal for a directive on public procurement replacing Directive 2004/18/EC, a proposal for a directive on procurement by utilities (entities operating in the water, energy, transport and postal services sector), replacing Directive 2004/17/EC and a new proposal for a directive on concessions. Next to the aim of increasing the simplicity and flexibility of EU public procurement law, a major aim of the proposals was to enlarge the possibilities for using public procurement in support of broader social and environmental goals.[77]

After long negotiations between the European Parliament and the Council, which amongst others disagreed on the desirability of extensive environmental and social provisions, the legislative package for modernisation of public procurement in the EU was finally adopted on 26 February 2014. The package is made up of a directive on public procurement,[78] a directive on procurement by entities operating in the utilities sectors[79] and a directive on the award of concession contracts.[80] This book deals

[76] European Commission, *Green Paper on the modernisation of EU public procurement policy: towards a more efficient European Procurement Market*, COM (2011) 15 final.

[77] European Commission, *Proposal for a directive on public procurement*, COM (2011) 896 final, 20 December 2011.

[78] Directive 2014/24/EU of the European Parliament and of the Council of 26 February 2014 on public procurement, OJ (L 94/65).

[79] Directive 2014/25/EU of the European Parliament and the Council of 26 February 2014 on procurement by entities operating in the water, energy, transport and postal services sectors, OJ (L 94/243).

[80] Directive 2014/23/EU of the European Parliament and of the Council of 26 February 2014 on the award of concession contracts, OJ (L 94/1).

primarily with the Public Sector Directive 2014/24/EU, leaving aside the special rules on utilities and concessions, although many of the same provisions apply under those regimes.

The Public Sector Directive has to be implemented into national law by 18 April 2016.[81] Even though the Directive provides notable opportunities for the promotion of environmental and social objectives through public procurement procedures, it also leaves a large amount of discretion to the Member States as to how they wish to transpose the relevant provisions into national law. It is crucial that national choices in the implementation procedure are preceded by an inclusive and open discussion and are backed up by thorough academic research. This book aims to contribute to the debate on whether and how to integrate so-called non-economic considerations in public purchasing procedures by discussing the most important innovations in the Directives from a sustainability perspective and thoroughly analysing the possibility for the inclusion of environmental and social considerations at the different stages of the procurement procedure.

As is well known, social and environmental goals can be included at different stages in the procurement process. First, non-economic objectives can be taken into account when defining eligibility criteria for participating in a tendering process. Contracting authorities have the possibility to refuse to consider bids from a tenderer which fails to satisfy certain minimum standards of financial, technical/professional or social capacity, for example compliance with basic labour standards. Second, environmental and social criteria, such as the renewable origin of materials can be integrated into the description of the subject or the technical specification of a contract. Third, contracting authorities can define environmental and social factors as contract award criteria, which will be taken into account and weighted in addition to the offered price. Last, social and environmental factors can play a role at the performance stage, where suppliers can be obliged to follow certain environmental or social standards as a contractual performance obligation.

The book focuses on specific aspects of Green and Social Public Procurement (which together make up Sustainable Public Procurement) that are of major importance in the new Directives or that have been neglected

[81] Art. 90 of Directive 2014/24/EU. For certain provisions, such as those on the transition to fully electronic procurement, a longer period for transposition is allowed up to 2017 or 2018.

in the existing body of literature. There are various elements in the Directive that foster sustainable public procurement. New opportunities have been created, for example, in respect of life-cycle costing and labelling. Dacian Dragos and Bogdana Neamtu illustrate in their chapter that life-cycle costing (LCC) is one of the pivotal elements of the reform of the new Public Sector Directive, and it may be regarded as a major novelty from the perspective of sustainable public procurement. The chapter critically analyses the legal and practical implications of the introduction of the LCC as a tool for sustainable public procurement in the European Union, based on existing experiences at the international level.

The potential for labels to serve as enablers of sustainable public procurement is explored by Roberto Caranta. He illustrates that the new provision on labelling in Directive 2014/24/EU is likely to raise problems in terms of practical application, due to its inherent tensions between the requirements of the internal market and the push towards sustainable public procurement. The chapter analyses the development of the case law on labelling and the legislation providing indications as to the interpretative problems the new rules present as well as highlighting the issues they have successfully addressed.

Another important feature of the Directive is its focus on improving the involvement of SMEs in the public procurement market. Sarah Schoenmaekers shows in her chapter that the combination of innovation and sustainability aspects in the Directive holds great potential for both SME involvement and the pursuit of environmental and social objectives. She shows how a greater involvement of SMEs can contribute to reaching key environmental objectives, on account of their specialism and potential for innovation as well as shorter approval routes and room for flexibility and customised solutions. At the same time, SMEs can benefit economically from a greater focus on sustainability in public procurement, which allows SMEs to adapt to upcoming markets and to unlock their growth and innovation potential.

Other provisions in the Directive that have great potential in terms of fostering sustainable public procurement practices are the so-called horizontal clause (Article 18(2)), the use of the best price–quality ratio in the award of contracts and the provisions on subcontracting. However, as shown by Anja Wiesbrock in her chapter, the effectiveness of these social provisions is undermined by the large amount of discretion left in the hands of Member States and contracting authorities. She provides three arguments for the use of a mandatory approach to the inclusion of social considerations, in particular, as far as basic labour rights and employment conditions are concerned: the EU's self-perception as a sustainable market economy and a 'social model', the normative choice for sustainable public procurements in the new Directives and the advantages of a mandatory approach in the light of simplification and internal market objectives.

Not only the Directive's discretionary approach, but also specific provisions appear to curtail the scope for pursuing indirect environmental or social benefits via the award of public contracts. This applies, for example, the link to the subject matter (LtSM) requirement, which has been expanded to apply to all stages of the procurement procedure under the 2014 Directives. Abby Semple argues in her chapter that the 'link to the subject matter' has emerged as a major limiting principle for sustainability considerations in the 2014 Directives. It effectively removes the ability to interrogate general corporate social or environmental responsibility policies to the extent that these address matters beyond the specific needs of the contracting authority. On the basis of an analysis of the origin and application of the concept in the Court's case law and the manner in which it has been expanded in the 2014 Directives, as well as interpretative efforts of the European Commission and the preparatory materials for the 2014 Directives, Semple evaluates how the link to the subject matter may restrict the effectiveness of sustainability criteria in public contracts and suggests alternative approaches, such as the application of the principles of proportionality and effectiveness.

Moreover, the book discusses a number of issues that, although important from a sustainability perspective, have so far received only limited attention in the academic literature. This is, for example, the case for the use of framework agreements, which may have important implications for sustainable public procurement due to their scale, broad scope and issues of control in an aggregated procurement. Marta Andrecka investigates the opportunities and challenges for including sustainable considerations in the procurement of framework agreements, discussing in particular the capacity of framework agreements, established through centralised purchasing bodies, to promote innovation and sustainable solutions and the risks regarding control of supply chains in framework agreements from a 'bottom-up' and 'top-down' perspective.

Finally, the book discusses the enforcement dimension of sustainable public procurement and its potential value as a driver for sustainable business. As we also argue in our conclusion, it is crucial to combine rules on sustainable public procurement with corresponding efforts in other areas of law. Public procurement law effectively only regulates a small portion of the market and does not impose any obligations upon companies that do not deliver goods, works or services to public bodies.

Company law, for example, has a crucial role to play in the transformation towards sustainability because it provides the legal framework for the internal workings of the company, including its decision-making. The relationship between public procurement and company law within the context of the overarching EU objective of sustainable development is discussed by Beate Sjåfjell in her chapter. Drawing on a research-based reform proposal for EU company law and corporate governance, she considers first, whether public procurement is a possible front-runner and a driver for the necessary change, second, whether there are any lessons to be learned from the insights derived from international company law research on how to internalise environmental and social externalities in the decision-making in companies and third, whether some of the innovative approaches in the new Public Procurement Directives can inspire a further development of the reform ideas for company law itself.

Moreover, the effectiveness of regulation by public procurement is restricted considerably compared to top-down regulation on account of its scope, length and the enforcement in case of non-compliance. This is highlighted by Anna Beckers in her chapter, who draws on evidence from the contracting practice between commercial parties and the debate in private law in order to reflect on the possibility to overcome these restrictions by means of a specific contract design and changes of contract law. Her chapter shows that it is difficult to use the same mechanisms for public procurement contracts and that the case for furthering sustainable procurement is inherently related to a fundamental decision between relaxing public procurement rules to allow the state to act as a true private actor and letting the state as a market actor use contracts in what may be perceived as a non-efficient way.

The challenges in using public procurement as a way of regulation and enforcing economic and social standards in public purchasing points to an important role to be played by the judiciary. The Court of Justice of the European Union (CJEU) in particular will have a crucial part in interpreting the sustainability provisions of the new Directive and ensuring its effective application and enforcement. Evidence from recent jurisprudence indicates a progressive stance of the CJEU in integrating environmental protection requirements into the EU's economic policies, in particular within the context of the current political prioritisation of economic goals in the EU. Suzanne Kingston shows in her chapter that the CJEU is indeed the most integrationist of the EU institutions. In recent cases, including in the area of public procurement law, the Court has shown a willingness to fulfil its role as the guardian of the Treaties, protecting the constitutional imperative of environmental protection.

Overall the book thus provides a mixed picture when it comes to the sustainability provisions in the new Public Procurement Directive. Although several provisions hold great potential for the integration of environmental and social consideration into public purchasing decisions, other developments, such as the extension of the link to the subject matter (LtSM) test, are likely to limit the use of sustainable public procurement. Crucially, as we argue in our conclusion, the effectiveness of the Directive in terms of fostering sustainable public procurement will depend on national implementing measures and on an effective enforcement by national and European courts.

2

The uneasy relationship between EU environmental and economic policies

The role of the Court of Justice

SUZANNE KINGSTON

1. Introduction: what unease?

On the face of it, it might be thought that the EU is doing a fairly good job of balancing its environmental and economic objectives. In contrast to most of its Member States' national constitutions,[1] the authors of the EU Treaties have expressly enshrined this balance at the highest level of EU law: as is well known, Article 3(3) TEU provides

> The Union shall establish an internal market. It shall work for the sustainable development of Europe based on balanced economic growth and price stability, a highly competitive social market economy, aiming at full employment and social progress, and a high level of protection and improvement of the quality of the environment.

Also of relevance is Article 11 TFEU, which provides

[1] A number of EU Member States' constitutions provide for some kind of constitutional environmental right: see, for instance, Art. 20a of the German Grundgesetz, '*Mindful also of its responsibility toward future generations, the state shall protect the natural bases of life by legislation and, in accordance with law and justice, by executive and judicial action, all within the framework of the constitutional order*'. However, very few provide for an express balancing of economic and environmental rights or goals. A notable exception is the Polish Constitution, Art. 5 of which provides, '*The Republic of Poland shall safeguard the independence and integrity of its territory and ensure the freedoms and rights of persons and citizens, the security of the citizens, safeguard the national heritage and shall ensure the protection of the natural environment pursuant to the principles of sustainable development*'. For an empirical analysis of environmental rights present in national constitutions across the globe, including EU Member States' constitutions, see C. Jeffords, *Constitutional environmental human rights: a descriptive analysis of 142 National Constitutions*, Working Paper 16/11, (University of Connecticut, August 2011).

> Environmental protection requirements must be integrated into the definition and implementation of the Union's policies and activities, in particular with a view to promoting sustainable development.

Further, Article 37 of the EU's Charter of Fundamental Rights (EUCFR) provides

> A high level of environmental protection and the improvement of the quality of the environment must be integrated into the policies of the Union and ensured in accordance with the principle of sustainable development.

While broadly similar in its terms to Article 11 TFEU, Article 37 EUCFR is a stronger formulation of the integration obligation: a duty to integrate a '*high level of environmental protection*' clearly goes further than a duty to integrate '*environmental protection requirements*'. Indeed, it is arguable that the very inclusion of the integration obligation within the EUCFR, and its consequent characterisation as a fundamental human right within the EU, denotes a recognition that environmental protection constitutes one of the core values upon which the Union is founded, within the meaning of Article 2 TEU.[2] The concept of a *value* of the Union is, it is reasonable to conclude from the post-Lisbon structure of the TEU, something distinct from (and perhaps even more fundamental than) an *aim* or *task* of the Union.

It is clear therefore that, as a matter of primary EU law, those drawing up and implementing EU economic *and* environmental policies have a legal duty to balance the EU's environmental and economic aims, with the ultimate objective of achieving a highly competitive social market economy at the same time as a high level of environmental protection.[3] Moreover, while the meaning of the concept of sustainable development

[2] See Art. 2 TEU, '*The Union is founded on the values of respect for human dignity, freedom, democracy, equality, the rule of law and respect for human rights, including the rights of persons belonging to minorities*'. Environmental protection is not otherwise mentioned as one of the fundamental values of the Union within this Art., but by virtue of the EUCFR the environmental integration obligation may be included within the concept of respect for human rights. On the history of the drafting of what is now the Art. 11 TFEU integration obligation, see J. Nowag, 'The sky is the limit: on the drafting of Article 11 TFEU's integration obligation and its intended reach', in B. Sjåfjell and A. Wiesbrock (eds), *The greening of European business under EU law: taking Article 11 TFEU seriously* (Routledge, 2015).

[3] For an analysis of the legal implications of Art. 11 TFEU, see S. Kingston, *Greening EU competition law and policy* (Cambridge University Press, 2012), Chapter 3 and B. Sjåfjell, 'The legal significance of Article TFEU for EU institutions and Member States', in B. Sjåfjell and A. Wiesbrock (eds), *The greening of European business under EU law: taking Article 11 TFEU seriously* (Routledge, 2015).

is highly contested,[4] the constitutionalisation of this concept in each of Article 3(3) TEU, Article 11 TFEU and Article 37 EUCFR may reasonably be understood as demonstrating a belief, at the highest political level within the EU, that it is *actually possible* to achieve economic, social and environmental goals at the same time. This is, in itself, by no means an ideologically neutral position. One might contrast, for instance, the influential 'limits to growth' movement (also variously described as a deep green or ecological position) which rejects the goal of constantly seeking economic growth as fundamentally in conflict with a high level of environmental protection.[5]

At a constitutional level, therefore, the EU not only acknowledges the important relationship between its economic and environmental policies, but proposes and indeed mandates a balance. As one would expect, this position as a matter of law can also be discerned in certain of the EU's policy positions. In the public procurement context, it is clear that the balancing of economic, environmental and social objectives was regarded as a major factor in the 2014 modernisation of the EU procurement regime. Indeed, the public procurement reform might be seen as a practical manifestation of the vision of the environment/economy interface set out by Commissioner Potočnik during his term as environmental Commissioner, which he termed as the 'new environmentalism'. By this he meant that:

> if 'old environmentalism' was about putting limits on the excesses of our old path to prosperity, the job of new environmentalists is to show that there is a possible new path to prosperity and well-being through a sustainable model of economy and society.[6]

It is notable that the '*essence*' of Potočnik's new environmentalism was, in his words:

> tackling environmental problems before they happen, building it into our economic policy, our industrial policy, our energy policy, our transport policy, our agricultural and fisheries policies.

[4] See M. Jacobs, 'Sustainable development as a contested concept', in A. Dobson, *Fairness and futurity: essays on environmental sustainability and social justice* (Oxford University Press, 1999).

[5] See, notably, D. Meadows, J. Randers and D. Meadows, *The limits to growth: 30 years update* (Taylor & Francis, 2005) and T. Jackson, *Prosperity without growth: economics for a finite planet* (Earthscan/Routledge, 2009).

[6] Potočnik, *New environmentalism*, SPEECH/13/554, Edinburgh, 20 June 2013.

At the very core of the environmental Commissioner's vision of EU environmental policy was, therefore, the recognition that much of that policy lay entirely outside his prerogative. The philosophy of 'new' environmentalism is therefore profoundly integrationist in approach and, in this sense, not so new at all.

In terms of integrating economic concerns into EU environmental policy, a decided turn towards emphasising the 'win-win' potential synergies between EU environmental and economic policies, and incorporating economic approaches into EU environmental policy, has been evident for some time. We see this, for instance, in the major shift towards use of (more economically efficient) market-based instruments, whether by their creation at EU level (e.g. emissions trading) or their promotion at national level (e.g. via the environmental State aid guidelines).[7] The encouragement of eco-innovation by promoting green public procurement within Member States, most recently in the 2014 legislative package on public procurement discussed below and elsewhere in this book, also fits this paradigm.[8] However, perhaps the *pièce de résistance* of new environmentalism in this sense is the Commission's proposal which led to EU's Seventh Environment Action Programme (EAP), on which political agreement was reached in June 2013. The Seventh EAP sets out the nine overarching priority objectives of the EU's environmental policy up to 2020.[9] The intense effort to repackage environmental aims as, at the same time, economic aims is striking throughout this document, particularly when contrasted with previous EAPs. Indeed, the very first recital of this, the EU's key environmental policy road map for seven years, leads not with the EU's environmental aims *per se*, but rather with the starting point that the '*Union has set itself the objective of becoming a smart, sustainable and inclusive economy by 2020*'. Even the EU's goals in biodiversity and nature conservation, a policy area which has not traditionally lent itself to an economic philosophy, has been rebranded in economic terms as the thematic priority of 'protecting, conserving and enhancing the Union's

[7] For an early policy document, see the Commission's *Green Paper on market-based instruments for environmental and other related policy purposes*, COM (2007) 140. See S. Kingston, *Greening EU competition policy*, Chapter 2.

[8] Namely, Directive 2014/24/EU on public procurement, OJ 2014 (L 94/65), Directive 2014/25/EU on procurement by entities operating in the water, energy, transport and postal services sectors, OJ 2014 (L 94/243) and Directive 2014/23/EU on the award of concession contracts, OJ 2014 (L 94/1).

[9] Decision 1386/2013/EU on a General Union Environment Action Programme to 2020, Living well, within the limits of our planet, OJ 2013 (L 354/171).

natural capital',[10] emphasising the role of biodiversity and ecosystems as a necessary input into the Union's economy. In fields as diverse as habitat protection to enforcement, the need for increased EU activity is now argued for by DG environment, therefore, on the basis of the economic benefits that such activity can bring, quantified in cash terms, with the intrinsic environmental value of the action typically relegated to a secondary line of argument.

This is not to say that the Seventh EAP necessarily in itself suggests a watered-down, 'paler green' environmental policy (although this may well be the result of the lack of substantive integration of environmental goals in other policy areas, as discussed below). Indeed, certain of the Seventh EAP's goals are unquestionably ambitious and, if followed through on, would revolutionise our relationship with the environment within Europe. These include the vision of a circular economy, meaning an economy where '*nothing is wasted and where natural resources are managed sustainably, and biodiversity is protected, valued and restored in ways that enhanced our society's resilience*',[11] and the goal of '*an absolute decoupling of economic growth and environmental protection*'.[12] Rather, what is remarkable about the Seventh EAP in this regard is its virtually wholesale repackaging of environmental goals in economic or partially economic terms. While this may be anathema to more traditional ecological political movements,[13] it is also couched in realism in view of the overwhelming concentration on economic goals in recent years in the EU, to which we now turn.

2. It's the economy, stupid

Despite this integration obligation at a constitutional level, picked up by the strong integration narrative within the EU's environmental policy, serious deficiencies remain in implementing the integration obligation in other EU policy areas, particularly where such integration could be viewed as compromising economic aims.[14] These tensions between the EU's economic and environmental goals have been expressed in notably

[10] Ibid., p. 178. [11] Ibid., p. 176. [12] Ibid., Recital 18.

[13] See, A. Dobson, *Green political thought*, 4th edn (Routledge, 2007).

[14] See L. Krämer, 'Giving a voice to the environment by challenging the practice of integrating environmental requirements into other EU policies', in S. Kingston (ed.), *European perspectives on environmental law and governance* (Routledge, 2013), and A. Jordan and A. Lenschow, 'Environmental policy integration: a state of the art review', *Environmental Policy and Governance*, 20 (2010), 147.

limited environmental ambition in fields where achieving a high(er) level of environmental protection might risk limiting economic growth. The commitment to integration of environmental and economic goals displayed in the EU's environmental policy in recent years has, in certain economically crucial EU policy areas, not been met with any serious reciprocal commitment to integration.

Foremost amongst these areas is the EU's macroeconomic policy. While the EU for many years had its own overarching Sustainable Development Strategy (the EU SDS), this has not been renewed since 2009, and has, according to the Commission, now been subsumed into the EU's general macroeconomic strategy, known as 'Europe 2020'.[15] Upon closer examination, however, the only elements of EU environmental policy meaningfully incorporated as part of the Europe 2020 Strategy are the EU's climate and energy goals.[16] At this, the highest policy level, therefore, the meaning of sustainable development, EU-style, does not extend to large tranches of traditional EU environmental policy.

Even more notable, from a practical perspective, is the lack of governance structures put in place to operationalise the environmental pillar of the EU's sustainability strategy, as contained in Europe 2020. As is well known, in the wake of the financial and subsequent economic crisis within Europe and beyond, the EU engaged in a large-scale reform of its economic governance model in the form of the European Semester process, entailing, *inter alia*, close monitoring of economic performance by means of the Annual Growth Survey, detailed reviews of Member States experiencing macroeconomic imbalances, reports on Member States' excessive deficits and Country Specific Recommendations.[17] In the case of the environmental aspects of sustainable development, while Eurostat

[15] European Commission, *Europe 2020: a strategy for smart, sustainable and inclusive growth*, COM (2010) 2020. See, stating that the Commission will implement its Rio+20 sustainable development goals through *Europe 2020*, European Commission, *A decent life for all: ending poverty and giving the world a sustainable future*, COM (2013) 92, at p. 6. See also, the discussion in M. Lee, *EU environmental law, governance and decision-making*, 2nd edn (Hart, 2014), Chapter 3. It should be noted that this move away from considering sustainable development in its own right is not peculiar to the EU, and mirrors similar moves at national level in the wake of the economic recession: see, for instance, the abolition of the Sustainable Development Council of Ireland (Comhar) in 2012, and the abolition of the Sustainable Development Commission of the UK in 2011.

[16] European Commission, *Europe 2020*, COM (2010) 2020, pp. 14–16.

[17] These documents are available per Member State and per year on http://ec.europa.eu/europe2020/index_en.htm.

continues to produce biennial reports on the EU's achievements in relation to the (more than 130) Sustainable Development Indicators set out in the EU SDS (which are divided into economic, social and environmental indicators), there is no specific follow-up to these reports. Similarly, while the European Environment Agency monitors over 200 environmental indicators, its four-yearly State of the European Environment and Outlook Report does not lead to any specific consequences or follow-up from EU institutions. Specifically, the advanced governance framework of the European Semester process does not apply to the non-economic elements of sustainability (although the Seventh EAP tentatively raises this possibility, by setting the goal by 2020 of '*assessing the appropriateness of the inclusion of a lead indicator and target in the European Semester*', and DG Environment is currently commissioning a report on Greening the European Semester).[18] As Lee has aptly commented,

> Almost by accident, monitoring and review of the environmental and the economic seem to have been separated, with all of the emphasis on the economic.[19]

Against this, it must be recognised that, in certain policy fields, a greater effort at genuine substantive integration between the EU's environmental and economic fields is evident. The EU's trade policy, for instance, has long accommodated environmental protection concerns,[20] and indeed the EU has used its external trade policy as an instrument to achieve its environmental sustainability goals, as illustrated by the EU's published negotiated position on the EU-US Transatlantic Trade and Investment Partnership, which includes a position paper devoted to sustainable development.[21] Nevertheless, even in the case of the EU's climate and energy policies, commonly vaunted as the greatest example of substantive environment/economic policy integration, the tension between these aims has been apparent in the context of the recent economic turndown, as evidenced by the removal of binding renewable energy targets for individual Member States in favour of an EU-level target in the EU's 2030 Climate and Energy Policy Framework, on which agreement was reached

[18] Seventh EAP, p. 186.

[19] Lee, *EU environmental law, governance and decision-making*, p. 76.

[20] See N. de Sadeleer, *EU environmental law and the internal market* (Oxford University Press, 2014).

[21] TTIP, *EU position paper on trade and sustainable development*, 7 January 2015, see available at www.ec.europa.eu/trade/.

in 2014.[22] It is striking that the very Council conclusions containing this Framework, which is the EU's central climate/energy strategy for the next 15 years, follows on by stating that '*the economic and employment situation remains our highest priority*'.

Perhaps the most widely contested example of the current trend to prioritise economic aims over environmental aims at the highest EU policy level, however, has come from the Commission itself. One of the first announcements of the Juncker Commission was the intention to withdraw certain important environmental proposals following review for consistency with, in particular, the EU's '*jobs and growth agenda*'.[23] These included the abandonment of the Circular Economy package which had been submitted by the previous Commission, and which was aimed at increasing recycling levels, reducing landfill and tightening rules on incineration.[24] This comes in the context of the institutional re-organisation of the Commission so that the Commissioner charged with the environmental portfolio, Commissioner Vella, is now answerable to the First Vice-President of the Commission, Commissioner Timmermans, who is tasked, *inter alia*, with furthering the EU's Better Regulation agenda. This agenda is aimed, *inter alia*, at reducing regulatory burdens for business, and is of course not an innovation of the Juncker Commission. The Barroso Commission had already indicated that this was a priority, which requires, amongst other things, regulatory impact assessments to be carried out on all EU initiatives expected to have significant direct economic, social or environmental impacts.[25]

[22] Conclusions of the European Council of 24 October 2014, EUCO 169/14. See, for example, the comment of the Polish Prime Minister Kopacz at the conclusion of the negotiations, '*I said that we will not return from this summit with new [financial] burdens, and indeed there are no new burdens*', Euractiv, *EU leaders adopt 'flexible' energy and climate targets for 2030*, 24 October 2014.

[23] Letter from Commission President Juncker to Commissioner for Environment, Maritime Affairs and Fisheries Vella, 1 November 2014, at p. 4, see http://ec.europa.eu/commission/sites/cwt/files/commissioner_mission_letters/vella_en.pdf.

[24] See Commission Communication, *Towards a circular economy: a zero waste programme for Europe*, COM (2014) 398 and, for the legislative proposal, COM (2014) 397. For the announcement of withdrawal of the proposal, see Annex to the Commission Work Programme for 2015: *A new start*, COM (2014) 910. Following widespread criticism of this withdrawal, the Commission has indicated that the package will be retabled in a different form.

[25] See the EU's Impact Assessment Guidelines, SEC (2009) 92, 15 January 2009, and the Seventh EAP, Preamble, Recital 34 and Art. 2(4): 'All measures, actions and targets set out in the 7th EAP shall be proposed and implemented in accordance with the principles of smart regulation and, where appropriate, subject to a comprehensive impact assessment'.

The EU's Better Regulation agenda has also led, through the Regulatory Fitness and Performance Programme (REFIT), the EU to map the entire EU legislative stock to identify burdens, gaps and inefficient or ineffective measures and identify possibilities for simplification or repeal. As part of this exercise, the costs of the environmental acquis were estimated at €1.18 billion per annum, or around 1 per cent of the total for all EU legislation.[26] In response to this, in 2012, the Commission released an action plan to reduce the costs for the seven most burdensome pieces of environmental legislation for business by around €300 million per annum.[27] From the outset, the Juncker Commission indicated its intention to continue as a priority an '*in-depth*' review of the legislative cornerstones of EU nature conservation policy, the Birds and Habitats Directives, again in the interests of the Better Regulation agenda.[28] Again, the economic lens through which any redrafting of these Directives would be done is apparent, as is clear from the narrative coming from DG Environment on this issue that '*protecting nature and maintaining Europe's competitiveness must go hand-in-hand as nature and biodiversity policy can play a key role in creating jobs and stimulating investment*'.[29]

It hardly needs to be said that this view of biodiversity as essentially an instrument of economic growth, coming from the Commissioner for the *environment*, is a highly controversial one from an environmental perspective.

In the public procurement context, the 2014 public procurement legislative package, which is the subject of this book, certainly contains elements representing progress in integrating environmental considerations within procurement procedures. In particular, the horizontal clause of Article 18(2) now means that Member States must ensure that, in the performance of public contracts, economic operators comply with, *inter alia*, EU environmental law; enterprises which do not respect environmental law may be excluded from the tender procedure,[30] or not awarded

[26] European Commission, *Regulatory fitness and performance programme (REFIT): initial results of the mapping of the acquis*, SWD(2013) 401, p. 59.

[27] European Commission, *Action programme for reducing administrative burdens in the EU – final report*, SWD(2012) 422. Specific burdens were identified in the fields of waste and chemicals, particularly REACH.

[28] Letter from Commission President Juncker to Commissioner for Environment, Maritime Affairs and Fisheries Vella, 1 November 2014, p. 4.

[29] This is the chosen topic of Commissioner Vella's speech at the EU's Green Week 2015, see www.greenweek2015.eu/.

[30] Note, however, that failure to comply with EU environmental law is not a mandatory ground for exclusion from the tender process (in contrast, for instance, with failure to

the contract or their tender rejected where it is abnormally low due to lack of compliance with these obligations.[31] Member States have also gained clarity on the conditions in which they can legitimately require products/services to have a specific eco-label (Article 43),[32] and on the conditions in which they can legitimately set criteria relating to the production process (Article 67(3)) and use life-cycle costing (Article 68).[33] However, the 2014 Directive still leaves the choice to contracting authorities whether or not they wish to include environmental considerations in their public procurement procedures. In particular, Recital (91) of the Directive, citing Article 11 TFEU, notes the Directive's aim of clarifying how the contracting authorities '*can* contribute to the protection of the environment and the promotion of sustainable development, whilst ensuring that they can obtain the best value for money for their contracts'. The Directive expressly declines to make green public procurement (GPP) mandatory, however, on the ground that, given '*the important differences between individual sectors and markets, it would . . . not be appropriate to set general mandatory requirements for environmental, social and innovation procurement*'.[34] This mirrors the weak language on this issue in the Seventh EAP, which noted only that Member States '*should take further steps*' to applying GPP standards to 50 per cent of their tenders.[35] The result is that the areas in which GPP is, as a matter of EU law, mandatory remain limited to office equipment and road transport vehicles.[36]

3. The CJEU's role in balancing economic and environmental goals

At a political level, this retreat from substantive integration of environmental protection within certain key EU economic policies is not difficult to explain. Europe has just been through, and indeed remains in, one of the most economically challenging periods in its history. Empirical

comply with national social security law), see Art. 57(1)-(2) of the 2014 Directive, although the Directive does allow for Member States to make this a mandatory ground of exclusion.

[31] For a critical perspective on the effectiveness of Art. 18(2), see Chapter 4 of this volume by Anja Wiesbrock.

[32] Contrast the situation under the previous Directive, Directive 2004/18/EC, OJ 2004 (L 134/14): see Case C-368/10 *Commission* v. *Netherlands* ECLI:EU:C:2012:284 (Max Havelaar), and on labels, see also Chapter 5 of this volume by Roberto Caranta.

[33] See Chapter 6 of this volume by Dacian C. Dragos and Bogdana Neamtu.

[34] Directive 2014/24, Recital (95).

[35] Seventh EAP, p. 184.

[36] See Regulation 106/2008 on a Community energy-efficiency labelling programme for office equipment, OJ 2008 (L 39/1) and Directive 2009/33/EC on the promotion of clean and energy-efficient road transport vehicles, OJ 2009 (L 120/5).

evidence demonstrates that concern for environmental issues amongst voters, including EU voters, tends to drop during periods of economic difficulty and corresponding higher unemployment.[37] In this context, the role of the CJEU in the economic/environment balance is thrown into sharp relief. In the absence of strong political leadership (not only within many Member States but also within the Commission) on the matter, the relevance of the CJEU's approach to integrating environmental protection into economic policies becomes even greater. In political science theory, this fits of course with the widely accepted analysis of the CJEU as a politically insulated, non-majoritarian institution charged with, in particular, upholding and enforcing the EU's ultimate constitutional norms. It is one of the features of the EU that elected politicians have voluntarily passed powers to unelected bodies, including the CJEU, in order to resolve collective action problems and, as Thatcher and Stone Sweet have noted, as a response to,

> the dilemma of political parties who agreed on the benefits of constitutional 'rules of the game', but disagreed, sometimes fundamentally, on the precise content of those rules.[38]

Such delegation, Egan observes, is not only designed to provide greater expertise, but also to enable decisions to be taken independently of the (politicised) policy process, with all the risks of regulatory capture that entails.[39]

Yet, at the same time, it is clear that courts, including the CJEU, must not intrude into the political process, at the risk of compromising the separation of powers and with it the court's own legitimacy.[40] As Lenaerts argues, the role of the courts is rather to determine what the law is, and

[37] See, for instance, L. Scruggs and S. Benegal, 'Declining public concern about climate change: can we blame the great recession?', *Global Environmental Change*, 22(2) (2012), 505; in the US context, M. Kahn and M. Kotchen, *Environmental concern and the business cycle: the chilling effect of recession*, Working Paper 16241 (National Bureau of Economic Research, July 2010).

[38] M. Thatcher and A.S. Sweet, 'Theory and practice of delegation to non-majoritarian institutions', *West European Politics*, 25(1) (2002), 9.

[39] M. Egan, 'Markets', in C. Rumford (ed.), *The SAGE handbook of European studies* (Sage, 2009), p. 135.

[40] See, in the CJEU context, K. Lenaerts, 'The court's outer and inner selves: exploring the external and internal legitimacy of the European Court of Justice', in M. Adams, H. de Waele, J. Meeusen and G. Straetmans (eds), *Judging Europe's judges: the legitimacy of the case law of the European Court of Justice* (Hart, 2013).

interpret it – indeed a '*risky venture*' as, in doing so, they are drawing the boundaries of their own legitimacy.[41]

While this debate is by no means novel, it is directly relevant to the present discussion, and to understanding the CJEU's role in balancing the EU's environmental and economic priorities. The CJEU's path-breaking role in establishing environmental protection as one of the Community's '*essential objectives*' in early judgments such as *ADBHU*, even before reference was made thereto in the founding Treaties, has been well-documented.[42] In not only upholding but also *implying* environmental constitutional objectives into the Treaties, the CJEU showed itself to be a leader in environmental governance within the EU in much the same way as its recognition of a general principle of respect for fundamental human rights within the Community.[43] As I have argued elsewhere,[44] the CJEU has by and large continued to demonstrate leadership in taking the EU's environmental objectives seriously, and in integrating them into the EU's economic policies, in a raft of case law including *Danish Bottles*,[45] *Walloon Waste*,[46] *Dusseldorp*,[47] *PreussenElektra*[48] and *Inn Valley*.[49]

The remainder of this contribution will not discuss these earlier cases, but instead focuses on some of the large number of recent cases in which the CJEU has again been asked to consider the economic/environment interface (with more than ten judgments handed down concerning this interface between the end of 2012 and the end of 2014). It is no accident that the CJEU is seeing increasing numbers of these cases on its docket: as the Member States and the EU have embraced market-based

[41] Lenaerts, ibid., p. 60.

[42] Case 240/85, *ADBHU*, ECLI:EU:C:1985:59. See F. Jacobs, 'The role of the European Court of Justice in the protection of the environment', *Journal of Environmental Law*, 18(2) (2006), 185.

[43] Indeed, as former Advocate General Jacobs has noted, the CJEU gave far more support for its conclusion that respect for human rights constituted a general principle of Community law than it did for its conclusion that objective of environmental protection had constitutional status, which conclusion '*appears to have considered... that environmental protection was so fundamental to the public interest that no explicit justification was required*'; in so concluding, the CJEU was '*undoubtedly acting in accordance with the spirit of the times*' (Jacobs, 'The role of the European Court of Justice in the protection of the environment', 188).

[44] S. Kingston, *Greening EU competition law and policy*, Chapter 3 and pp. 133–8.

[45] Case 302/86 *Commission* v. *Denmark* ECLI:EU:C:1988:421.

[46] Case C-2/90 *Commission* v. *Belgium* ECLI:EU:C:1992:310.

[47] Case C-203/96 *Dusseldorp* ECLI:EU:C:1998:316.

[48] Case C-379/98 *PreussenElektra* ECLI:EU:C:2001:160.

[49] Case C-320/03 *Commission* v. *Austria* ECLI:EU:C:2005:684.

environmental instruments, which use economic means to achieve environmental goals, it is natural that the legislation creating such instruments finds its way before the CJEU, where it falls within the scope of EU law. Indeed, the CJEU's recent judgments cover the whole gamut of different policy options/instruments available to the EU and to its Member States, including:

- (National) laws aimed at promoting greener products/energy via green certificate schemes, where the CJEU applies Article 34 TFEU (for instance, *Vindkraft*, *Essent Belgium*, *Industrie du Bois* and *Green Network*);[50]
- (National) measures aimed at promoting greener products/energy by granting financial support (for instance, *Vent de Colère*);[51]
- (National) laws aimed at promoting good environmental performance by granting exclusive or special rights (for instance, *Ragn Sells*)[52] or by (national or European) GPP measures (for instance, *Max Havelaar* and *Evropaïki Dynamiki*);[53]
- (National or European) emissions trading schemes (for instance, *Commission* v. *Estonia*, *Iberdrola*, *Billerud*, *ŠKO-ENERGO*).[54]

From a policy perspective, Member States and/or the EU very often have a choice between some or all of these policy instruments when deciding how best to achieve their (environmental/economic) aims.[55] It is therefore useful to consider the CJEU's approaches to these cases together. By contrast, it is worth noting that the CJEU has not yet had the opportunity to make any significant ruling on the environmental policy instrument which leaves most to the private sector, and has the least formal role for the State, namely voluntary private environmental initiatives undertaken

[50] Case C-573/12 *Vindkraft* ECLI:EU:C:2014:2037, Joined Cases C-204/12 to C-208/12 *Essent Belgium* ECLI:EU:C:2014:2192, Case C-195/12 *Industrie du Bois* ECLI:EU:C:2013:598, Case C-66/13 *Green Network* ECLI:EU:C:2014:2399.

[51] Case C-262/12 *Vent de Colère* ECLI:EU:C:2013:851.

[52] Case C-292/12 *Ragn-Sells* ECLI:EU:C:2013:820.

[53] Case C-462/10 P *Evropaïki Dynamiki* ECLI:EU:C:2012:14.

[54] Case C-505/09 P *Commission* v. *Estonia* ECLI:EU:C:2012:179, Joined Cases C-566/11 etc *Iberdrola* ECLI:EU:C:2013:660, Case C-203/12 *Billerud* ECLI:EU:C:2013:664, Case C-43/14 *ŠKO-ENERGO* ECLI:EU:C:2015:120.

[55] On the evolution of these so-called new environmental policy instruments in Europe, see R. Wurzel, A. Zito and A. Jordan, *Environmental governance in Europe: a comparative analysis of new environmental policy instruments* (Elgar, 2013).

by corporations, such as environmental agreements or covenants.[56] Taken together, the cases to date show that as Member States increasingly rely on various shades of environmental market-based instruments to achieve their policy aims, the CJEU is becoming a key forum in setting the legal boundaries of the environment/economic interface within the EU.

3.1. *(National) laws aimed at promoting greener products/energy via green certificate schemes*

Perhaps the most significant, and interesting, of the recent judgments is the July 2014 judgment of the Grand Chamber of the CJEU in *Vindkraft*.[57] This case concerned the compatibility with the Treaty free movement of goods provisions of the way in which Sweden chose to transpose part of the EU's 2009 Renewable Energy (RES) Directive.[58] The RES Directive formed a key plank of the 2009 climate and energy package, setting mandatory individual national targets for Member States with the aim of reaching a 20 per cent EU-wide share of energy from renewable sources by 2020 overall, and a mandatory 10 per cent target for each Member State in the transport sector.[59] (As noted above, mandatory national renewables targets have, however, been removed from the EU's 2030 Climate and Energy Strategy.) Under the RES Directive, this was to be done, *inter alia*, via the adoption of national renewable energy action plans to cover the period to 2020, which were to be notified to the Commission by June 2010. In contrast to the position in relation to ETS national allocation plans in Phases I/II, however, the Commission was only granted the power to issue a recommendation on foot of an evaluation of national renewable energy action plans – and not the power of approval *per se*.[60] The RES Directive also contained various innovative methods of encouraging cooperation

[56] The few cases where potential environmental justifications have been given for *prima facie* anti-competitive action have not, upon examination, shown that such action was necessary or proportionate to environmental aims: see, for instance, Case C-385/07 P *DSD* ECLI:EU:C:2009:456 (Art. 102 TFEU). See Kingston, *Greening EU competition law and policy*.

[57] Case C-573/12 *Vindkraft* ECLI:EU:C:2014:2037.

[58] Directive 2009/28/EC on the promotion of the use of energy from renewable sources, OJ 2009 (L 140/16).

[59] RES Directive, note 13 *supra*, Art. 3. See also, Art. 7d(6) of the Fuel Quality Directive, Directive 2009/30/EC, OJ 2009 (L 140/88), which introduced the mandatory target of achieving by 2020 a 6 per cent reduction in the greenhouse gas intensity of fuels used in road transport and non-road mobile machinery.

[60] RES Directive, Art. 3(5).

between Member States in meeting their targets, via statistical transfers of renewable energy between Member States,[61] joint projects between Member States and between Member States and third countries[62] and joint national (financial) support schemes.[63] These methods must be viewed in the context of the broader efforts to achieve an EU internal market in electricity, in line with the EU's three successive legislative packages to achieve a single market for gas and electricity in the EU.[64] In its 2013 progress report on the RES Directive, the Commission noted that the total share of renewables in the EU was 12.5 per cent and that, if current renewables growth rates remained in place until 2020, 11 countries would fail to meet their binding national targets.[65]

In the situation considered in *Vindkraft*, Sweden had chosen to implement the RES Directive by, *inter alia*, passing legislation on electricity certificates in 2011, by which approved producers are awarded an electricity certificate for each megawatt-hour (MWh) of green electricity produced. These certificates are tradable on an open competitive market. Electricity suppliers, and some users, are legally obliged to hold, and to surrender to the Swedish State in April each year, a certain quota of certificates corresponding to a proportion of their total quantity of electricity supplied or consumed in the previous year (failing which surrender a penalty was payable). Importantly, while the Swedish legislation did not say so expressly, the referring court stated that in fact approval for the award of green electricity certificates was reserved to green electricity production installations located in Sweden. Further, while in principle other States' green electricity certificates could be used to fulfil a producer/consumer's quota where an international agreement was in place with that State, no such agreement existed at the relevant time with Finland.

In the facts at issue in *Vindkraft*, the plaintiff (Vindkraft), a wind farm located in Finland, sought and was refused approval from the Swedish Energy Agency to be awarded green electricity certificates for the energy that it produced, and challenged this refusal in the Swedish courts on grounds, *inter alia*, of infringement of Article 34 TFEU on free movement of goods, arguing that the effect of the Swedish scheme was to reserve around 18 per cent of the Swedish electricity market (i.e. the portion

[61] Ibid., Art. 6. [62] Ibid., Arts. 7–10. [63] Ibid., Art. 11.

[64] See, in relation to electricity, the most recent Directive, Directive 2009/72/EC of the European Parliament and of the Council of 13 July 2009 concerning common rules for the internal market in electricity and repealing Directive 2003/54/EC, OJ 2009 (L 211/55).

[65] COM (2013) 175.

subject to the quota) to Swedish electricity producers. Understandably, the referring court was unsure how to proceed, given that, in particular, the RES Directive provides that Member States may meet their binding renewables obligations by applying '*support schemes*' (Article 3(3) RES Directive), defined to include any instrument that promotes the use of renewable energy, including green certificate schemes, and expressly provides that

> without prejudice to Articles [107 TFEU and 108 TFEU], Member States shall have the right to decide, in accordance with Articles 5 to 11 of this Directive, to which extent they support energy from renewable sources which is produced in a different Member State.

Further, Article 15 of the RES Directive requires Member States to ensure that proof of the renewable source of energy in an energy supplier's energy mix must be proven by guarantees of origin, 'in accordance with objective, transparent and non-discriminatory criteria'.

Vindkraft, therefore, raised the important question whether the CJEU's position on the role of environmental factors in EU internal market law had changed since its key 2001 judgment on national renewables support schemes, in that case the German feed-in tariff scheme, *PreussenElektra*.[66] In *PreussenElektra*, the feed-in tariff scheme obliged electricity supply undertakings to purchase electricity produced in their area of supply from renewable sources, and specified the price to be paid for this electricity. The CJEU held this to be compatible with what is now Article 34 TFEU, on the ground that the discrimination against imported renewable energy inherent in the German scheme was justified and proportionate given that, because the internal renewable energy market had not yet been fully achieved, the environmental objectives of the scheme could not be achieved in a less restrictive manner.[67] In *Vindkraft*, the CJEU was confronted with a broadly similar issue, in circumstances where the internal market had been further harmonised in the interim by, amongst other things, the RES Directive.

Nevertheless, one view of *Vindkraft* might be that the problem from a free movement perspective stemmed not so much from the Swedish legislation at issue, but rather from Article 3(3) of the RES Directive itself which, as stated above, expressly allowed Member States to distinguish between domestically and foreign-produced renewable energy. This indeed was Advocate General Bot's approach, who proposed that

[66] Case C-379/98 *PreussenElektra* ECLI:EU:C:2001:160. [67] Ibid., paras 68–81.

Article 3(3) be declared invalid (although this had not been raised in the referring court's Order for Reference). The CJEU, however, did not follow this approach, but instead noted first that, while the RES Directive clarified that Member States have the right to decide to what extent they support green energy produced in another Member State, it did not fully harmonise national support schemes such as to exclude the application of Article 34 TFEU.[68] Next, the CJEU held that, while the Swedish rules constituted a measure having equivalent effect to a quantitative restriction and, as such, was prima facie contrary to Article 34 TFEU, promoting the use of renewable energy sources for the production of electricity constituted a legitimate objective which was in principle capable of justifying barriers to the free movement of goods.[69]

The crux of the judgment, however, lies in its reasoning on proportionality, where it adopts what can be termed a 'close-look' approach. Here, considering the proportionality of the territorial restriction as such, the CJEU reasoned that, while the internal market in renewable energy had moved on since *PreussenElektra*, the Swedish scheme at issue was nevertheless proportionate '*as EU law currently stands*'.[70] In particular, despite the fact that the RES Directive provided for guarantees of origin of renewable energy (Article 15), the '*systematic identification*' of green electricity was still '*difficult to put into practice*' at the distribution and consumption stages,[71] and national support schemes for green electricity had not yet been fully harmonised,[72] with different Member States having different RES targets and different renewable energy potentials (and costs).

Thus far, the CJEU's reasoning was fully in line with its jurisprudence to date and, while interesting for its acknowledgement of the continued imperfections in the EU internal market for renewable energy, unremarkable from a legal perspective. Indeed, had the judgment ended there, this would hardly have been surprising. In an unusual twist, however, the CJEU went on to consider the proportionality of the Swedish legislation as a whole, and specifically of its use of a market mechanism to achieve Sweden's environmental/energy goals. Here, the CJEU noted that, in designing its national support scheme so that consumers bear the additional cost of producing renewable energy, Sweden was validly exercising its discretion in pursuit of the legitimate aim of increasing green electricity production;

[68] *Vindkraft*, paras 61–3.

[69] Citing *PreussenElektra*, the Kyoto Protocol and Art. 194(1)(c), inserted by the Treaty of Lisbon.

[70] Ibid., para 105. [71] Ibid., paras 90, 96. [72] Ibid., para 94.

further, the ability of the scheme to achieve that aim was proven.[73] Nevertheless, in order to be proportionate, such a market must be proven to function effectively and fairly such that traders subject to renewables obligations can in fact '*obtain certificates effectively and under fair terms*'.[74] To this end, it was

> important that mechanisms be established which ensure the creation of a genuine market for certificates in which supply can match demand, reaching some kind of balance, so that it is actually possible for the relevant suppliers and users to obtain certificates under fair terms.

Further, the CJEU added, the method for determining the penalty for non-compliance with the quota and the amount of that penalty must not go beyond what is necessary to provide an incentive to comply, and must not be '*excessive*'.[75]

This aspect of the judgment is fascinating in that it shows the CJEU's willingness to embrace a Member State's effort to use a market-based approach in achieving its environmental/energy goals, but only if the Member State proves that the market is actually functioning the way that *the CJEU considers* it should. As such, it represents a curious *mélange* of economic liberalism (leave it to the market) and paternalism (as long as the market works the way we, the judges, want it to). The CJEU's acceptance of this example of market-based environmental policy instrument, therefore, is resoundingly conditional. From the economically liberal perspective, the idea that any institution, much less a court (which is not a regulator, nor equipped with particular economic expertise), would be tasked with deciding what 'kind of balance' is 'fair' enough to constitute a 'genuine' market is rather strange. What is a 'fair' balance? Who should decide, and on what (presumably value-laden) criteria? Why should the 'fairness' of a market determine whether it is 'genuine'? These questions certainly do not admit of easy answers, and may cause serious problems of (economic) uncertainty. In another sense, however, the (market-environmental-social) tensions in *Vindkraft* find their source in the very model of constitutionally embedded economic liberalism provided for in the EU Treaties themselves, which of course the CJEU is tasked with upholding. In this sense, the linguistic and conceptual tensions in *Vindkraft* can be traced to the indeterminacy of the very

[73] Ibid., paras 109–12. [74] Ibid., para 113. [75] Ibid., para 116.

notion of a social market economy which lies at the foundation of the EU Treaties.

Some months later, the Fourth Chamber effectively repeated its *Vindkraft* position in *Essent Belgium*, this time in the context of the previous RES Directive,[76] and concerning the Belgian scheme whereby only Belgian-produced renewable energy could be taken into account in determining whether Belgian electricity producers had satisfied their renewable obligations. Again, the CJEU declined to follow the Opinion of Advocate General Bot,[77] who had concluded that the Belgian scheme breached EU internal market law, as the EU internal electricity market had now developed far enough to make it possible to verify whether electricity produced in other Member States comes from renewable sources, and that *PreussenElektra* was no longer good law.[78]

Aside from territoriality restrictions on the grant of green electricity certificates, the CJEU has also considered the compatibility of other limitations on the grant of such certificates by Member States. In its 2013 judgment in *Industrie du Bois*, the plaintiff challenged the compatibility of the restrictions placed by the Walloon region of Belgium on the grant of green certificates to cogeneration plants powered by wood (as opposed to, in particular, biomass), on the ground that these restrictions breached the principle of equal treatment and the EU Charter of Fundamental Rights. The CJEU was not convinced by this argument, holding that, in the present state of EU law, Member States were entitled, when introducing national support schemes for cogenerations and renewable energy production, to provide for enhanced support measures of particular benefit to cogeneration plants principally using biomass.[79]

While under the RES Directive, Member States now have express competence to cooperate with other Member States and with third States to achieve their national RES targets (Article 3(3)(b)), this does not mean that Member States have the competence to enter into agreements with third States recognising the renewable source of energy produced in that State. Rather, as the CJEU held in December 2014 in *Green Network*, the guarantees of origin provided for in the RES Directive apply only to EU-produced green electricity. In that case, therefore, an Italian law enabling

[76] Directive 2001/77 on the promotion of electricity produced from renewable energy sources in the internal electricity market, OJ 2001 (L 283/33).

[77] Opinion of AG Bot, ECLI:EU:C:2013:294.

[78] Opinion, paras 100 *et infra*.

[79] *Industrie du Bois*, paras 53 *et infra*.

Italy to exempt from its green certificates scheme green electricity produced in a third State (in that case, Switzerland) where an agreement between Italy and Switzerland had been signed was held to be contrary to the EU Treaty. Specifically, applying Article 3(2) TFEU, the CJEU held that the EU provisions on guarantees of origin (in that case, applying the prior RES Directive, Directive 2001/77) had been harmonised such that, if Italy were to sign an agreement on the topic with Switzerland, this would be liable to '*alter the scope of common rules*' within the meaning of the CJEU's case law on the EU's exclusive competence.[80] *Green Network*, therefore, emphasises the important distinction between the EU rules on guarantees of origin (which, according to *Green Network*, are harmonised) and national support schemes in the form of green electricity certificates (which, according to *Vindkraft* and *Essent Belgium*, are not).

3.2. (National) measures aimed at promoting greener products/energy by granting financial support

A further important judgment on the renewable energy/internal market interface is the Second Chamber's December 2013 judgment in *Vent de Colère*. This case concerned the question whether French legislation obliging electricity distributors to purchase wind energy at a higher price than the normal market price constitutes State aid within the meaning of Article 107(1) TFEU (and therefore should have been notified to the Commission prior to grant), where the costs ensuing from this purchase obligation are compensated by a public fund to which electricity producers, suppliers and distributors contribute, and are passed on to consumers via a uniform and generally applicable charge. In finding that the French mechanism constituted an '*intervention through State resources*' (in that case, the key question in evaluating whether the law entailed State aid), the CJEU distinguished the German feed-in tariff at issue in *PreussenElektra*, which had been held not to entail State sources, on the ground that the charge intended to offset the extra costs from the French purchase obligation was collected from all final consumers of electricity in France and entrusted to the French *Caisse des dépôts et consignations*, a public body.[81] Further, the French Minister for Energy determined the amount of that charge, and French law provided for an administrative penalty for failure to pay the charge, with the French State ultimately guaranteeing

[80] *Green Network*, para 49. [81] Ibid., para 22.

that any shortfall in sums collected as compared to the additional costs of the purchase obligation for electricity undertakings would be made up by the State. As a consequence of the CJEU's judgment, the French wind energy promotion scheme, which had been in operation since 2000, constituted illegal aid, meaning that in principle it should be repaid along with interest on the amounts due. The CJEU refused to limit the temporal effects of the judgment following argument as to its serious financial consequences for the economic actors at issue.[82]

3.3. (National) laws aimed at promoting good environmental performance by granting exclusive or special rights or by (national or European) GPP measures

Outside the context of national renewable energy schemes, the CJEU has also considered the legality of other national policy instruments aimed at promoting good environmental performance. In *Max Havelaar*, the CJEU held that the way in which the province of North Holland had included an eco-label requirement in its technical specifications for a tender for the supply and management of automatic coffee machines breached the 2004 Public Procurement Directive.[83] Specifically, the province had referred to two particular eco-labels in the award criteria, the EKO label (an organic produce label) and the MAX HAVELAAR label (a fair-trade label). Drawing on its jurisprudence in *Concordia Bus* and *Wienstrom*,[84] the CJEU recalled that the contracting authority's decision to award a contract to the tenderer who submits the most economically advantageous tender must be based on criteria which are in compliance with the requirements of the Directive, which award criteria may in principle be not only economic but also qualitative, including environmental characteristics (Article 53(1) of the 2004 Directive).[85] The CJEU also recalled, however, that the award criteria must be linked to the subject matter of the contract,[86] and must be objective, with the award procedure in compliance with the principles of equality, non-discrimination and transparency. In the present case, the award criteria at issue concerned environmental and social characteristics within the meaning of the Directive, and related to products to be supplied

[82] *Vent de Colère*, para 44. [83] OJ 2004 (L 134/114).
[84] Case C-513/99 *Concordia Bus Finland* ECLI:EU:C:2002:495, Case C-448/01 *Wienstrom* ECLI:EU:C:2003:651.
[85] *Dutch Coffee*, para 85. [86] See Chapter 3 of this volume by Abby Semple.

as part of the subject matter of the contract. Further, as regards the fair trade criterion, there is no requirement that an award criterion relates to an '*intrinsic characteristic of a product*' as opposed to the way in which the product was produced.[87] Nevertheless, the Directive did not entitle a contracting authority to make use of a specific eco-label as a technical specification of the tender. Rather, use of such a label was allowed only to create a presumption that the products bearing the label comply with the characteristics defined, but other appropriate means of proof must also be allowed.[88]

In *Evropaïki Dynamiki*, the General Court rejected the plaintiff's argument that the European Environment Agency (EEA) had, in the context of an award criterion referring to the '*general environmental policy of the company*', wrongly awarded a tender to the only tenderer which had submitted a certified environmental management scheme. Pursuant to the relevant rules for the award of contracts for Community institutions in force at the time, which were in turn based on the 2004 Public Procurement Directive, the criteria justified by the subject of the contract included the environmental characteristics of the product. It will be recalled that, in contrast to the general rule under that Directive excluding criteria or conditions relating to a general corporate policy, proof of the environmental policy of the company constitutes a legitimate way of adducing evidence as to the environmental characteristics of the product.[89] The plaintiff argued that, rather than relying on the certificate, the EEA should have had regard to the actual environmental performance of the company. Rejecting this argument, the General Court held that the general wording of the award criterion enabled tenderers to present their environmental policy as they wish and to supply the evidence they consider to be appropriate. Submission of an environmental management certificate was '*one of a number of conventional ways of providing*' such evidence.[90] Importantly, the evidence showed that, in that case, the evaluation committee had actually made a comparative assessment of the tenders and had evaluated whether the environmental policies submitted by the tenderers were '*genuine*', and had not simply accepted the environmental management certificate without more.[91]

In effect, therefore, the CJEU's reasoning in the context of public procurement mirrors, albeit applied in a partially codified legislative context, the 'close-look' proportionality seen in the free movement context

[87] Ibid., para 91. [88] Ibid., para 94.
[89] See Chapter 5 in this volume by Roberto Caranta. [90] Para 75. [91] Ibid., para 76.

considered above: the means used to achieve the environmental/social goal at issue must not be more restrictive than actually necessary to achieve those goals.

3.4. The judicial role in the EU carbon market: the case of the ETS

While space precludes detailed discussion of the field, no discussion of the CJEU's role in striking the economic/environment balance is complete without mention of the Court's growing jurisprudence of the CJEU relating to the EU's Emissions Trading Scheme (ETS).[92] The first generation of EU ETS cases that found their way before the CJEU comprised Member State challenges to Commission decisions on their national allocation plans proposed for Phases I and II of the EU ETS. While these cases remain interesting in demonstrating how intensively the CJEU was willing to review Commission decisions of an essentially economic nature *qua* market regulator (answer: rather surprisingly intensively),[93] they are generally now of less direct significance with regard to the post-Phase II, centralised allocation and regulatory framework.[94] However, we are already now seeing judgments on the Phase III regulatory framework starting to appear. One of the first of these was the General Court's 2013 judgment in *Poland* v. *Commission*, in which Poland sought unsuccessfully to challenge the Commission's decision as to the transitional measures for harmonised free allocation of allowances, taken pursuant to Article 10a of the ETS Directive.[95] In rejecting Poland's arguments that the Commission had not sufficiently taken into account differences between Member States and regions (in particular, Polish dependency on coal) and had gone beyond what was necessary to achieve the Directive's aims, the GC

[92] For greater discussion of the role of the CJEU in governing the EU ETS, see G. Dari-Mattiacci and J. Van Zeben, 'Legal and market uncertainty in market-based instruments: the case of the EU ETS', *NYU Environmental Law Journal*, 19 (2012), 415.

[93] See, for example, Case T-183/07 *Poland* v. *Commission* ECLI:EU:T:2009:350 (Commission reduction of industry emission caps by 26.7 per cent annulled – appeal to CJEU dismissed March 2012 in Case C-504/09 P) Case T-263/07 *Estonia* v. *Commission* ECLI:EU:T:2009:351 (Commission reduction of industry emission caps by 47.8 per cent annulled – appeal to CJEU dismissed March 2012 in Case C-505/09 P).

[94] Some earlier cases are, however, clearly still relevant: see, for instance, Case C-524/09 *Ville de Lyon* ECLI:EU:C:2010:822, where the Fourth Chamber of the CJEU rejected, on confidentiality grounds, the claim that an administrator of a national registry of ETS allowances should be obliged to give out details of ETS trading data, account holders and the like in the medium term after completion of the relevant transactions.

[95] Case T-370/11 *Poland* v. *Commission* ECLI:EU:T:2013:113.

distinguished its Phase I and II judgments on the basis that, in these Phases, the margin of discretion left to Member States in transposing the ETS Directive was far greater.[96]

Despite the specific legislative context of the CJEU's judgments on the ETS, a parallelism of argument is clear in the CJEU's ETS cases and many of the other cases concerning the environment/economic interface discussed above. In *Commission* v. *Estonia*,[97] for instance, in arguing that it should have been allowed to set maximum total quantities of greenhouse gas emissions allowances, the Commission made precisely the same argument that the CJEU subsequently adopted in *Vindkraft*, that is, that the environmental objective of the scheme could only be achieved if demand in the market outstrips supply.[98] Due to the narrow role attributed to the Commission under the 2003 ETS Directive,[99] however, the CJEU rejected that argument.

Similarly, in *Iberdrola*, the CJEU interpreted the 2003 ETS Directive as compatible with a Spanish law aimed at reducing the 'windfall profits' earned by electricity producers due to the initial structure of the ETS whereby such producers were allocated allowances for free, and could subsequently sell them on the allowance market. In holding that the Spanish law to reduce the price that such producers received for their electricity was compatible with the ETS Directive, the CJEU emphasised that free allocation of allowances was not directly related to the ETS's environmental aims, and that the Spanish rules did not affect the functioning of the allowances market, but only the level of profit of the electricity producers, and did not compromise the environmental aims of the ETS.[100] Notably, however, the CJEU accepted the electricity producers' claim that the way that the Spanish scheme worked in fact could in some cases reduce the incentive to reduce greenhouse gas emissions, but held that this did not mean the scheme was contrary to the ETS Directive, as long as it did not '*remove that incentive entirely*'.[101] Here, therefore, the CJEU accepts that, however well designed, markets, including those with environmental objectives, do not always work perfectly. In *ŠKO-ENERGO*, the CJEU again noted that Member States are free to adopt measures which may affect the economic implications of using ETS emissions allowances, as

[96] Ibid., paras 52–3. [97] Case C-505/09 P *Commission* v. *Estonia* ECLI:EU:C:2012:179.

[98] Ibid., para 72.

[99] Directive 2003/83 establishing a scheme for greenhouse gas emission allowance trading within the Community, OJ 2003 (L 275/32).

[100] Paras 35–58. [101] Ibid., para 58.

long as such measures do not neutralise the principle of free allocation of allowances, which was temporarily applicable in Phases I and II of the EU's ETS, or undermine the Directive's aims. In that case, a Czech law imposing a gift tax of 32 per cent on freely allocated emission allowances, with an exemption for photovoltaic power stations, was held in principle to be contrary to the Directive (although this was ultimately for the national court to decide).

The most notable CJEU judgment on the EU ETS to date, however, is indisputably the *ATAA* judgment,[102] where a challenge by the Air Transport Association of America and a number of US airlines to the inclusion of third-country airlines within the scope of the ETS failed. In a lengthy and complex judgment, the Grand Chamber of the CJEU held that the application of the EU ETS to third-country airlines was compatible with international law and, in particular, with the principle of territoriality, given that the scheme only applies to commercial aircraft that arrive at or depart from a Member State airport.[103] Nor did the fact that the ETS applied to the whole of the aircraft's journey (not just that which occurred over EU territory) affect this conclusion, given the EU's objective under Article 191(2) TFEU of achieving a high level of environmental protection and its status as a party to the UNFCCC.[104] The CJEU also considered that the extension to third-country operators did not infringe the more specific relevant instruments of international law, namely the Chicago Convention (on the ground that the validity of EU law cannot be reviewed in the light of that Convention)[105] and the Open Skies Agreement between the USA and EU (on the ground that the extension was compatible with the EU's obligation to exempt the fuel load from taxes, fees and charges on fuel).[106] The judgment was highly controversial, and has contributed to a major dispute with the vast majority of members of the International Civil Aviation Organization (ICAO), leading to the EU's 2013 decision to 'stop the clock' on the application of the ETS to flights between EU airports and third countries, and the EU's 2014 Regulation suspending such application between 2013 and 2016, in view of the ICAO's roadmap to develop a global market-based mechanism to tackle aviation emissions by 2016, to be implemented by 2020.[107]

[102] Case C-366/10 *ATAA* ECLI:EU:C:2011:864. [103] Ibid., para 127.

[104] Ibid., para 128. [105] Ibid., para 72. [106] Ibid., para 145.

[107] Regulation 421/2014 establishing a scheme for greenhouse gas emission allowance trading within the Community, in view of the implementation by 2020 of an international agreement applying a single global market-based measure to international aviation emissions, OJ 2014 (L 129/1).

4. Conclusion

These are critical times for the environment/economy interface within the EU. Its commitment to sustainable development at a constitutional level cannot be doubted. Yet the meaning of sustainable development, EU-style, is still unclear, and the past years, with their economic difficulties, have seen a shift at political and policy levels towards prioritising development over sustainability. At the same time, the popularity, at Member State and EU levels, of environmental market-based instruments to achieve environmental goals[108] has brought a striking increase in cases coming before the CJEU in which the Court is asked to balance environmental and economic goals. In this context, the CJEU is becoming a key forum in setting the legal boundaries of the environment/economic interface within the EU, and its role as a non-majoritarian, independent and politically insulated institution, focused on interpreting and upholding the EU Treaties, is thrown into sharp relief.

While the case law is still rapidly developing, overall the CJEU has demonstrated itself to be a constitutionalist actor which is serious about the requirement to achieve real, substantive integration of environmental protection requirements into the EU's economic policies, as required by Article 11 TFEU. This has meant that, in important cases (*Vindkraft*, *Essent Belgium*), its acceptance of market mechanisms to achieve environmental goals has been markedly conditional. Markets are not sacred, inviolable spaces to be protected from political or policy interference; rather, they are a means to a (political/policy) end and, where that end is not in fact being achieved, the legislator or regulator must step in. Specifically, the CJEU has used what can be termed a 'close look' proportionality analysis, closely examining whether the purported environmental aims were actually being realised, and in the least restrictive manner. Moreover, a welcome parallelism of approach can be discerned in the CJEU's jurisprudence on different types of environmental market-based instruments, from markets in renewable energy (green certificate schemes), to markets trading rights to pollute (the ETS), to financial incentives, to GPP measures. Nevertheless, of course, the CJEU's role as an actor in environmental integration is ultimately limited by legislation, where such legislation exists, and the legislative context to the cases before it. After all – in contrast to the constitutional prohibition on restrictions to trade

[108] See also, for instance, Directive 2012/27/EU on energy efficiency, OJ 2012 (L 315/n1), Art. 7.

within the internal market – there is no constitutional prohibition on environmental damage, even the most serious and flagrant environmental damage, in the EU Treaties. In this sense, the implied prioritisation of economic over environmental goals in the EU Treaties will, despite the CJEU's integrationist efforts, persist. The resultant tensions remain visible in the CJEU's case law, including in the field of public procurement.

3

The link to the subject matter

A glass ceiling for sustainable public contracts?

ABBY SEMPLE

1. Introduction

Originating in a dictum of the Court of Justice in the *Concordia Bus Finland* case, the 'link to the subject matter' (LtSM) has emerged as a major limiting principle for sustainability considerations in the 2014 EU Procurement Directives. It is intended to delimit the scope of legitimate requirements or preferences which can be expressed in procurement procedures and applied in contract performance clauses. It effectively removes the ability to interrogate general corporate social or environmental responsibility policies to the extent that these address matters beyond the specific needs of the contracting authority. This chapter analyses the origin and application of the concept in the Court's case law and the manner in which it has been expanded in the 2014 Directives. As cases applying the test are few, additional sources such as interpretative efforts of the European Commission and the preparatory materials for the 2014 Directives are drawn upon for better understanding of its scope.

The chapter then turns to an analysis of how the LtSM may restrict the effectiveness of sustainability criteria in public contracts, drawing on examples related to renewable energy generation, transport emissions and fair-trade products. Application of a strict version of the test may create difficulties in achieving the objectives of such criteria, due to the complexity of supply chains and the prevalence of 'upstream' environmental and social impacts. On the other hand, abandoning or loosening the link may also pose problems in terms of verification of criteria and the additionality of the benefits they target. The use of sustainability criteria in procurement decisions is distinguished from the role of regulation, with the former being particularly well placed to test the effectiveness of different approaches to achieve and refine environmental and social policy goals. The chapter concludes by proposing a loose LtSM test combined with application of the principles of proportionality and transparency as an appropriate way for the Court to review sustainability measures in public procurement.

2. Sustainable public procurement

Sustainable public procurement (SPP) is a means of ensuring that public contracts contribute to broader environmental and social policy goals espoused by governments – such as reduction of greenhouse gas emissions, energy and resource efficiency, or promotion of employment, social inclusion and equality.[1] SPP may contribute to such objectives either directly in the performance of the contract (e.g. where a supplier reduces the carbon emissions associated with production or delivery of a product or service, or a works contractor employs disadvantaged workers or trains apprentices), or indirectly by encouraging companies to change general corporate practices. As will be seen below, the scope for pursuing indirect environmental or social benefits via the award of public contracts appears to have been curtailed under the 2014 Directives by the expansion of the LtSM requirement, although significant room for interpretation remains within the legislative text. This chapter aims to highlight the likely consequences of the various possible interpretations of the requirement.

Large-scale research has indicated that contracting authorities in Europe routinely incorporate environmental and social criteria into contracts advertised in the Official Journal, including at least one such

[1] For background on SPP, see S. Arrowsmith and P. Kunzlik (eds), *Social and environmental policies in EC procurement law: new directives and new directions* (Cambridge University Press, 2009); R. Caranta and M. Trybus (eds), *The law of green and social procurement in Europe* (DJØF Publishing, 2010); N. François, 'La place des considérations d'ordre non strictement économique dans l'attribution des marchés publics – Essai sur la prise en compte de considérations d'ordre environnemental, social, éthique et de genre dans les critères de sélection et d'attribution des marchés publics', *Chroniques de Droit Public*, 13 (2009), 621–44; A. Semple, 'Reform of the EU procurement directives and WTO GPA: forward steps for sustainability?', in *Charting a course in public procurement innovation and knowledge sharing* (Academics Press, 2012). See also *The procura+manual: a guide to implementing sustainable public procurement*, 3rd edn (ICLEI – Local Governments for Sustainability, 2015); A. O'Rourke, C. Leire and T. Bowden, *Sustainable public procurement: a global review* (United Nations Environment Programme, 2013); *Buying green: a handbook on environmental public procurement*, 2nd edn (European Commission, 2011) and *Buying social: a guide to taking account of social considerations in public procurement* (European Commission, 2010). The Commission has produced a range of procurement criteria and other resources for green public procurement, see http://ec/europa.eu/environment/gpp.

criterion in more than half of contracts.[2] These levels fall short of EU targets and there is as yet little hard evidence regarding the impact of these criteria on contractual outcomes.[3] This does not however distinguish SPP from other policies pursued via procurement, where the evidence base is often poor both at organisational level and in the aggregate. It does appear that SPP has become more prevalent both at local and central government level and across Europe, despite the effects of the financial crisis.[4] This is driven not only by legal requirements to ensure that contractors obey basic environmental and social obligations (such as safe work practices, handling of waste and hazardous substances or payment of tax and social security) but also by a broader desire to leverage public contracts to achieve societal gains. This practice has a long pedigree, for example, the use of public works contracts during the 1930s to reduce unemployment may be seen as a forebear of more recent SPP practices.[5] Some SPP practices also have a direct financial return to the contracting authority, such as where energy-efficient lighting or equipment reduces running costs, or the payment of higher wages increases local tax revenue and reduces claims for social assistance.

Beyond direct and indirect impacts, there is also a third means by which SPP may contribute to environmental and social objectives, and

[2] A 2011 study found that at least one environmental criterion was included in 55 per cent of the last contracts signed by 850 public authorities in 26 Member States, with a full set of such criteria included in 26 per cent of the contracts studied. Centre for European policy studies and College of Europe, *Monitoring the uptake of green public procurement in the EU27* (European Commission, 2012). In terms of social criteria, some 23 per cent of contracting authorities reported including these in tenders either 'regularly' or 'as much as possible' in 2011 (M. Essig, J. Frijdal, W. Kahlenborn and C. Moser, *Strategic use of public procurement in Europe: final report to the European Commission* (European Commission, 2011).

[3] A 2009 study found an average 1.2 per cent reduction in life-cycle costs and 25 per cent reduction in CO2 emissions based on the application of GPP criteria for nine product and service groups in seven EU countries. PricewaterhouseCoopers, Significant and Ecofys, *Collection of statistical information on green public procurement in the EU* (European Commission, 2009). However, there are methodological difficulties associated with studies which rely upon voluntary participation of contracting authorities and/or award notices published in the Official Journal, both in terms of the quality of data and achieving a representative sample.

[4] Centre for European Policy Studies and College of Europe (2012) – the study cross-referenced the sample of 850 contracts signed in 2011 with 230,000 contracts signed by public authorities in 2009–10, finding that the proportion of contracts including at least one green criterion had increased from 29 per cent to 55 per cent.

[5] See C. McCrudden, *Buying social justice: equality, government procurement and legal change* (Oxford University Press, 2007), pp. 37–48, who also traces the history of procurement linkages further back to the 1830s.

this is by bringing greater scrutiny to the policies themselves. It is broadly recognised that significant challenges exist in policy formation and implementation in the fields of climate change and poverty alleviation, to take two examples.[6] These are areas in which the private sector inevitably has a role to play in securing advancements – and decisions by public authorities about how to contract with them may be of equal importance to decisions about regulation or taxation. Various policy approaches have been applied in both fields; however, serious problems remain both in the conception and execution of policy. Climate change policies face hazards linked to inadequate accounting mechanisms and the risks of subsidising particular technologies to the exclusion of others.[7] Poverty alleviation is plagued by ideological precepts and in some cases political opportunism or corruption.[8] One of the most exciting potential roles for SPP is as a means of identifying and addressing such hazards, by a combination of demand-side scrutiny and supply-side competition. The provisions of the 2014 Directives which deal with verification and means of proof are particularly relevant here. However, it is also possible that the LtSM requirement will adversely affect pursuit of such policies via procurement, not least due to legal uncertainty regarding its meaning.

3. Reform of the EU Procurement Directives

The most recent reform of the EU Procurement Directives resulted in the adoption by the Council and Parliament of three new directives in 2014.[9]

[6] See sources cited below for specific challenges in both fields. On the nexus between the two, see Y. Le Bouthillier, M. Cohen, J. Gonzalez Marquez, A. Mumma and S. Smith (eds), *Poverty alleviation and environmental law* (Edward Elgar, 2012).

[7] See, for example: A. Kander, M. Jiborn, D. Moran and T. Weidmann, 'National greenhouse-gas accounting for effective climate policy on international trade', *Nature Climate Change*, 5 (2015), 431–5; R. Falkner, *Business power and conflict in international environmental politics* (Palgrave Macmillan, 2009); C. Rohde, J. Rosenow, N. Eyre and L.-G. Giraudet, 'Energy saving obligations – cutting the Gordian knot of leverage?', *Energy Efficiency*, 8 (2015), 129–40.

[8] See for example: A. Banerjee and E. Duflo, *Poor economics: a radical rethinking of the way to fight global poverty*, (PublicAffairs, 2011); J. Spencer, 'People, places and policy: a politically relevant framework for efforts to reduce concentrated poverty', *The Policy Studies Journal*, 32 (2004), 545–68.

[9] Directive 2014/23/EU of the European Parliament and of the Council on the award of concession contracts (the 'Concessions Directive'); Directive 2014/24/EU of the European Parliament and of the Council on public procurement and repealing Directive 2004/18/EC (the 'Public Sector Directive'); and Directive 2014/25/EU on procurement by entities operating in the water, energy, transport and postal services sector and repealing Directive 2004/17/EC (the 'Utilities Directive').

Member States have until April 2016 to implement these Directives into national law, with the vast majority of provisions being mandatory for implementation. One of the stated ambitions of the reform was to facilitate greater 'strategic' use of public procurement, in particular to pursue environmental, social and economic objectives.[10] This in part reflects the timing of the reform process which began in early 2011, with pressure rising on governments to address the consequences of the financial crisis and to achieve more with a lower level of expenditure. The approximately €2 trillion spent by the public sector on goods and services was repeatedly invoked as if it were a fungible asset, rather than being extremely dispersed and variable. Nevertheless, the momentum associated with strategic procurement – and in particular the social agenda adopted by the European Parliament rapporteur, succeeded in placing these issues on the table. Negotiations among the Commission, Parliament and Council took place over a period of two years, with the final text of the Directives being adopted in February 2014.

As with the previous revision completed in 2004, the text of the 2014 Directives bears the hallmarks of compromise. The possibilities for contracting authorities to procure sustainably are balanced – sometimes precariously – against the imperatives of competition and transparency. The result clearly fails to deliver against one of the other ambitions of the reform process: simplification. Rather we are left with provisions which invoke esoteric concepts such as 'characteristics which do not form part of the material substance' of goods or services being purchased, 'factors which are not attributable to an economic operator' and the LtSM test which is the focus of this chapter. The purpose of drawing attention to these problematic terms is not to denigrate the efforts of the EU legislators, but rather to highlight that the task of determining how the various objectives of public procurement may be reconciled is only partially fulfilled by the text of the Directives. Considerable work remains to be done first by national legislators in their implementation of the Directives, and then by contracting authorities, their advisors and the courts.

There were several perceptible tensions underlying the reform process: the desire to strengthen the internal market,[11] against the desire to use

[10] European Commission, *Green Paper on modernisation of EU public procurement policy: towards a more efficient European Procurement Market*, COM (2011) 15.

[11] These ambitions are set out in M. Monti, *A new strategy for the single market: at the service of Europe's economy and society* (European Commission, 2010) and COM (2010) 608, Towards a single market act.

public procurement to achieve other policy objectives; the need to maintain common procedures, against the need to give contracting authorities greater flexibility and choice and the imperative to meet international commitments such as those under the WTO Government Procurement Agreement, against the imperative to use European procurement to foster European growth.[12] It is too early to comment upon the impact which the 2014 Directives will have on these various objectives. It is possible to observe that the scope of EU procurement regulation has probably increased, rather than decreased as was called for by some Member States and commentators.[13] This is due to the explicit regulation of concessions, which include a number of high value contracts, and the hardening of rules on modifications to contracts and public–public cooperation.[14] While these rules arose from the Court's case law, their inclusion in the Directives means that they are more likely to be applied and enforced widely throughout the 28 Member States. This makes it more important than ever to ask how contracting authorities can effectively address sustainability issues in contracts which are regulated by the EU Directives.

Amongst the 'headline' reforms intended to support SPP, the provisions on technical specifications and award criteria, and in particular the rules on life-cycle costing and references to labels, have attracted considerable commentary.[15] However, the use of environmental or social specifications and award criteria remains entirely voluntary on the part of contracting

[12] Not all of these aims may in fact be oppositional; however, their different prioritisation by the various European institutions, national governments and other stakeholders suggested different legislative directions. For example, some advocates of horizontal policies suggested that lowest price should be removed as a basis for awarding contracts, but this was seen both as an excessive interference with the ability of contracting authorities to choose their award criteria and potentially undermining price competition, for example, for commodities. The resulting compromise adopts the 'most economically advantageous tender' (MEAT) as the sole formal award basis, but it is still possible to exclude factors other than price or cost from the evaluation unless this is restricted by national governments (Art. 67(1) and (2) Public Sector Directive; Art. 82 (1) and (2) Utilities Directive).

[13] The United Kingdom, for example, argued for an overall raising of the thresholds above which the Directives apply. Arrowsmith called for a simplification of the regime by adopting a single directive on the model of the old Utilities Directive (2004/17/EC), see S. Arrowsmith, 'Modernising the European Union's public procurement regime: a blueprint for real simplicity and flexibility', *Public Procurement Law Review*, 3 (2012), 71–82.

[14] In contrast, the introduction of a lighter regime for social and other specific services and a number of new exclusions (such as for certain types of legal services and oil and gas exploration) may result in some decrease in the value of contracts advertised in the OJEU.

[15] In this volume, see Chapter 5 by Roberto Caranta and Chapter 6 by Dacian C. Dragos and Bogdana Neamtu on these topics.

authorities.[16] Of potentially broader significance are the mandatory provisions regarding the identification of subcontractors and the rejection of abnormally low tenders where these are found not to comply with applicable environmental, social or labour law.[17] While detailed consideration of these provisions falls outside of the scope of this chapter, discussion of the LtSM requirement should take account of the other provisions within the Directives which facilitate, mandate and limit SPP. This is important both from the perspective of contracting authorities seeking the most effective way to implement policies, and from the perspective of courts seeking to determine the legality of various approaches within the overall scheme of the Directives and Treaty.

4. The link to the subject matter–requirement

4.1. *Origin of the link to the subject matter–requirement*

The Court of Justice first identified a requirement for award criteria to be linked to the subject matter of the contract in the *Concordia* case, concerning the procurement of bus transport services by the City of Helsinki.[18] The City had included emissions of nitrogen oxide and noise amongst the criteria used to identify the most economically advantageous tender. The Court held that such award criteria were legitimate provided that they were linked to the subject matter of the contract; did not confer an unrestricted freedom of choice on the contracting authority; were explicitly mentioned in the contract notice or tender documents and complied with

[16] With one exception: for all procurement which is intended for use by natural persons, technical specifications must take into account accessibility criteria for persons with disabilities or design for all users (Art. 42(1) Public Sector Directive; Art. 60(1) Utilities Directive).

[17] Set out respectively in Arts. 71(5) and 69(3) of the Public Sector Directive – see Chapter 4 of this volume by Anja Wiesbrock. The Directives do not themselves define 'abnormally low tender' – so that it is only where a contracting authority itself decides to investigate (or is compelled to do so under national law) that the requirement to reject tenders which do not comply with such laws arises. It is also important to note the use of the term 'applicable', which is significant in light of the CJEU's jurisprudence on the enforceability of wage agreements in the context of public contracts (see Case C-346/06 *Dirk Rüffert* v. *Land Niedersachsen* ('*Rüffert*') [2008] ECLI:EU:C:2008:189; Case C-549/13 *Bundesdruckerei GmbH* v. *Stadt Dortmund*, not yet reported). Arguably the use of the term 'applicable' in Art. 18(2) of the Public Sector Directive implies a stricter test than the LtSM.

[18] Case C-513/99 *Concordia Bus Finland* v. *Helsingin kaupunki and HKL-Bussiliikenne* [2002] ECLI:EU:C:2002:495.

the fundamental Treaty principles, in particular non-discrimination.[19] At the time, there was no mention of environmental criteria in the Directives and so the case was welcomed as affirmation that non-economic considerations might form part of procurement decisions. This position, including the link to the subject matter (LtSM) requirement for award criteria, was subsequently written into the 2004 Directives.[20]

In identifying the requirement for a LtSM, the Court applied questionable logic:

> Since a tender necessarily relates to the subject-matter of the contract, it follows that the award criteria which may be applied in accordance with [the provisions on award criteria set out in the directives] must themselves also be linked to the subject-matter of the contract.[21]

While it is true that tenders relate to the subject matter of a contract, they may also relate to many other matters. For example, it is common for tenders (particularly in open procedures) to contain extensive background information about the company or grouping submitting the bid, as well as statements of compliance with various conditions set forth in the invitation to tender. The Court's statement thus appears to be a false syllogism. There may however be other reasons to consider that award criteria must relate to the subject matter of a contract.

EU Procurement Directives have long drawn a distinction between criteria for exclusion or selection, which are aimed at determining the capacity and suitability of economic operators to carry out a contract, and award criteria which are aimed at determining either the lowest priced or most economically advantageous tender.[22] Roughly, exclusion or selection criteria should concern the past or present situation of an operator, whereas award criteria should concern its proposals for the future performance of the contract. However, this distinction is not strictly maintained within the 2014 Directives. It is, for example, possible to assess at the selection stage the environmental and supply chain management measures which an operator *will be able* to apply in performance of a contract, and award criteria may now also concern qualifications and

[19] Case C-513/99 *Concordia*, para 64.

[20] Art. 53(1) of Directive 2004/18/EC; Recital 1 of Directive 2004/17/EC.

[21] Case C-513/99 *Concordia*, para 59.

[22] Under the 2014 Directives, MEAT is the only acceptable award basis – although it is still technically possible to exclude criteria other than price or cost unless this is prohibited by national implementing legislation.

experience of staff in certain circumstances.[23] The latter provision in particular represents a move away from the more rigid separation between selection and award criteria which the Court seemed to endorse in the *Lianakis* case, and which attracted much criticism.[24]

4.2. Interpretation of the LtSM requirement

The Court in *Concordia* held that criteria targeting the emissions and noise levels of buses were linked to the subject matter of a contract for the provision of bus services. It was soon given another opportunity to consider whether an environmental award criterion satisfied this test, in *EVN and Wienstrom.*[25] In that case the contracting authority had allocated 45 per cent of the available marks at the award stage for bidders' ability to produce renewable electricity in amounts which exceeded the volume required under the contract. The award criteria were challenged on a number of grounds, and the Court looked to the then recent *Concordia* judgment to assess their validity. It upheld the 45 per cent weighting for the renewable energy criterion but found that the focus on volumes of electricity which exceeded the authority's requirements meant that the criterion was not linked to the subject matter of the contract. It also held that the absence of effective verification provisions contravened the Directive.[26] The contracting authority in *EVN* argued that the focus of the award criterion made sense due to the seasonal variation in production capacity for renewable electricity: assessing production volumes in excess of its total annual requirement was aimed at ensuring reliability of supply.

The Court seemed to accept this argument in principle, but held that the formulation of the award criterion – higher renewable electricity production leading to higher marks without any upper ceiling – was likely to give an undue advantage to larger operators.[27] A proportionality test is implicit in the Court's assessment. If the authority had instead awarded

[23] As authorised under Annex XII, Part II (d) and (g) and Art. 67(2)(d) of the Public Sector Directive.

[24] Case C-532/06 *Lianakis* v. *Dimos Alexandroupolis* [2008] ECLI:EU:C:2008:40. See Public Procurement Law Review 2009–10 for assorted critiques of the judgment, and C. Bovis and G. Calzolari 'Dialogue', and P. Lee 'Implications of the *Lianakis* decision', in G. Piga and S. Treumer (eds), *The applied law and economics of public procurement* (Routledge, 2013), Chapters 5–9. See also S. Arrowsmith, *The law of public and utilities procurement* (Sweet & Maxwell, 2014), vol. I, 7-183–7-194 for arguments in favour of a degree of overlap being permissible between selection and award criteria.

[25] Case C-448/01 *EVN and Wienstrom* [2003] ECLI:EU:C:2003:651.

[26] Case C 448/01 *EVN*, paras 67–72.

[27] Case C 448/01 *EVN*, para 69.

marks based on a defined margin above its requirements, provided this was accompanied by verification, this may well have withstood the Court's scrutiny. The Court specifically disavowed the requirement that the criterion be effective in attaining its objective,[28] in this case increasing the proportion of renewable electricity available on the market. This contrasts with the more pragmatic approach which the Court has displayed in cases concerned with supply-side schemes which support renewable energy generation, notably *PreussenElektra*, *Ålands Vindkraft* and *Essent Belgium*.[29] In each of those cases, the Court considered that measures restricting free movement could be justified based upon the Treaty commitment to environmental protection and the specific need to increase renewable energy production.

To date, *EVN* is the only case in which the Court has ruled that the LtSM requirement was not met. It again considered the scope of the requirement in its influential *Max Havelaar* judgment, issued during the period when the 2014 Directives were under negotiation.[30] That case concerned an attempt by the North Holland region to include criteria targeting organic and fair-trade products in a contract for the supply of tea and coffee vending machines. The criteria themselves were problematic in that they referred only to the names of labels and not the criteria underlying them, and were otherwise lacking in transparency.[31] However, the Court upheld the principle that criteria which relate to a particular means of production (e.g. organic agriculture) or distribution (e.g. fair trade purchasing terms) could be considered to be linked to the subject matter of a contract for supply of products.[32] In doing so, it appeared to endorse a looser version of the LtSM requirement than that which was applied in *EVN*: the fair-trade criteria in question included a requirement for

[28] Case C 448/01 *EVN*, para 53. The Court considered that the effectiveness of the criterion in achieving its objectives was not relevant to determine its compatibility with EU law.

[29] Case C-379/98 *PreussenElektra AG* v. *Schleswag AG, in the presence of Windpark Reußenköge III GmbH and Land Schleswig-Holstein* [2001] ECLI:EU:C:2001:160; Case C-573/12 *Ålands Vindkraft AB* v. *Energimyndigheten*, judgment of the Court (Grand Chamber) of 1 July 2014, not yet reported and Joined Cases C-204/12 to C-208/12 *Essent Belgium NV* v. *Vlaamse Reguleringsinstantie voor de Elektriciteits- en Gasmarkt*, judgment of 11 September 2014, not yet reported. See M. Syzdło, 'How to reconcile national support for renewable energy with internal market obligations? The task for the EU legislature after Ålands Vindkraft and Essent', *Common Market Law Review*, 52 (2015), 489–510, discussing these cases.

[30] Case C-368/10 *Commission* v. *Kingdom of the Netherlands* ('*Max Havelaar*'), not yet reported.

[31] Case C-368/10 *Max Havelaar*, paras 93–7.

[32] Case C-368/10 *Max Havelaar*, paras 89–92.

'long-term trading relationships' with producers. The existence of a long-term relationship by definition goes beyond the immediate needs of the contracting authority.[33] While this seems to represent a looser approach to the LtSM requirement than was applied in *EVN*, it is possible that if the long-term trading requirement had been viewed as disproportionate then it would not have survived scrutiny.

The Court also held that there was no requirement for award criteria to relate to an intrinsic characteristic of a product or something which alters its material substance – thus putting to rest an invidious distinction once championed by the Commission.[34] In relation to fair-trade certification, the Court held that this could constitute an award criterion but not a technical specification – a position which is now (arguably) reflected in the 2014 Directives.[35] The distinction between technical specifications, award criteria and contract performance clauses has been a significant one for SPP, with the formulation of technical specifications being more tightly regulated and greater flexibility existing in relation to award criteria and contract performance clauses. As will be seen this distinction has been partly eroded by the inclusion of the LtSM requirement at all stages under the 2014 Directives. However, technical specifications continue to play a distinct role within procedures in that contracting authorities are obliged to reject tenders which do not comply with them.[36] This means that they are appropriate for enforcing minimum standards where it is possible to verify compliance during the procurement process, but not

[33] Case C-368/10 *Max Havelaar*, para 37.

[34] For a discussion and refutation of the 'material substance' theory, see P. Kunzlik, 'The procurement of "green" energy', in S. Arrowsmith and P. Kunzlik (eds), *Social and environmental policies in EC procurement law: new directives and directions* (Cambridge University Press, 2009), pp. 392–401.

[35] Recital 99 of the Public Sector Directive indicates that technical specifications may only address end-user social criteria, as opposed to those which relate to conditions of trade or employment. However, it is not clear why such a distinction should be drawn based upon the definition of technical specifications, which refer to methods of production and provision for both supplies and services and which allow references to both social and environmental labels. For discussion of these points, see A. Semple, *A practical guide to public procurement* (Oxford University Press, 2015), 4.33–4.39. See also M. Martens and S. de Margerie, 'The link to the subject-matter of the contract in green and social procurement', *European Procurement & Public Private Partnership Law Review*, 8 (2013), 15–6 and ClientEarth, *The link to the subject matter – a question of importance for sustainable public procurement* (2013), see www.clientearth.org/public-procurement/publications/.

[36] Art. 56(1)(a) Public Sector Directive; and Art. 76(5) Utilities Directive. The obligation to reject tenders which do not meet the technical specifications was highlighted by the Court in Case C-243/89 *Commission* v. *Kingdom of Denmark* ('*Storebaelt*') [1993] ECLI:EU:C:1993:257, para 37 and Case C-561/12 *Nordecon AS and Ramboll Eesti AS* v. *Rahandusministeerium* ('*Nordecon*'), not yet reported, paras 37–9.

usually for targeting optimum performance levels if these are not known in advance. For this reason contracting authorities may combine technical specifications setting minimum standards with award criteria and/or contract performance clauses which incentivise better performance on sustainability issues.

4.3. *LtSM under the 2014 Directives*

The LtSM requirement appears in six separate provisions in the Public Sector Directive:[37]

- In relation to technical specifications (Article 42(1))
- In relation to the criteria underlying labels (Article 43(1)(a))
- In relation to variants (Article 45(1))
- In relation to selection criteria (Article 58(1))
- In relation to award criteria (Article 67(2))
- In relation to contract performance clauses (Article 70)

Article 67 also contains a (partial) definition of concept, drawing upon the *Max Havelaar* judgment:

> Award criteria shall be considered to be linked to the subject-matter of the public contract where they relate to the works, supplies or services to be provided under that contract in any respect and at any stage of their life cycle, including factors involved in:
> (a) the specific process of production, provision or trading of those works, supplies or services; or
> (b) a specific process for another stage of their life cycle, even where such factors do not form part of their material substance.[38]

This must be read in conjunction with Recital 97 of the Public Sector Directive, which states:

> [T]he condition of a link with the subject-matter of the contract excludes criteria and conditions relating to general corporate policy, which cannot be considered as a factor characterising the specific process of production or provision of the purchased works, supplies or services.

[37] Equivalent provisions exist under the Utilities Directive, with the exception of the provision on variants, which are not required to be linked to the subject-matter of the contract under Art. 64 Utilities Directive. In relation to selection criteria, under Art. 80 Utilities Directive, the LtSM requirement only applies inasmuch as a contracting entity chooses to apply the criteria for qualitative selection set out in the Public Sector Directive.

[38] Art. 67(3) Public Sector Directive; Art. 82(3) Utilities Directive. See footnote 30 on the 'material substance' part.

> Contracting authorities should hence not be allowed to require tenderers to have a certain corporate social or environmental responsibility policy in place.

Although the recitals are not in themselves binding, they do express the intention of the legislator and should inform interpretation of the Directives' substantive provisions. The combined effect of Article 67(3) and Recital 97 is to emphasise that specifications, criteria and contract performance clauses must relate to the goods, services or works being purchased, and not concern matters which fall outside of the scope of the contract at hand. The reasons for the inclusion of the LtSM requirement in the 2014 Directives were expressed in the Commission's *Green Paper* published at the outset of the reform process:

> Relaxation of [the link to the subject-matter] requirement might enable public authorities to go further in pursuing Europe 2020 policy objectives through public procurement. Among others, it would allow contracting authorities to influence the behaviour of undertakings regardless of the product or service purchased, e.g. in order to encourage more environmental responsibility or greater attention to corporate social responsibility.
>
> However, when considering such a possibility, the trade-offs with other policy considerations must be carefully assessed. The link with the subject-matter of the contract ensures that the purchase itself remains central to the process in which taxpayers' money is used. This is an important guarantee to ensure that contracting authorities obtain the best possible offer with efficient use of public monies.[39]

The *Green Paper* went on to cite several other reasons for maintaining the LtSM requirement, including the greater possibility of state aid arising in public procurement procedures where this link was not applied and the potential for criteria which are not linked to the subject matter to result in discrimination against operators from other Member States. The Commission also considered that it could be more difficult for economic operators, and particularly small- and medium-sized enterprises (SMEs), to meet criteria which are not linked to the subject matter of the contract, as they

> might be asked to comply with different requirements (with regard to the percentage of women, number of unemployed people recruited, child care facilities available for employees, environmental or waste management measures, eco-labels, etc.) for every procurement or for each contracting authority.[40]

[39] *Green Paper*, COM (2011) 15, p. 39.

[40] *Green Paper*, COM (2011) 15, p. 40.

Finally, it cited the potential for requirements which are not linked to the subject matter to impede innovation in public procurement, as companies would be competing on the basis of corporate policy rather than on the basis of offering the best product or service.[41] While all of these arguments bear at least some plausibility in theory, it is unfortunate that this aspect of the Commission's proposals was not accompanied by any evidence regarding the alleged effects of loosening, maintaining or expanding the subject matter test. At the time of issuing its synthesis of the *Green Paper* consultation, the Commission published a series of six studies examining the impact of the 2004 Directives, including one which focused specifically on the use of procurement to further environmental, social and innovation policy.[42] However, none of these studies, nor the impact assessment published at the same time, contained any evidence regarding the alleged impacts of the LtSM requirement.[43]

To take each of the Commission's arguments in turn, it is difficult to see how the LtSM acts as a 'guarantee that contracting authorities obtain the best possible offer with efficient use of public monies' – or that this forms one of the legitimate or attainable objectives of EU procurement regulation. Presumably contracting authorities do not include criteria in procurement decisions unless they in some way contribute to value from their perspective. Regarding state aid the Commission's argument appears to be that loosening the LtSM requirement would create a risk of undue economic advantage being conferred upon private operators through the award of public contracts. However, given that the Court has clearly ruled that not all procurement criteria must be economic in nature, it seems strange to cite the LtSM requirement as a bulwark against such an advantage being conferred. A contracting authority might equally confer such an advantage by attaching a very low weighting to cost in its award criteria. This is not prevented by the Directives, nor indeed is the award of a public contract in which price or cost have been fixed in advance.[44]

41 Ibid.

42 W. Kahlenborn, C. Moser, J. Frijdal and M. Essig, Strategic use of public procurement in Europe: Final Report to the European Commission MARKT/2010/02/C (Berlin, 2011).

43 European Commission (2011) *Evaluation report: impact and effectiveness of EU public procurement legislation*, SEC (2011) 853 final. For all six reports, see http://ec.europa.eu/growth/single-market/public-procurement/modernising-rules/evaluation/index_en.htm.

44 This possibility is set out in Art. 67(2) of Directive 2014/24/EU, which states that in such situations economic operators will compete on quality criteria only.

The idea that bidders, and particularly SMEs, would struggle more to meet requirements or preferences which are not linked to the subject matter of the contract also appears illogical. Bidders are more likely to encounter diverse and contradictory requirements where these are specific to each contract, rather than those which target general corporate responsibility. An example of this can be seen in the new provisions regarding the use of environmental and social labels, which state that contracting authorities may only require a specific label where its requirements only concern criteria which are linked to the subject matter of the contract.[45] In practice, labelling schemes typically cover a range of sustainability criteria relevant to the industry in question, many of which can only be meaningfully enforced at organisation level rather than for a particular product or service. A small factory producing paper products may have to choose between a general environmental certification for its facility and specific labels for each type of paper it produces. If the LtSM requirement is interpreted strictly, contracting authorities will hesitate to refer to the more general certification scheme which may also contain requirements not linked to their specific purchase. For the small operator, this may require a higher level of investment in certification with a lower return (because it is not relevant to other customers). Importantly, it would also interfere with economic operators choosing certifications which will deliver the greatest environmental or social benefits based on their overall activities – a point which is revisited below.

The Commission considered that loosening the LtSM requirement could deter innovation procurement as it would cause companies to compete based on qualities other than those of the specific goods or services they offer. However, one of the main difficulties with innovation procurement – acknowledged by the creation of the innovation partnership procedure in the 2014 Directives – is that the goods and services in question may not exist on the market yet. How is a contracting authority to select operators, or evaluate the quality of their proposals in this situation? By definition, the 'subject matter' of the contract will remain somewhat uncertain – most likely defined in terms of performance or functionality rather than a detailed description of the goods or services to be provided. A strict interpretation of the LtSM requirement would make innovation procurement even more difficult, in that it would rule out the

[45] Art. 43(1) Public Sector Directive; Art 61(1) Utilities Directive.

possibility of evaluating factors which are generally conducive to innovation. For example, it would make it more difficult to give companies credit at selection stage for research carried out in neighbouring fields or to include contract conditions which relate to intellectual property above and beyond the scope of the initial contract (such as open licensing agreements or shared ownership provisions which only come into effect if the developed product is successful).

The *Green Paper* also appeared to overstate the scope of the LtSM requirement under the 2004 Directives, describing this as 'a fundamental condition that has to be taken into account when introducing into the public procurement process any considerations that relate to other policies' which applied 'throughout the successive stages of the procurement process'.[46] As outlined above, the subject matter link only appeared in relation to award criteria under the 2004 Directives, and had only been referred to by the Court in this context – amongst several other requirements for award criteria. What we are faced with under the 2014 Directives then is a radical extension of the LtSM requirement, apparently based upon the problematic reasoning put forward by the Commission in the *Green Paper*. Interestingly, while both the European Parliament and Council were influential in ensuring the possibility to address social considerations in particular under the 2014 Directives, both ultimately accepted the expansion of the LtSM requirement in the manner proposed by the Commission.[47] Conceivably, this was seen as a point of compromise, balanced against the stronger ability to address social concerns through reservation of certain contracts for companies employing a minimum percentage of disabled or disadvantaged workers or which have a public service mission,[48] and the provisions on abnormally low tenders and subcontracting mentioned above, which provide some ability to enforce environmental, social and labour obligations. However,

[46] *Green Paper*, COM (2011) 15, p. 39.

[47] Rapporteur Marc Tarabella put forward some 750 proposed amendments to the draft text of the Public Sector Directive, a large proportion of which aimed to ensure the possibility for contracting authorities to take social considerations into account. However, the proposed amendments did not seek to remove the LtSM requirement from the draft provisions on selection criteria, technical specifications, labels or contract performance clauses (European Parliament, Committee on the Internal Market and Consumer Protection, *Draft report on the proposal for a directive of the Parliament and Council on public procurement* of 3 May 2012, 2011/0438/(COD)).

[48] As provided for in Arts. 20 and 77 of the Public Sector Directive.

these provisions only apply where specifically invoked by the contracting authority, whereas the LtSM requirement applies to every procedure regulated by the Directives.

5. Arguments in favour of a loose LtSM requirement

5.1. Problems with a strict interpretation

The LtSM requirement, if strictly construed, can be detrimental both to the inclusion of environmental and social objectives in tenders and to the ability of the market to deliver these. To understand this it is worth taking a few examples of how environmental and social criteria can affect the market in the context of procurement procedures.

5.1.1. Renewable energy generation

In the case of renewable electricity, the requirement that selection criteria, specifications, award criteria and contract performance clauses be linked to the subject matter of the contract limits schemes designed to encourage investment in renewable energy via the award of public contracts. A contracting authority is free to insist that all or a given percentage of the electricity it purchases is produced from renewable sources. It may not however use its award of contract as a means of distinguishing between suppliers who produce or supply a greater percentage of renewable energy overall, or who invest in new generation capacity – unless this in some way affects the electricity which it is purchasing. Public sector demand for renewable electricity may push prices up, due to limitations on production capacity. Eventually supply should increase to meet this demand, however, as is well recognised by the Court in its case law on green certificates, the normal rules of supply and demand are not sufficient to develop the level of renewable energy capacity needed to meet Europe's 2020 target.[49] Award criteria or contract performance clauses which target the development of additional renewable energy capacity may be more

[49] The Renewable Energy Directive (2009/28/EC) sets a binding target for 20 per cent of final energy consumption to be from renewable sources by 2020, due to rise to at least 27 per cent by 2030. Recent figures indicate an EU average of 14 per cent had been achieved by 2012 (European Environment Agency, *Share of renewable energy in gross final energy consumption* (ENER 028) – Assessment, published Oct 2014).

effective[50] than those which relate solely to the electricity consumed by the authority.

5.1.2. Carbon footprint calculation

A second example of how a narrow LtSM requirement can be detrimental is where a direct comparison of greenhouse gas emissions is undertaken between tenders, as part of life-cycle costing or another award criterion. For a supply contract, this may include the emissions associated with transport of the goods from a warehouse or production facility to the point of consumption. A tenderer who moves their warehouse or production facility closer to the point of consumption would therefore attain higher marks than they would otherwise – notwithstanding that this may increase their overall emissions due to longer transport routes to other customers. However, such 'external' emissions could not be taken into account if they are not considered linked to the subject matter – thereby both rendering the award criterion counterproductive and allowing discrimination against suppliers who are located at a greater geographic distance to the contracting authority, even where they are more environmentally efficient overall. The same situation applies if the tenderer is located closer to the authority in the first place, although in that case a strict LtSM requirement for emissions would merely give them an unfair advantage, rather than actually increase net emissions.[51]

5.1.3. Fair-trade criteria

On the social side, similarly counterproductive effects can be seen to arise where contracting authorities are not able to take general corporate practices into account. Some commentators questioned whether, even after the *Max Havelaar* judgment, fair-trade criteria requiring democratic governance structures to be in place and restricting certification to small

[50] In this example, criteria targeting overall production capacity or investment in new capacity may be more effective both in contributing to the broader policy goal (i.e. meeting the 2020 target) and in ensuring the contracting authority can consume according to its own preferences over the longer term. There is a separate question of whether procurement is an *efficient* means of realising either goal, for example, compared to subsidies, regulation, taxation or other market interventions.

[51] This situation could still arise if the authority is careful to include the pre-production stage in its calculations, that is, the transfer of raw materials to the factory. Even if emissions are higher at this stage for the operator who has moved their facility closer to the point of consumption, the contracting authority is only entitled to take a small portion of those emissions into account – those which are linked to the subject-matter of its contract.

operators could be applied where an intermediary existed between the producer and the company bidding for a public contract.[52] One of the arguments made against living wage or fair-trade schemes is that they may push local costs and prices up, with a negative impact on those who are not covered by such schemes. This effect – which admittedly is difficult to measure – would be compounded where contracting authorities are obliged to focus only on the goods, services or works they are purchasing, as opposed to looking at the broader practices of tendering firms. As for schemes promoting employment or apprenticeships, award criteria or contract clauses which only concern these to the extent that they are specific to the contract being awarded are both less likely to be efficient in promoting their objectives (as it may make more sense for firms to employ apprentices or long-term unemployed people on another contract), and more likely to be discriminatory against non-domestic undertakings than those which allow 'credit' for the operation of such schemes elsewhere.

5.1.4. Shifting the burden

A final potential effect of a strict interpretation of the LtSM requirement – and one which runs directly counter to one of the intentions of the reform – is that it may prompt contracting authorities to apply stricter approach at the exclusion stage. Although the LtSM requirement also applies to selection criteria, it is not included in the provisions on mandatory and discretionary exclusion of operators.[53] These include the ability to exclude operators for non-payment of tax and social security or for violations of environmental, social and labour law. There is likely to be a trade-off between the strictness with which the subject matter link is interpreted, and the strictness with which exclusion grounds are applied. This tendency will be reinforced where the LtSM requirement is interpreted as meaning that matters relating to general corporate practices cannot be revisited later in the process – for example, in contract performance clauses which create a general requirement for an operator

[52] M. Martens and S. de Margerie, 'The link to the subject-matter', 15–16. Recital 97 of the Public Sector Directive now affords some limited comfort in this regard, although it refers to fair-trade *products* rather than *practices*.

[53] Art. 57 Public Sector Directive; Art. 80 Utilities Directive. The exclusion grounds are accompanied by provision for the 'self-cleaning' of economic operators and maximum periods for exclusion (Art. 57(6) and (7) Public Sector Directive) – however, contracting authorities have discretion to determine if any measures taken by an operator to demonstrate its reliability are sufficient in the circumstances.

to pay its taxes or observe environmental law, as opposed to just doing these things in respect of the contract awarded.[54] This runs contrary to the aim of the 2014 Directives to streamline selection processes and reduce the burden placed on suppliers at this stage. The inability of contracting authorities to address general corporate sustainability issues prospectively as well as retrospectively may detract from competition and transparency in the award of public contracts, if exclusion criteria become a proxy for enquiries into general corporate policy.

There are at least three reasons then for questioning the value of a strict LtSM requirement. The first is that it may specifically undermine the environmental or social objectives which contracting authorities wish to pursue via their procurement, many of which are endorsed at Union level. The second is that it tends to counteract attempts to reduce the burdens placed on suppliers at the pre-tender stage. The third is that it is more likely to result in market fragmentation and to impede the free movement of goods and services, as well as the efficient allocation of resources which is the ultimate aim of these freedoms, than approaches which are not specific to the subject matter of the contract. This third effect arises where the LtSM requirement narrows the scope of sustainability criteria so that companies who genuinely perform well against the targeted objectives are only evaluated based on the limited range of activities which form the subject matter of the contract, which are more likely to be local in character. Decisions about certification and labelling may also be more narrowly based on the need to demonstrate sustainability characteristics of individual products or services, rather than improving overall environmental and social performance.

One further point which should be addressed is the idea that the LtSM requirement does not restrict the scope of sustainability considerations which may be addressed in procurement procedures because contracting authorities are free to define the subject matter of their contracts. Carried to its logical conclusion, this would imply for example that a public authority could simply choose to say that it was purchasing 'renewable electricity and investment in renewable energy generating capacity' or 'construction of a school and training of apprentices'. This may indeed

[54] It is possible that the general duty placed on Member States to ensure observance of applicable environmental, social and labour laws in the execution of public contracts under Art. 18(2) could be cited as justification for such conditions. However, the requirement for a subject-matter link in Art. 70 may be considered to be a more specific obligation, and one which rests directly on contracting authorities.

be one approach to broadening the scope of sustainability criteria which contracting authorities can legitimately apply, while affording a high degree of transparency to the market regarding the implementation of horizontal policies. However, in this context the LtSM might be read as a minimum requirement as well as a limiting condition: selection criteria, technical specifications, award criteria and contract performance clauses would all have to relate to the *whole* subject matter of the contract, including any such additional elements. Moreover, attempts to subvert the intention of the legislator in including the LtSM requirement may be met with the Court's customary purposive approach to interpretation.

5.2. *Is a looser LtSM test problematic?*

Arguments against a strict LtSM requirement may be put aside by those who consider that the purpose of procurement is not to influence the general corporate policies of undertakings delivering public contracts but simply to obtain goods, services or works on specific terms. This view has some conceptual appeal and may even be endorsed by those who support the application of contract-specific sustainability measures. It must be recognised, however, that this narrower view of the function of public procurement has its conceptual origins in comparisons with private consumption, relying on the premise that in its commercial function government should behave as a private actor on the market does. It need only be pointed out that concerns about overall corporate social responsibility – from tax compliance to environmental stewardship and community benefits – are increasingly prevalent both within procurement decisions by private companies and consumption decisions by private citizens. A broader approach to corporate social responsibility is also supported by the EU definition of the concept.[55] The idea that the public

[55] The European Commission defines CSR as 'the responsibility of enterprises for their impact on society', COM (2011) 681, *A renewed EU strategy 2011–14 for corporate social responsibility*, s. 3.1. There is an obvious disconnect between this broad concept and limitation of public procurement measures to a narrow temporal and topical focus, if the LtSM requirement is strictly construed. For discussion of the scope of CSR, see B. Sjåfjell and L. Anker-Sørensen, 'Directors' duties and corporate social responsibility (CSR) in H. Birkmose, M. Neville and K. Engsig Sørensen (eds), *Boards of directors in European companies – reshaping and harmonising their organisation and duties* (Kluwer Law International, 2013).

sector should be uniquely restrained from acting on such concerns in its purchasing is anomalous.

5.2.1. Additionality and verification

A better argument against loosening the LtSM requirement might be that it puts the 'additionality' of sustainable procurement measures at risk. For example, if marks can be awarded for a supplier's overall production of renewable energy instead of just that which is produced for a particular contract, can it be claimed that there is an additional positive impact from the award of the contract itself? This depends on whether criteria which target general corporate practices are combined with those which apply to the specific goods, services or works being purchased, or replace them. Obligations imposed at the organisational level do require a robust approach to verification to ensure that they are not met by vague policies which are effectively business-as-usual. In cases where they reinforce contract-specific sustainability commitments and help to avoid the problems which a narrow view of the subject matter engenders, they can be of clear additional benefit. A commitment on the part of a contractor to reduce its overall carbon footprint in addition to that associated with a particular contract makes it less likely that 'leakage' will occur as discussed at Section 5.1.2 above.

Ultimately, given that the Directives aim to facilitate rather than mandate sustainable procurement, the additionality of benefits achieved may be considered to fall within the purview of the contracting authority. However, the 2014 Directives do provide a number of mechanisms for ensuring that claims made by tenderers (whether relating to sustainability considerations or otherwise) can be effectively verified. Amongst these are the provisions on labels, life-cycle costing, test reports and conformity assessment procedures. Although the 2014 Directives also require contracting authorities to accept a self-declaration (in the form of the European Single Procurement Document) as preliminary evidence of compliance with certain criteria, it is clear that the authority may request certificates confirming compliance at any moment in the procedure where this is deemed necessary.[56] There is, however, a risk that the complexity of verifying sustainability claims leads to an overreliance on self-declarations. This risk

[56] Art. 59(4) Public Sector Directive. At time of writing, the standard electronic format for the ESPD has not yet been published, so it is difficult to judge the extent to which it will replace other forms of evidence in practice.

would be compounded if authorities consider they are precluded from requesting certain forms of evidence by a strict interpretation of the LtSM test.

5.2.2. Consumption is not regulation

Preferences, or even requirements which are applied by public authorities in their own purchasing, should also not be equated to a form of market regulation.[57] Regulation of markets implies that undertakings cannot operate without meeting the requirements expressed in the regulation or facing sanctions. A requirement or preference on the part of a hospital to only purchase uniforms from companies which apply social audits throughout their supply chains, for example, does not prohibit such companies from operating on the market. Even if such an approach were mandatory under the procurement directives, it would still not constitute regulation in the sense of setting rules which all undertakings in a sector must apply. If a company does not wish to engage in social audits, it could still offer its products on the private market. Although government contracts are extremely important in several market sectors, it is worth remembering that the total value of goods and services purchased by the public sector accounts for under 20 per cent of GDP, and the value of procurement which is subject to the EU Directives is much lower.[58] Including general corporate sustainability criteria in tenders is more accurately seen as a lever than as a hammer.

A further distinction between procurement decisions and regulation is that the putative 'regulator' (the contracting authority) may alter, apply or disapply rules with each contract – with the exception of the very few

[57] See J. Hettne, 'Sustainable public procurement and the single market: is there a conflict of interest?', *European Procurement & Public Private Partnership Law Review*, 1 (2013), 31–40. Hettne refers to the Court's judgments in *Medipac* and *Rüffert* in support of the proposition that the scope for applying sustainability considerations in procurement is limited where harmonised EU regulation applies. While it is true that the Court found that the contracting authority in both cases was not entitled to apply requirements which conflicted with harmonised EU legislation, this followed from the obligation of the authorities to apply that legislation in the particular situations which the cases concerned, rather than from a general restraint on procurement decisions as a form of regulation themselves. The basic argument made by Hettne, that the procurement rules must be seen as part of the broader *acquis communautaire* and that the Treaty principles also apply to procurement decisions, is uncontroversial. However, for an alternative view of procurement as a form of (quasi) regulation, see Chapter 10 of this volume by Anna Beckers.

[58] The most recently published estimates from the European Commission show that some €425 billion was advertised in the OJEU in 2011, or about 3.4 per cent of EU GDP (European Commission, *Annual Public Procurement Implementation Review 2013*).

mandatory exclusion grounds required under the procurement directives. This characteristic of procurement decisions makes them both unsuited to the task of general market regulation and well suited to the pursuit of specific objectives which the contracting authority has identified for a particular contract. It is also this feature which makes sustainability criteria in procurement amenable to policy experimentation – to test the effects which various requirements or preferences have on the market and use this data to inform future development of policy, including regulation. The increased use of electronic means to manage procurement procedures and outcomes, as well as the move to greater transparency in government contracting, opens a potentially exciting field for such experimentation.

5.2.3. Measuring the effects

Regardless of the distinction which should be made between the conditions under which public authorities buy goods and services and the conditions which regulate a market sector, it is legitimate to ask what the broader impact of SPP measures on the market may be. Do such policies exert a discernible 'demand pull' – encouraging broader adoption of the standards applied? This question, critical from the policymaker's point of view, might be considered less relevant to the individual contracting authority whose primary concern is to meet its own procurement needs in a way which reflects its environmental and social obligations. However, if demand pull effects are real, they may be of interest to the individual contracting authority even if it takes a narrow view of the impact of its own procurement. Most obviously, prices for environmentally and socially responsible goods and services will fall if more companies decide to produce them, or investments are made in more efficient supply chains. In order to determine the links between public procurement and such effects further research is needed – taking account of the methodological difficulties faced by large-scale studies of procurement.

6. Conclusion

The enhanced presence of the LtSM requirement in the 2014 EU Procurement Directives reflects the tensions and compromises within the revision process. Far from providing a straitjacket for sustainability criteria, it is open to interpretation within the scope of the CJEU's prior case law and the partial definition provided in Article 67(3) of the Public Sector Directive. However, there are distinct risks associated with an overly narrow interpretation of the requirement, as highlighted above.

Unfortunately these risks may lead contracting authorities to apply alternative approaches to implementing SPP that will be more restrictive of competition and less conducive to the transparent and effective pursuit of complex environmental and social objectives. Unless courts are prepared to uphold a wider interpretation of the test, it may come to act as a glass ceiling for sustainable procurement, contrary to the intention of the reform of the Directives. Support for a looser version of the test may be found in the CJEU's *Max Havelaar* judgment, while its case law on green certificates in particular suggests that the environmental objectives of measures should be taken into account in judging their compatibility with internal market principles.

As suggested above, a looser approach to the LtSM is not without some of its own hazards. In particular, this may threaten the additionality of the gains targeted by SPP and may in some cases make verification more difficult. However, such risks fall squarely within the discretion granted to contracting authorities by the 2014 Directives, and the Directives contain a number of provisions such as those on labels and life-cycle costing which may well assist them in meeting these challenges. Applying a loose LtSM test would bring it closer to the general proportionality test applied by the Court in many areas, including in its procurement case law.[59] Indeed, the Court's approach to the LtSM in *EVN* and *Max Havelaar* bears close resemblance to proportionality review. Combined with the robust application of the transparency principle evident in *Max Havelaar*, this approach has much to recommend it as a means of interpreting the LtSM requirement.

[59] For discussion of the Court's application of proportionality in procurement cases, see A. Semple, *A practical guide*, 2.39–2.50.

4

Socially responsible public procurement

European value or national choice?

ANJA WIESBROCK

1. The new EU Procurement Directive: promoting socially responsible public procurement?

According to the United Nations Environment Programme, sustainable procurement seeks to 'achieve the appropriate balance between the three pillars of sustainable development, i.e. economic, social and environmental'.[1] This means that procurement decisions should be guided by a combination of economic factors (such as the costs of products and services), environmental factors (such as emissions, climate change and biodiversity) and social factors (such as social justice, human rights and employment conditions). The EU has adopted a similar definition of sustainable public procurement, which equally reflects the importance of balancing economic, social and environmental factors at all stages of a procurement procedure.[2]

This balanced and inclusive notion of sustainable public procurement is in line with the overarching EU objective of *sustainable development*, which is enshrined in the EU Treaties.[3] Sustainable development and the related principle of integration require by definition a simultaneous and coherent incorporation of economic, social and environmental concerns into policy development and decision-making procedures.[4] The

[1] United Nations Environment Programme (UNEP), Sustainable Consumption and Production Branch (2012), see www.unep.fr/scp/procurement/whatisspp/.

[2] The European Commission, Sustainable Public Procurement, see http://ec.europa.eu/environment/gpp/glossary_en.htm.

[3] See, Arts. 3 and 21 TEU, Arts. 11 and 191 TFEU and Art. 37 of the Charter of Fundamental Rights.

[4] See further A. Wiesbrock and B. Sjåfjell, 'The jigsaw puzzle of sustainability', in B. Sjåfjell and A. Wiesbrock (eds), *The greening of European business under EU law: taking Article 11 TFEU seriously* (Routledge, 2015), pp. 181–92.

importance of taking into account, on equal footing, all three pillars of sustainable development when procuring goods, services or works is, however, to date not reflected in European or national procurement legislation. As a consequence of being part of the legal framework on free movement of goods and services, EU public procurement rules are first and foremost examined through the lens of the principles of non-discrimination, competition and transparency.[5] This implies that free competition is equated to the main goal of public procurement decisions, whilst social and environmental objectives are often referred to as 'secondary' policies.[6] Moreover, in most countries the 'green' aspects of sustainable procurement policies are slightly more developed than the 'social' elements, especially at the level of central governments.[7]

In particular, the improvement of labour standards through public procurement procedures has long proved a difficult and vexed issue for legislators, contracting authorities and tendering companies alike. This is primarily due to the overriding requirement to prevent discrimination against tenders on non-economic grounds that are unrelated to the subject matter of the contract. The difficulty of proving that social standards are intrinsic to the delivery of the good or service procured has led contracting authorities to avoid the inclusion of social criteria in tender specifications, with the exception of criteria linked to the performance monitoring stage.

The new EU Public Procurement Directives, adopted in February 2014,[8] open several opportunities for public authorities to show greater consideration for social standards. Alongside the objective of increasing the simplicity and flexibility of EU public procurement law, a major aim of the new Directive is to enlarge the possibilities for using public procurement in support of broader social and environmental goals.[9] In the media and amongst non-governmental organisations (NGOs) and

[5] C.H. Bovis, 'Developing public procurement regulation: jurisprudence and conceptual directions', *Common Market Law Review*, 49(1) (2006), 461–95, at 461.

[6] For a critical perspective on this approach, see also F. Losada, 'The Green Paper on the modernization of public procurement of the EU: towards a socially-concerned market or towards a market-oriented society?', *Oñati Socio-Legal Series*, 2(4) (2012), 60–82.

[7] See W. Kahlenborn, C. Moser, J. Frijdal and M. Essig, *Strategic use of public procurement in Europe: final report to the European Commission MARKT/2010/02/C* (Berlin, 2011). Many local contracting authorities do, however, take account of SME participation and effects on local employment which lie at the intersection of the social and economic pillars.

[8] This chapter (as the book in general) focuses on the provisions contained in the new Public Sector Directive 2014/24/EU (hereafter 'the Directive') and leaves aside the special regimes for Concessions (Directive 2014/23/EU) and Utilities (Directive 2014/25/EU) – although many of the same provisions apply under those regimes.

[9] European Commission, *Proposal for a directive on public procurement*, COM (2011) 896 final, 20 December 2011, p. 2.

interest groups, the new Directive has been celebrated as 'a step forward for green and social public procurement',[10] 'good news for socially responsible public procurement'[11] and for introducing 'positive developments from the trade union perspective'.[12]

This chapter argues that even though the Directive provides notable opportunities for the promotion of social objectives through procurement procedures, its potential effect is undermined by the discretionary nature of most sustainability provisions. It illustrates how the large margin of discretion granted to Member States and contracting authorities threatens to undermine the effectiveness of the Directive's social clauses. A detailed analysis of the new 'horizontal clause', possible award criteria and the rules on subcontracting is followed by a reflection on how too much discretion in the use of social clauses can lead to legal uncertainty and a tendency amongst contracting authorities not to make use of such measures (Section 2).

The chapter proceeds by suggesting a mandatory approach to the inclusion of social considerations in public procurement procedures. It provides three arguments for such a mandatory approach: First, behind the background of the EU's objectives of fostering sustainable development and of serving as a 'social model' for other countries, respect for basic social standards and labour rights should be part of any procurement activity, not something left to the policy choice of the Member States or the contracting authorities. Second, regardless of whether one agrees with the argument made above: as soon as the normative choice to make use of public procurement to foster other objectives is made (as it is in the case of the new Directive), individual provisions should no longer deal with the question of *whether* such an approach is desirable, but regulate *how* it can be achieved effectively. Third, mandatory social standards are not contradictory to other procurement objectives: a mandatory approach can in fact aid simplification and transparency and contribute to single market aims by creating a level playing field (Section 3). Section 4 concludes the chapter with some reflections on the status quo and the way forward for socially responsible public procurement.

10 European Federation of Public Services Unions, *New EU Directive: a step forward for green and social public procurement*, see www.epsu.org/a/10125.

11 *New EU Directive: good news for socially responsible public procurement*, 29 January 2014, see http://electronicswatch.org/en/new-eu-directive-good-news-for-socially-responsible-public-procurement_24085.

12 ETUC, *New EU framework on public procurement. ETUC key points for the transposition of Directive 2014/24/EU* (2015), see www.etuc.org/sites/www.etuc.org/files/publication/files/ces-brochure_transpo_edited_03.pdf.

2. How discretion undermines the effectiveness of social clauses

As mentioned above, the references to social standards in the newly adopted Public Procurement Directives certainly provide for an *opportunity* to foster socially responsible purchasing decisions of public authorities and to balance economic, social and environmental aspects at the different stages of the procurement procedure. However, in spite of high expectations raised by the explicit objective in the Commission proposal to make greater strategic use of public procurement to further environmental and social policies,[13] the relevant provisions in the Directive contain few concrete obligations in this respect. Instead, the Directive relies to a great extent on the discretion of the Member States and contracting authorities to apply social criteria at the different stages of the procurement process, without being required to do so. Arguably, this discretionary approach undermines the effectiveness of the Directive's social provisions and runs counter to the objective of enhancing the strategic use of public procurement to further non-economic goals. This holds true in particular for the so-called 'horizontal clause', the use of the best price–quality ratio in the award of contracts and the provisions on subcontracting. All these provisions would benefit greatly from a mandatory approach, establishing minimum standards for the inclusion of social considerations in public procurement procedures.

2.1. The horizontal clause

Arguably the most important innovation in the Directive from a social and labour law perspective is the insertion of an overriding obligation of the Member States to take 'appropriate measures' to ensure that in the performance of public contracts the applicable environmental, social and labour law obligations are duly respected (Article 18(2)). In this context, the Directive refers to international, EU and national law, including collective agreements. The international standards to be followed are listed in Annex X to the Directive and include the eight ILO core conventions.[14]

[13] COM (2011) 896 final, 20 December 2011, p. 2.

[14] It has been criticised, however, that the list of relevant international conventions contained in Annex X is limited and does not contain several important conventions that form the cornerstone of social and employment provisions, such as the ILO Conventions on labour inspections (No. 81), on protection of wages (No. 95), on minimum standards of social security (No. 102), on employment policy (No. 122) and on occupational safety and health (No. 155). It is particularly notable that ILO Convention 94 on labour clauses in public contracts is not part of that list. See E. Van den Abeele, 'Integrating social and environmental dimensions in public procurement: one small step for the internal market, one giant leap for the EU?', *ETUI Working Paper*, 2014.08.

Recital 37 of the preamble to the Directive further strengthens the provision by underlining that it is of *particular importance* that Member States and contracting authorities take relevant measures to ensure compliance with applicable environmental, social and labour law in order to ensure the appropriate integration of such requirements into public procurement procedures.

Article 18(2) thus differs notably from the scarce references to social requirements in Directive 2004/18. Whereas the old Directive restricted itself to providing for a *possibility* for contracting authorities to lay down social and environmental obligations relating to the *performance* of a contract,[15] Article 18(2) is all-encompassing and legally binding for the Member States. The legally binding nature of the provision is significant, in particular considering the reluctance of the Council in the negotiation procedure to agree to such a horizontal clause. Moreover, whereas the application of social conditions was previously largely confined to the contract performance stage, the new Directive provides for compliance with minimum social standards and legislation at various stages of the procurement procedure. According to recital 40 of the preamble to the Directive, control of the observance of the environmental, social and labour law provisions should be performed at the relevant stages of the procurement procedure: when applying the general principles governing the choice of participants and the award of contracts, when applying the exclusion criteria and when applying the provisions concerning abnormally low tenders. In fact, the generally worded requirement contained in Article 18(2) is substantiated in other parts of the Directive, spelling out the ability and in some cases obligation to reject a tenderer, subcontractor or tender where they do not comply with the applicable obligations. The new Directive furthermore introduces an obligation on Member States to ensure respect for applicable working conditions of the place of work.[16] This is a major success for trade unions, who have long lobbied for an explicit recognition of the principle of equal treatment and respect for collective agreements at the workplace.

Article 18(2) thus features three major innovations in comparison with the old regime: it is legally binding and it establishes a principle of equal

[15] Art. 26 of Directive 2004/18/EC.

[16] In respect of services, recital 38 specifies that those should be considered to be provided at the place at which the characteristic performances are executed. Services provided at distance should be considered to be provided at the place where the services are executed, rather than the places to which the services are directed.

treatment at the workplace, at least in domestic situations.[17] However, a closer look at the provision raises doubts regarding its effectiveness in strengthening social and labour law principles in a procurement context. First of all, even though being in principle legally binding, Article 18(2) is formulated vaguely, depending essentially on national implementing measures in order to be applied and enforced effectively. The provision does not impose any obligation upon contracting authorities, but it is directed at the Member States. Even though it is stated in Recital 37 of the Preamble that Member States *and* contracting authorities are required to take measures to ensure that economic operators comply with applicable social and labour law provision, it follows from the legislative history of Article 18(2) that the legislator intentionally placed this responsibility in the hands of the Member States, so as to avoid imposing an excessive burden upon contracting authorities. This means that contracting authorities across the Union will be faced with divergent obligations depending on the implementing measures of the respective Member States. It is particularly problematic that Article 18(2) merely requires Member States to take 'appropriate measures' to ensure compliance with applicable social and labour law, without being more specific. Different interpretations of what is considered 'appropriate' at the national level could thus lead to vastly divergent implementing measures. Moreover, the fact that the provision is addressed to the Member States, rather than contracting authorities may have important implications in terms of enforcement. Whereas the Commission could bring an action against a Member State for non-compliance with Article 18(2), it is doubtful whether a private applicant could bring a case against a contracting authority under this heading.[18]

Since Article 18(2) does not prescribe any specific measures to be taken, a literal transposition of the provision into national law is likely to be of little effect in changing the status quo. This is because Article 18(2) does not by itself create any additional legal ground for the enforcement of the rules to which it refers; it simply clarifies that the Member States should seek to ensure compliance.[19] The effectiveness of the clause thus depends essentially on the willingness of the Member States to not only include

[17] See also ETUC, *New EU framework on public procurement. ETUC key points for the transposition of Directive 2014/24/EU* (2015), see www.etuc.org/sites/www.etuc.org/files/publication/files/ces-brochure_transpo_edited_03.pdf, pp. 9–11.

[18] Thanks to Abby Semple for making this point.

[19] A. Sánchez Graells, *How to crack a nut*, Blogpost, see http://howtocrackanut.blogspot.no/2014/09/cjeu-continues-reducing-scope-of.html.

in their national legislation the general principle of compliance with applicable social and labour law, but to ensure its actual application by spelling out specific enforcement measures. Recital 39 of the Preamble to the Directive indicates how such measures could look like by referring to contract clauses as well as to the possibility of considering non-compliance with the relevant obligations to be grave misconduct on the part of the economic operator concerned, liable to exclusion from the award of a public contract. It does not, however, impose any obligations in this respect upon the Member States.

Notwithstanding the argument made above, it is important to note that the horizontal clause is substantiated in other parts of the Directive, which spell out specific obligations of contracting authorities to ensure compliance with applicable social and labour laws. Yet, these obligations do not encompass *all* stages of the procurement process. In fact, they only apply to very specific situations and are not always mandatory. An obligation of contracting authorities to ensure compliance with applicable social and labour law provisions applies only in relation to subcontracting (Article 71(1), see Section 2.3 below) and to the rejection of abnormally low tenders, where the low price or cost is due to non-compliance with these laws.[20]

Contracting authorities *may* be required by Member States or *may* decide on their own initiative to exclude economic operators from participating in a public procurement procedure, where they can demonstrate by 'appropriate means' a violation of applicable social or labour law obligations.[21] In addition, contracting authorities have *discretion* not to award a contract to a tenderer, where the tender does not comply with the applicable social and labour law and collective agreements.[22] No mention of Article 18(2) is made at the stage of technical specifications (Article 42), even though this is a key stage in the procurement procedure, where the required characteristics of the work or service are defined.

Hence, in spite of the mandatory wording of Article 18(2), ensuring compliance with the applicable social and labour law/collective agreements is not explicitly required at the stage of technical specifications, is discretionary at the selection and award stage (unless a tender is found to be abnormally low due to non-compliance with applicable obligations) and is only mandatory with regards to subcontracting at the performance stage. Thus, whereas it follows from recital 40 of the preamble that

20 Art. 69(3) of the Directive.

21 Art. 57(4) of the Directive.

22 Art. 56(1) of the Directive.

Article 18(2) in principle applies to various stages of the procurement procedure, the Directive fails to spell out its mandatory effect at those stages and leaves it up to the Member States and contracting authorities to effectively apply mandatory social considerations when selecting/excluding economic operators, when defining technical specifications and award criteria and when monitoring performance with the contract.

Finally, as regards equal treatment, it is important to note that the Directive contains an exception to Article 18(2) for posted workers, where the principle of equal treatment must be applied in accordance with the Posted Workers Directive 96/71/EC. This is in particular relevant for the imposition of minimum wages and similar labour law provisions, where the conditions laid down in the *Rüffert* judgment[23] continue to apply. The Court held in that case that contracting authorities can only impose labour provisions on foreign undertakings if they are based either on statutory regulation or on universally binding collective agreements (rather than collective agreements that are not generally applicable).

Moreover, the CJEU recently clarified in the *Bundesdruckerei* case[24] that derogations from the application of domestic labour provisions may equally apply to public contracts, which are not governed by the rules on posted workers, but nevertheless involve the use of foreign employees. According to the Court, Article 56 TFEU precludes the application of a minimum wage requirement contained in the legislation of the Member State to which the contracting authority belongs to subcontractors established in another EU Member State. The Court did not *per se* rule out the imposition of minimum wage requirements in a public procurement context.[25] Rather, it dealt specifically with the application of minimum wage legislation on an extra-territorial basis to tenderers relying exclusively on workers in another Member State. Moreover, the Court actually confirmed that even in relation to subcontractors established in another Member State, the imposition of a minimum wage requirement could in principle be justified on the basis of the objectives of protecting employees and preventing social dumping, but that the measure was disproportionate in the case at hand.[26] Since the case was decided on the basis of the then

[23] Case C-346/06 *Rüffert* [2008] ECLI:EU:C:2008:189.

[24] Case C-549/13 *Bundesdruckerei* [2014], not yet reported.

[25] For a different opinion, see A. Sánchez Graells, *How to crack a nut*, Blogpost, see http://howtocrackanut.blogspot.no/2014/09/cjeu-continues-reducing-scope-of.html.

[26] The minimum wage requirement in *Bundesdruckerei* was considered disproportionate because it only applied to public sector contracts (not universally applicable) and bore no relation to the cost of living in the other Member State.

applicable Directive,[27] the Court does not mention Article 18(2). It will be interesting to see to what extent the horizontal provision will play a role in similar cases in the future.

The *Rüffert* and *Bundesdruckerei* cases not only limit the use of minimum wage requirements in cross-border tendering situations, they also raise questions concerning the possibility for Member States to comply with their obligations under ILO Convention 94 while consistently applying the case law of the Court.[28] It appears that Member States that observe the standards for labour clauses in public contracts contained in ILO Convention No 94 are in danger of violating EU public procurement rules[29] and vice versa. The Convention provides that all procurement contracts awarded by central public authorities must include clauses ensuring wages, hours of work and other conditions of labour which are no less favourable than those established for work of the same character in the trade or industry concerned, in the district where the work is carried out.

The potential conflict of Member States following the standards of ILO Convention No 94 with EU law, including for the three EFTA states that apply EU law through the European Economic Area (EEA) agreement,[30] is apparent from a letter sent to Norway by the EFTA Surveillance Authority (ESA) in the aftermath of the *Rüffert* judgment.[31] ESA challenged the Norwegian rules on pay and working conditions in public contracts that are based on the ILO Convention for non-compliance with the EEA rules on free provision of services and the Posted Workers Directive. This was primarily based on the Norwegian rules requiring compliance with rates of pay and other working conditions at least as favourable as those provided for by the applicable collective agreement, irrespective of whether it had been declared generally applicable or not. The regulation did thus

[27] The case concerned in particular an interpretation of Art. 26 of Directive 2004/18/EC (corresponding to Art. 70 of Directive 2014/24/EU).

[28] ILO Convention 94 has been ratified by Austria, Belgium, Bulgaria, Denmark, Finland, France, Italy, the Netherlands, Norway and Spain. See also N. Bruun, A. Jacobs and M. Schmidt, 'ILO Convention No. 94 in the aftermath of the Rüffert case', *European Review of Labour and Research*, 16(4) (2010), 473ff.

[29] In fact, the Swedish government was warned in 1998 by the DG Internal market that a ratification of ILO Convention 94 might be contrary to EU law on public procurement and posting of workers. See K. Ahlberg, 'Kommissionens tjänstemän varnar för ratifikation ILO-konvention hindrar konkurrens', *EU & arbetsrätt*, 1 (1998), 1.

[30] Being part of the provisions on the internal market, the EEA states are bound by EU rules on public procurement. See in particular Art. 65 (1) and Annex XVI of the EEA Agreement.

[31] Letter of formal notice to Norway for failure to ensure compliance with Art. 36 EEA and Directive 96/71/EC, 15 July 2009.

neither specify a minimum rate of pay, nor did it make direct reference to specific collective agreements that had been declared universally applicable. Moreover, the fact that the regulation applied only to public and not to private contracts was considered to constitute a restriction on the freedom to provide services that could not be justified on the basis of the objective of preventing social dumping and the protection of workers. In the light of the unresolved underlying question of a possible incompatibility of rules stemming from the ILO Convention and the EU procurement regime, it is surprising that the Convention is not mentioned at all in the new Directive.

Arguably, ILO Convention 94 establishes a general principle of law,[32] which should not only serve as a basis for the decisions of the CJEU in its case law, but should also be reflected in EU secondary legislation, in particular Directive 2014/24/EU. The Directive should explicitly allow contracting authorities to oblige economic operators to apply working and employment conditions not less favourable than those established in the trade or industry concerned in the place where the contract is carried out, and indicate that the Directive does not affect the application of ILO Convention No 94 or prevent a Member State from ratifying it.[33]

2.2. *Contract award criteria: the best price–quality ratio*

The use of award criteria relating to social, employment or environmental objectives can be a powerful tool for contracting authorities to promote sustainable development by giving preference to sustainable tenders. Moreover, award criteria can encourage tenderers to reach beyond established sustainability standards, thereby facilitating sustainable public procurement and constituting a driver for more sustainable markets.[34] In cases such as *Concordia Bus Finland*,[35] *EVN and*

[32] W. Däubler, *Sind die Mindestlohnvorgaben des TVgG NRW für öffentliche Auftragnehmer und deren Nachunternehmer mit dem Unionsrecht vereinbar?*, Rechtsgutachten im Auftrag des WSI, 20 January 2014, see www.boeckler.de/pdf/wsi_ta_rechtsgutachten_daeubler_2014.pdf.

[33] During the negotiations of the previously applicable Directive 2004/18/EC, the Swedish delegation already proposed this change, but it was opposed by the Commission and the UK delegation on the grounds that the implementation of ILO Conventions had to respect European law. See J.M. Hebly, *European public procurement – legislative history of the classic Directive 2004/18/EC* (Kluwer Law International, 2007), p. 313.

[34] ClientEarth, *Identifying opportunities for sustainable public procurement: award criteria*, (2011), p. 2.

[35] Case C-513/99 *Concordia Bus Finland* [2002] ECLI:EU:C:2002:495.

Wienstrom[36] and *Max Havelaar*,[37] the CJEU has confirmed that tenders may be compared and chosen on the basis of previously defined and weighted economic and quality award criteria, rather than by reference to price alone. Indeed, environmental or social considerations that are of importance to the contracting authority provide an indication of the quality of the tenders and are therefore crucial in determining best value for money.[38] Whereas most of the cases referred to above deal with environmental considerations, also social aspects of the sustainable development concept, which may concern the persons using or receiving the works, supplies or services or other persons, can be taken into account.[39]

The new Directive allows for the use of non-economic award criteria by referring to the 'best price–quality ratio'. Whilst price or cost is a mandatory element to be assessed by contracting authorities, they may in addition take into account qualitative criteria, which can include social, environmental and innovative characteristics.[40] Contracting authorities can thus decide to award contracts on the basis of price or cost alone,[41] or by combining those elements with qualitative criteria, including social criteria. This means that contracts are to be awarded under similar conditions than under the previously applicable regime (Directive 2004/18/EC), whilst mainly the wording has changed. The term 'most economically advantageous tender' (MEAT), which previously referred to an award decision based on a combination of economic and non-economic criteria, is now used in order to refer to the best solution from the point of view of the contracting authority, which may also include a contract award on the basis of price alone.[42] The new Directive is thus far from following the suggestion by the European Parliament to remove lowest price as an award criterion. The price of a product, service or work is in principle acceptable as the sole award criterion, whereas quality considerations must always be combined with a price element.

[36] Case C-448/01 *EVN and Wienstrom* [2003] ECLI:EU:C:2003:651.

[37] Case C-368/10 *Commission* v. *Kingdom of the Netherlands* ('*Max Havelaar*'), not yet reported.

[38] Case C-368/10 *Max Havelaar*, not yet reported, para 83.

[39] Ibid., para 85.

[40] Art. 67(2) of the Directive.

[41] As opposed to price, the cost of a product or service is based on a cost effectiveness approach, such as the use of life-cycle cost calculation. See Chapter 6 of this volume by Dacian C. Dragos and Bogdana Neamtu.

[42] The term 'best price–quality ratio' replaces the previously used expression 'most economically advantageous tender' (MEAT), which is now used in order to indicate the best solution for the contracting authority, including contracts awarded on the basis of price only and a combination of price and qualitative criteria.

Yet, the Directive does contain one major innovation: Member States may decide to forbid the use of lowest-price award, or to limit its use for certain categories of contracts or authorities. Moreover, the preamble to the Directive focuses on qualitative aspects by encouraging contracting authorities to choose award criteria that allow them to obtain high-quality works, supplies and services that are optimally suited to their needs.[43] Examples of such criteria include the social integration of disadvantaged persons or members of vulnerable groups,[44] the implementation of measures for the promotion of equality of women in the labour market, reconciliation of work and private life, compliance with fundamental ILO Conventions, recruitment of disadvantaged persons,[45] employment of long-term job-seekers and the implementation of training measures for unemployed or young persons and accessibility for disabled persons.[46] Award criteria may also relate to the qualification and experience of the staff assigned to performance of the contract.[47]

However, in addition to being limited by the requirement that any such criteria must be linked to the subject matter of the contract,[48] the application of qualitative award criteria remains completely discretionary. Also the option of abandoning the lowest price criterion, although encouraged as a way of ensuring 'a greater quality orientation of public procurement',[49] is entirely up to the discretion of the Member States. This is likely to lead to major differences in the Member States' procurement regimes. Whereas some countries, such as the Netherlands and Austria,[50] are already applying or are about to introduce legislation that makes the application of the best price–quality ratio mandatory, at least for certain types of contracts,

[43] Recital 92. [44] Recital 93. [45] Recital 98. [46] Recital 99.

[47] This is in particular the case where the performance of the contract is intellectual in nature, such as consultancy or architectural services, where the quality of the staff employed is relevant to the level of performance of the contract and, as a result, the economic value of the tender. See Art. 67(2) and recital 94 of the Directive and Case C-601/13 *Ambisig*, paras 31–4.

[48] See further Chapter 3 of this volume by Abby Semple. Interestingly, the production process used in the manufacture of a supplied good is specifically defined as linked to the subject matter of the contract (Art. 67(3) of the Directive).

[49] Recital 90.

[50] In the Netherlands, the 'most economically advantageous tender' (i.e. a combination of economic, social and environmental considerations) has become the standard award procedure. Awarding a contract on the basis of price or costs alone is only possible under exceptional circumstances and must be justified (see Art. 2.114 of the Procurement Law 2012 (*Aanbestedingswet* 2012)). The Austrian government is about to introduce an amendment to the Federal Procurement Act that will make use of the best price/quality ratio mandatory for construction contracts above EUR 1 million.

in other countries, such as Norway, the use of non-economic criteria in public procurement procedures is controversial.[51]

2.3. *Subcontracting*

The Directive's provisions on subcontracting are equally characterised by deference to national preferences and depend in their effectiveness to a large extent on the discretion of Member States and contracting authorities. Even though, as indicated above, Article 71(1) of the Directives requires that the mandatory social and labour law provisions referred to in Article 18(2) are to be observed by subcontractors, and that national authorities are responsible to guarantee compliance, it does not stipulate what kind of measures national authorities must take in order to do so. Similar to the vague wording of Article 18(2), the provision on subcontracting merely refers to 'appropriate action' by the competent authorities acting 'within the scope of their responsibility and remit'. The Directive thus again depends on national implementing measures to specify what kind of actions contracting authorities have to take in order to ensure subcontractors' compliance with social and labour law provisions.

Article 71(6) contains two examples of measures that are considered appropriate in this context, but does not oblige contracting authorities to apply them. These are (1) a system of joint and several liability throughout the subcontracting chain and (2) the application of the exclusion grounds provided for in Article 57 to subcontractors. Arguably, both types of measures are key mechanisms necessary to ensure compliance with applicable social and employment conditions and should be applied in all cases where Article 18(2) obligations are at stake. Yet, the discretionary wording of Article 71(6) is likely to result in considerable divergence across Member States and fails to guarantee an effective compliance with mandatory social and labour law by subcontractors. Moreover, a potential limitation to the effectiveness of Article 57 is that contractors and subcontractors are able to rely upon self-declarations in the first instance. The Directive provides for the mandatory acceptance of the self-declaration of candidates at the

[51] See the recommendation of the 'Simplification Committee' on 'Simpler rules – better procurement' to largely eliminate references to non-economic criteria from the public procurement regime as well as the attempt to reach a middle way by the Economic and Fisheries department (Forenklingsutvalget, *Enklere regler – bedre anskaffelser. Forenkling av det norske anskaffelsesregelverket*, NOU 2014:4, pp. 85–94; Nærings- og fiskeridepartementet, *Høring – endring av lov og forskrifter om offentlige anskaffelser*, see www.regjeringen.no/nb/dokumenter/horing--endring-av-lov-om-offentlige-anskaffelser/id2401043/).

time of tender submission as preliminary evidence for compliance with, *inter alia*, Article 18(2).[52] In practice this may lead to some non-compliant contractors/subcontractors obtaining public contracts. It should also be noted that Member States must specify the maximum period of exclusion based on prior non-compliance, which may not be longer than three years from the date of the relevant event (the demonstrated violation of Article 18(2)).[53]

Another significant challenge in the control of supply chains, in particular where a number of levels of subcontractors are involved, is a lack of transparency over these subcontractors, their working practices and their adherence to social and labour law standards. The Directive provides Member States and contracting authorities with an opportunity to further transparency and oversight of the subcontracting chain, but contains few obligations in this respect. In respect of certain types of contracts, the contracting authorities are obliged to require the main contractor to indicate the name, contact details and legal representative of its subcontracts and to notify any changes to this information during the course of the contract.[54] However, apart from the fact that this obligation is only relevant for works contracts and services to be provided at a facility under the direct oversight of the contracting authority,[55] it starts to apply only *after* the award of the contract or even as late as the start of performance and is limited to information known by the main contractor at 'this point of time'. This is problematic in so far as contracting authorities ought to have an overview over the amount of subcontracting involved in a tender when awarding the contract, not least in view of their obligation to ensure compliance with mandatory social and labour law. It is also possible, but by no means obligatory, to request at the selection stage evidence of the supply chain management measures that the main contractor will be able to put in place.[56]

It is, up to national authorities (at Member State or contracting authority level) to decide on whether they wish to oblige the tenderer to indicate already in its tender the share of the contract it intends to subcontract and any proposed subcontractors.[57] Moreover, it appears that the obligation applies only to the direct subcontractor of the main

52 Art. 59(1) of the Directive.

53 Art. 57(7) of the Directive.

54 Art. 71(5) of the Directive.

55 The Member States or contracting authorities may, however, decide to extend the obligation to other types of contracts, such as supply contracts and other types of service contracts.

56 Annex XII, Part II (d) of Directive 2014/24/EU.

57 Art. 71(2) of the Directive.

subcontractor, as extending the information requirement further down the subcontracting chain is discretionary.[58]

Member States are allowed to go further than what is specified in the Directive, for instance by extending the transparency obligations, by enabling direct payment to subcontractors or by enabling or requiring contracting authorities to verify that subcontractors are not in any of the situations in which exclusion of economic operators would be warranted.[59] However, they are at the same time permitted to limit the applicability of information and enforcement requirements in respect of certain types of contracts, certain categories of contracting authorities or economic operators or as of certain amounts.[60]

The effectiveness of the Directive's provision on subcontracting in furthering transparency and ensuring compliance with mandatory social and labour law will thus to a great extent depend on national implementing measures as well as on decisions taken by individual contracting authorities. First indications from national discussions on the transposition of Directive 2014/24/EU indicate that the Member States are likely to take vastly divergent perspectives on this. Whereas Austria, for instance, has recently introduced relatively strict rules in relation to the involvement and nomination of subcontractors, requiring full disclosure of all proposed subcontractors during the tender procedure,[61] the UK Cabinet Office has chosen not to impose any new information obligations on subcontractors, or on main contractors in relation to their subcontractors, as such requirements are considered to limit flexibility.[62]

2.4. *The consequences of discretion*

The preceding analysis of the most important provisions from a social and labour law perspective in the new Directive show that the potential effectiveness of the relevant social clauses depends to a large extent upon

[58] Art. 71(5)(b). [59] Recital 105 of the preamble. [60] Art. 71(8).

[61] J. Stalzer, *Austria: fair procurement – initiative requires MEAT as sole award criterion for construction contracts*, see www.schoenherr.eu/knowledge/knowledge-detail/austria-fair-procurement-initiative-requires-meat-as-sole-award-criterion-for-construction-cont/.

[62] The Public Contracts Regulations 2015, which implement the 2014 EU Public Sector Procurement Directive entered into force on 26 February 2015. With regard to subcontractors (Section 6), the UK has chosen not to make it compulsory for contracting authorities to ask bidders to indicate in their proposal the share of the contract they may intend to subcontract and to provide the details of any subcontractors or to make the main contractor directly obliged to provide information about its subcontractors and supply chain, other than in the situations where this is required by Directive 2014/24/EU.

the discretion of national authorities. This is likely to lead to enormous diversity amongst the Member States in their sustainable procurement regime. Even though a certain degree of national divergence is acceptable and perhaps even desirable, major differences in the regulation of social criteria in the award of public contracts will arguably lead to an inherently complex regime liable to run counter to simplification objectives and preventing the establishment of a level playing field.

Already before the transposition of the new Directive, purchasing authorities in the Member States differed widely in both the extent to which social clauses were used and their legal form. A study carried out in 2007 revealed that certain Member States (Belgium, France, the Netherlands and Sweden) had adopted high-profile national policies aimed at encouraging purchasing linked to the pursuit of a range of environmental and social goals.[63] Others had left such activities to subnational levels of government (Germany), taken the path of facilitation rather than positive encouragement (Italy) or expressed commitments to labour standards in terms of compliance with prevailing standards where the work was to be carried out.[64] Moreover, differences exist not only between Member States, but may also exist at the regional level, such as in Germany, where the Federal States (*Bundesländer*) have individual procurement laws, which are highly divergent regarding the number and type of social criteria as well as their mode of regulation.[65] As indicated above, evidence from national discussions on the transposition of the horizontal clause, award criteria and subcontracting confirms the likelihood of widely divergent implementing measures.

The uncertainty and lack of knowledge resulting from this diversity of rules has led to a situation where contracting authorities are reluctant to make use of social considerations. Evidence from the Netherlands on tendering in the phones, natural stone, coffee and work clothing sectors shows that, in spite of a relatively strong emphasis on socially responsible public procurement at the national level, the majority of tenders do not make use of any social criteria whatsoever.[66] Considering

[63] Public World, *EU public procurement regulations and core labour standards: a report for DFID*, (2007), see www.publicworld.org/files/dfid2007.pdf.

[64] See also the comparative study by T. Schulten, K. Alsos, P. Purgess and K. Pedersen, *Pay and other social clauses in European public procurement* (2012), see www.boeckler.de/pdf/wsi_schulten_pay_and_other_social_causes.pdf.

[65] For an overview see E.K. Sarter, D. Sack and S. Fuchs, 'Public procurement as social policy? An introduction to social criteria in public procurement in Germany', *Hans Böckler Stiftung: Working Paper Series Comparative Governance* (2014).

[66] G. ten Kate, 'A review of Dutch policy for socially responsible public procurement', *SOMO Paper* (March 2014), see www.uzp.gov.pl/cmsws/page/GetFile1.aspx?attid=8077.

the predominant focus on free competition by the Union institutions and the Court, economic criteria for awarding a contract are mostly considered as the 'safest' options in order to prevent complex assessment procedures and future legal challenges. Contracting authorities thus resort to a 'precautionary principle' as the use of social criteria and conditions is considered complex and time-consuming and bears the risk of delay caused by a judicial procedure.[67]

3. A mandatory approach towards socially responsible public procurement

Suggesting a mandatory approach towards socially responsible public procurement has been tantamount to breaking a taboo. The mantra that the 'primary' objectives of EU procurement rules are to guarantee the free movement of goods and the free provision of services in the EU internal market as well as to ensure the non-discrimination against tenderers and contractors from other Member States, and the dominance of financial and competition authorities in the implementation and supervision of EU procurement law (with only a marginal involvement of labour ministries),[68] has made it difficult to argue for mandatory observance of social requirements. Social considerations are often considered to be contradictory to the economically inspired objectives of the EU procurement regime. Mandatory provisions are seen as an excessive burden for contracting authorities, limiting their flexibility and requiring a disproportionate amount of resources and know-how. Considering the reluctance of many stakeholders, especially business, to the idea of using public procurement in support of social policy objectives,[69] it is therefore not surprising that the new Directives fall short of embracing a mandatory approach.[70]

Before going into three arguments for the use of a mandatory approach, it is important to underline that not all types of criteria that contracting authorities can possibly use should have a mandatory character.

[67] For examples from Sweden, Germany and Denmark, see N. Bruun and K. Ahlberg, 'Public procurement and labour rights: governing by scaremongering', in S. Evju (ed.), *Regulating transnational labour in Europe: the quandaries of multilevel governance* (Privatrettsfondet, 2014), pp. 263–79.

[68] N. Bruun and K. Ahlberg, 'Public procurement and labour rights: governing by scaremongering', pp. 263–79.

[69] European Commission, *Green Paper on the modernization of EU public procurement policy: towards a more efficient European Procurement Market*, Synthesis of replies (2011), p. 7.

[70] A. Semple, 'Mixed offerings for sustainability in a new European Union procurement directive', *Public Procurement Law Review*, 21 (2012), 106–8.

Contracting authorities should primarily be obliged (1) to secure that contractors and subcontractors delivering products or carrying out works or services on their behalf comply with elementary social and labour rights and (2) to combine economic, social and environmental elements in their procurement decisions. The latter obligation implies that EU law should explicitly ban the use of price-only and cost-only assessment, or at the very least restrict it to specific cases such as highly standardised products which do not leave room for quality assessment.[71]

Conversely, the weighting and balancing of economic considerations (price) and qualitative criteria should lie within the discretion of the contracting authority, as long as the possibility to rely on price alone is ruled out. Moreover, where and to what extent contracting authorities make use of different types of social considerations that go beyond minimum standards at the various stages of the procurement procedure should remain optional. The Directive contains a number of different possibilities in this respect, all of which can be used separately or in combination. This includes the possibility to require social characteristics as technical specifications, as long as they are linked to the subject matter of the contract and proportionate to its value and objectives,[72] the possibility to require a specific social label in the technical specifications, the award criteria or the contract performance conditions[73] and the possible inclusion of social considerations in the conditions for performance of the contract.[74]

3.1. *The EU as a social model and a sustainable market economy*

Given the EU's objectives of fostering sustainable development of being a social market economy and of serving as a social model for other countries, respect for basic social standards and labour rights should be part of any procurement activity, not left to the policy choice of the Member States or the contracting authorities. In addition to a number of sustainability provisions in the EU Treaties,[75] EU economic strategies aim at 'sustainable economic growth with more and better jobs and greater social cohesion'[76] and at becoming a 'smart, sustainable and inclusive economy'.[77] Such

[71] Irish Congress of Trade Unions, *Response to the public consultation on public procurement*, (December 2014), see www.ictu.ie/download/pdf/public_procurement_response_to_consultation.pdf.

[72] Art. 42. [73] Art. 43. [74] Art. 70.

[75] See Chapter 1 of this volume by Beate Sjåfjell and Anja Wiesbrock.

[76] Lisbon European Council 23 and 24 March 2000, Presidency Conclusions, point 5.

[77] European Commission Communication, *Europe 2020: a strategy for smart, sustainable and inclusive growth*, COM (2010) 2020 final (3 March 2010).

objectives are also reflected in the preamble to Directive 2014/24/EU, which emphasises the importance of fully exploiting the potential of public procurement to achieve the objectives of the Europe 2020 strategy for smart, sustainable and inclusive growth.[78]

Even though the EU public procurement rules are aimed at guaranteeing the free movement of goods and services in the EU internal market, it would be misguided to narrowly construe the objective of the EU procurement rules as being limited to fulfilling economic purposes of a strictly commercial nature.[79] Instead, the focus on sustainability requires by definition an integrated approach, taking into account economic, social and environmental objectives when designing and implement procurement policies. It is in the long run impossible to ensure sustainable economic growth without taking the social and employment dimension into account. Social progress and social solidarity must thus form an integral part of the European approach to competitiveness. Hence, the EU's self-perception as a social market economy that aims at sustainable growth warrants a proper balancing of economic, social and environmental objectives in procurement procedures as well as the establishment of certain mandatory minimum standards.

The importance of balancing economic and social considerations in procurement procedures in order to foster sustainable growth has long been recognised by the European Commission, which stated already in 1993 that public procurement should be targeted to promote sustainable growth.[80] In its 2010 'Buying Social Guide', the Commission emphasised the complementarity of the EU objectives of achieving best value for money and of using public procurement to support common societal goals.[81] Moreover, the claim of representing a unique social model that successfully combines economic and social principles has dominated EU discourse for at least a decade. According to the European Commission, a socially responsible procurement policy must be seen as an instrument to foster the European social model as a vision of society that combines sustainable economic growth with improved living and working conditions.[82] Strong and effective provisions on controlling and

[78] Recital 95, see also recital 123.

[79] See also R. Nielsen, 'EU public procurement law and nordic labour law – recent developments and future challenges', in P. Wahlgren (ed.), *What is Scandinavian law?: social private law* (Stockholm Institute for Scandinavian Law, 2007), pp. 185–220.

[80] COM (93) 700 final.

[81] European Commission, *Buying social: a guide to taking account of social considerations in public procurement* (European Commission, 2010).

[82] Ibid., p. 10.

safeguarding fair working conditions along the supply chain are particularly important in the light of the EU's self-perception of presenting a successful 'social model' that can serve as an example for third countries.

In spite of this, the European Commission and the Council[83] have up to now, including in the new Directive, failed to recognise the importance of including certain minimum social standards in public procurement legislation in order to contribute effectively to the objective of sustainable economic growth in a social market economy. Moreover, leaving the discretion on whether or not to award contracts on the basis of a price–quality ratio, to contracting authorities or Member States effectively means that many contracting authorities are likely to prefer the simplicity of economic considerations, to the detriment of social and environmental objectives, unless this is ruled out at the national level.

In this respect, the Directive clearly represents a missed opportunity. An effective and truly mandatory horizontal clause, an obligation to award contracts on the basis of the best price–quality ratio and strong provisions on transparency and monitoring in subcontracting could have potentially boosted the impact of public procurement rules on sustainability objectives, without compromising economic growth.[84] Moreover, ensuring the effective implementation and enforcement of mandatory labour rights would have sent an important message to the Member States as well as to third countries of the strength of the European social model, counteracting recent challenges to Social Europe resulting from the consequences of the Viking/Laval series of judgments and the impact of the Eurozone crisis.[85]

3.2. The normative choice of using public contracting to reach socio-economic objectives

Even though it might be controversial whether and to what extent public contracting should be used as a means to encourage companies to design their activities in conformity with socio-economic objectives, it appears that this value judgment has already been made with the adoption of

[83] The European Parliament has largely embraced and contributed positively to the inclusion of non-economic considerations in the new Directive.

[84] See also below Section 3.3.

[85] A. Hug, 'Introduction', in A. Hug and O. Tudor (eds), *Single market, equal rights? UK perspectives on EU employment and social law* (The Foreign Policy Centre, 2012), p. 6. See also Chapter 2 of this volume by Suzanne Kingston.

the new Procurement Directives. Recital 2 of the Preamble of Directive 2014/24/EU makes it crystal clear that a major objective of the new regime is to 'make better use of public procurement in support of common societal goals'. Moreover, Recital 91 provides that the Directive clarifies *how* the contracting authorities can contribute to the protection of the environment and the promotion of sustainable development, rather than leaving open the question of *whether* such an approach is desirable.

Arguably, the EU institutions have taken the decision to make use of public procurement in order to foster social and environmental objectives. This normative choice should accordingly be reflected in the provisions of the Directive. This implies that the discretion of the contracting authorities and Member States within the context of the Directive should be limited to the question of how and to what extent they wish to integrate social considerations in public procurement procedures. The choice of *whether* to pursue such an approach has been taken at the EU level and should no longer be left in the hands of national authorities. Even though a contrasting perspective might emphasise that the Directive aims primarily at facilitating rather than mandating socially procurement, in light of the major EU objective to foster the strategic use of public procurement, Member States and contracting authorities should no longer be able to completely disregard non-economic considerations in public procurement procedures.

Hence, compliance with international and national social and labour law standards – whether contained in legislation or collective agreements – should be non-negotiable and made a compulsory factor at all stages of the procurement procedure. The obligations of contracting authorities to this effect should be stated clearly in the various provisions of the Directive, rather than depending on Member States or contracting authorities to guarantee their effectiveness. Moreover, contracting authorities should be obliged to integrate social considerations into their award decisions, while continuing to decide on the type and the weighting of economic, environmental and social criteria to be used.

3.3. *Simplification, transparency and competitive tendering*

Finally, mandatory social standards are not contradictory to other procurement objectives: a mandatory approach can in fact aid simplification and transparency and contribute to single market aims by creating a level playing field. Contrary to the perception that the need for simplification provides an argument against the furtherance of social and environmental factors, enhancing sustainability criteria does not necessarily lead to a more complex and costly procurement regime.

When sustainability considerations are stated clearly and formulated as requirements for contracting authorities, they do not lead to a more complicated regime, but can actually simplify the procurement process. It will be much easier for economic operators across the EU to understand and comply with relevant social and labour law standards if those are included as minimum mandatory clauses in all Member States and at all stages of the procurement procedure. An example of simplification resulting from clear and unambiguous mandatory standards can be found in the rules on subcontracting of the state of Belize. It is stated in the Belize Labour Act that 'a subcontractor shall be bound in all cases to conform to the conditions of the main contract and the main contractor shall be responsible for the observance of all contract conditions on the part of the subcontractors'.[86] In contrast to the long and complicated provisions on subcontracting contained in the EU Directive, the Belize Labour Act simply demands that main contractors take responsibility for the observance of all contract conditions by its subcontractors, including labour and social requirements. Even though this obligation does not explicitly contain an information requirement, contractors are bound to guarantee transparency along the supply chain in their own interest. Such a relatively broad wording that nonetheless prescribes responsibility of the main contractor for all actions related to performance of the contract along the supply chain leaves room for further implementing measures at the national level that take account of national rules on joint liability and so forth.

The abandonment of the use of the lowest price as the sole award criterion would also simplify the current regime, albeit that this deprives contracting authorities of the possibility to completely disregard the environmental and social implications of a tendering procedure. Taking away the lowest-price option means that contracting authorities will no longer have to choose between divergent award procedures, but should rather in all cases award a contract on the basis of a combination of economic, social and environmental considerations. The advantages of such an approach become apparent when looking at the 2012 Procurement Law of the Netherlands, which provides for the application of a standard award procedure, which combines economic, social and environmental elements in all cases. Awarding a contract on the basis of price or costs alone is

[86] Art. 143(1) Belize Labour Act (Cap. 297), revised edn 2000.

only possible under exceptional circumstances and must be justified.[87] As mentioned above, Member States have the possibility to introduce such a simplified regime that provides for a single award procedure combining economic and qualitative criteria when implementing the Directive.

Moreover, the introduction of social clauses is not necessarily detrimental to internal market or economic objectives. There has long been an awareness that certain working conditions have to be guaranteed in order to secure a frictionless and satisfying completion of public orders.[88] Social requirements are thus not an alien factor within procurement, but are inherent to economic considerations, as the quality of the work or service supplied is closely linked to the quality of working conditions.[89] Consequently, the question of whether or not the goods, services or works to be supplied were purchased and produced on the basis of fair working conditions can be an important factor in determining best value for money.[90]

Moreover, the mandatory observance of certain social and labour standards in the performance of public contracts can contribute to creating a level playing field. As pointed out by the European Working Group on Ethical Public Procurement, the current rules make it possible for suppliers to achieve unfair competitive advantages through the abuse of human rights and the practice of indecent working conditions, which allows them to offer a lower price than suppliers operating in compliance with national and international labour legislation.[91] The Commission itself has highlighted that socially responsible procurement can help create a level playing field by influencing the marketplace in order to give companies real incentives to develop socially responsible management.[92] It can contribute to developing a market in socially beneficial products and serve as a model for other consumers and companies. Mandatory social standards can thus contribute to simplification and internal market objectives by

[87] See Art. 2.114 of the Procurement Law (Aanbestedingswet) 2012.

[88] T. Schulten, K. Alsos, P. Purgess and K. Pedersen, *Pay and other social clauses in European public procurement* (2012).

[89] See also C. McCrudden, 'Using public procurement to achieve social outcomes', *Natural Resources Forum*, 28 (2004), 257–67.

[90] To this effect see also the opinion of AG Kokott in the *Max Havelaar* Case C-368/10, delivered on 15 December 2011.

[91] European Working Group on Ethical Public Procurement, *Proposals for a European Commission strategy on socially responsible public procurement*, see https://noharm-europe.org/Proposal_for_a_EU_strategy_on_Socially_Responsible_Public_Procurement_final.pdf.

[92] European Commission, *Buying social: a guide to taking account of social considerations in public procurement* (European Commission, 2010), p. 5.

allowing for the formulation of simple and transparent rules setting clear and unambiguous minimum standards, and by creating a level playing field that constitutes the basis for free and fair competition.

4. Concluding Remarks

The argument that an effective observance of social and labour standards in public procurement procedures requires mandatory provisions is not new. Indeed, the European Parliament stated in 2011 in its resolution on the modernisation of public procurement that 'the effective functioning of sustainable public procurement requires *clear and unambiguous* EU rules precisely defining the framework of Member States' legislation and implementation'.[93] Awareness of the benefits of mandatory standards from a social and economic perspective is, however, to date not reflected in the EU legal framework.

The new Directive provides opportunities to public authorities to achieve sustainable development objectives when they buy goods, services and works from external parties, but the relevant provisions are likely to have a limited practical effect on purchasing decisions due to the large amount of discretion granted to Member States and contracting authorities. A mandatory approach would have been preferable for several reasons including the self-perception of the EU as social model and sustainable market economy, the importance of effectively ensuring compliance with minimum standards once the value judgment of using public procurement to promote non-economic objectives is made, and the potential of mandatory social standards to contribute to simplification and internal market aims.

However, despite the absence of truly mandatory elements, Directive 2014/24/EU does constitute an important opportunity to allow for a greater consideration of social considerations in public procurement procedures. It is now up to the Member States to make use of this opportunity and to provide for precise and enforceable environmental, social and labour provisions when they implement the Directive in national laws.

[93] European Parliament resolution of 25 October 2011 on the modernisation of public procurement (2011/2048(INI)), paras 14 and 19.

5

Labels as enablers of sustainable public procurement

ROBERTO CARANTA

Whether and to what extent environmental and social considerations may be taken into account and, in particular, reference may be made to environmental and fair trade labels, is a question of fundamental importance for the further development of the public procurement law. In giving its answer, the Court is faced with the challenge of finding an equitable balance between the requirements of the internal market and environmental and social concerns, without, however, ignoring the practical requirements of award procedures. On the one hand, there can be no discrimination between potential tenderers or partitioning of markets. On the other hand, contracting authorities must be allowed to procure environmentally friendly, organic and fair trade products without excessive administrative burdens.

AK Kokott, conclusions to Case C-368/10, *Commission* v. *Netherlands*, paragraph 3

1. Introduction

In March 2015, I was travelling to Cardiff to attend the 2015 Procurement Week, a yearly not-to-be-missed event organised by Bangor University. I was flying KLM and served a sandwich. Airplane food, but not bad considering what you normally get. And labelled. The package bore a number of labels: that of 'Green palm' for sustainable palm oil;[1] that of 'Caring dairy' on sustainable farming;[2] the one specific to the cheese used (Beemster) which is itself 'Caring Dairy' labelled;[3] the one stressing the strive of KLM towards sustainability – KLM takes care.[4] And of course the package itself was made of paper from sustainable forestry and bore the Forest Stewardship Council – FSC label.[5]

[1] See http://greenpalm.org/. [2] See www.benjerry.com/caringdairy/.
[3] See www.beemster.ca/en-us/the-beemster-story/premium-gourmet-dutch-cheese/.
[4] See https://klmtakescare.com/. [5] See https://ic.fsc.org/fsc-certification.4.htm.

While this is somewhat reminiscent of the proud chests of Soviet era generals brimming with medals, my sandwich bears witness to how important labels have become. Labels are information shortcuts. Through a symbol, maybe a few words, they convey the message that a given product or service present a number of valuable characters.[6] This may include desirable environmental or sustainability features (eco-labels) concerning the product or service itself and its life cycle.[7]

In a way, labels are visual symbols standing for certificates. As such labels are especially useful today given the information overload we all are experiencing thanks to the media and the internet. They may act as powerful enablers of consumers' choices.[8] Indeed, eco-labels may 'provide consumers with information about the environmental costs of food choices, resulting in changes in consumer preferences and buying practices'.[9]

The information provided often refers to what in the public procurement jargon are known as technical specifications and award criteria.[10] Social labels are usually more about the contractor than about just the goods or services which are the subject matter of the contract, so that may be linked to management schemes. They may also deal with the way the contract is implemented, and as such may be treated as contract performance conditions.[11] In other words, labels may potentially provide information as to all aspects of the life cycle of what is being bought. For instance, '[a]n effective environmental life-cycle eco-labelling system for food would inform consumers about the environmental costs of their food purchases'.[12]

Not normally having an 'official' imprimatur – meaning not corresponding to a certification from a State or an international institution – labels do often represent different and possibly competing standards at

[6] M. Cetik, 'Do Europe's product labels converge? The case of EU ecolabel, EU energy label and CE marking', *TILEC Discussion Paper*, see http://dx.doi.org/10.2139/ssrn.1949080.

[7] M. Cetik, 'Do Europe's product labels converge?', 3.

[8] See, specifically concerning foodstuff, J.J. Czarnezki, *Everyday environmentalism, law, nature and individual behavior* (Environmental Law Institute, 2011), Chapter 4; see also D. Wilsher, 'Reconciling national autonomy and trade integration in the context of eco-labelling', in S. Arrowsmith and P. Kunzlik (eds), *Social and environmental policies in EC procurement law* (Cambridge University Press, 2009), p. 408.

[9] J.J. Czarnezki, 'The future of food eco-labelling: organic, carbon footprint, and environmental life-cycle analysis', *Stanford Environmental Law Journal*, 30 (2011), 5; critically B. Neamtu and D.C. Dragos, 'Sustainable public procurement: the use of eco-labels', *European Procurement & Public Private Partnership Law Review*, 2 (2015), 100.

[10] D. Wilsher, 'Reconciling national autonomy and trade integration in the context of eco-labelling', p. 408.

[11] Case C–368/10 *Commission* v. *Netherlands* [2012] ECLI:EU:C:2012:284.

[12] J.J. Czarnezki, 'The future of food eco-labelling', 39.

international, regional and national level[13] – not to mention so-called 'first-party' or 'self-declared' labels which do not correspond to any third-party independent certification scheme.[14] As it has been remarked, 'eco-labelling schemes have grown enormously at national level over the last thirty years'.[15] Further differentiation may be due to different coverage of the various labels, so much so that energy labels may be considered as crypto-eco-labels even if they may also be taken to indicate more limited operation costs: not only energy savings translated into money savings but also the other way round.[16]

Diversity is not in itself a bad thing since harmonisation tends to stifle innovation in fast-moving areas.[17] The risk is, however, that specific labels are referred to by the contracting authorities with the intention or at least the result of distorting competition. Adding to diversity, in fact, manufacturers and providers are usually not under a legal obligation to have their products and services labelled,[18] and may choose not to have them to save the costs and hassles coming with a certification process.[19]

This chapter will discuss how contracting authorities and entities may refer to labels in their procurement documents. The law as it was until the judgment in the *Max Havelaar* case will be analysed first (Section 2). The provisions in the 2014 Directives will be examined next (Section 3), while Section 4 concludes the chapter.

2. The law up to *Max Havelaar*

When writing about sustainable public procurement under EU law, different bodies of rules must be taken into account.[20] The first is obviously

[13] See A. Semple, *A practical guide to public procurement* (Oxford University Press, 2015), 7.032; see also the classification in B. Neamtu and D.C. Dragos, 'Sustainable public procurement', 94f.

[14] J.J. Czarnezki, A. Homan and M. Jeans, 'Greenwashing & self-declared seafood eco-label', see http://dx.doi.org/10.2139/ssrn.2421530.

[15] D. Wilsher, 'Reconciling national autonomy and trade integration in the context of eco-labelling', p. 412.

[16] Cfr. the discussion in M. Cetik, 'Do Europe's product labels converge?', 4f.

[17] D. Wilsher, 'Reconciling national autonomy and trade integration in the context of eco-labelling', p. 412.

[18] B. Neamtu and D.C. Dragos, 'Sustainable public procurement', 94; M. Cetik, 'Do Europe's product labels converge?', 6.

[19] 'Self-labelling' could however land them in troubles when this involves unsubstantiated claims; see, with reference to the US experience, J.J. Czarnezki, A. Homan and M. Jeans, 'Greenwashing & self-declared seafood eco-label', 7ff.

[20] See A. Semple, *A practical guide*, especially table 7.1. therein with a full list of relevant legislation, and (also referring to soft law instruments) D.C. Dragos and B. Neamtu,

made up of the Public or Classic Sector, Utilities and (today) Concessions Directives. Other pieces of legislation may however have to be considered as well. Regulation (EC) No 66/2010 on the EU Eco-label is relevant here, as well as Regulation (EU) No 174/2013 amending Regulation (EC) No 106/2008 on a Community energy-efficiency labelling programme for office equipment, and Directive 2012/27/EU on energy efficiency.[21] The latter is a framework directive, meaning that it sets out the aims, functions and common principles but the specific details are enacted by the Commission through delegated regulations.[22] The legislation making up the EU's second body of rules is not public procurement specific in that it applies to all products, including those used for private consumption, and as such it is also relevant in buying decisions of contracting authorities and entities.[23]

A main feature of EU public procurement rules on eco-labels is that contracting authorities and entities are free to decide whether or not to refer to labels. This corresponds to a general pattern in EU sustainable public procurement law, which is to be seen rather as enabler than a set of mandatory standards.[24] This approach was discussed in the *Green Paper on the modernisation of EU public procurement policy: towards a more efficient European Procurement Market.*[25] The 2014 Directives, however, still cling to it. The important differences between individual sectors and markets were considered to make it inappropriate to set general mandatory requirements for environmental, social and innovation procurement.[26] It

'Sustainable public procurement in the EU: experiences and prospects', in F. Lichère, R. Caranta and S. Treumer (eds), *Modernising public procurement: the new directive* (DJØF Publishing, 2014), 308ff.; also refer to R. Caranta, 'Sustainable procurement', in M. Trybus, R. Caranta and G. Edelstam (eds), *EU public contract law: public procurement and beyond* (Bruylant, 2014), 168f.

21 A. Semple, *A practical guide*, para 7.07; see also the Commission guide, *Buying green! A handbook on green public procurement*, 2nd edn (2011), p. 6.

22 See the analysis by P. Kunzlik, 'The procurement of "green" energy', in S. Arrowsmith and P. Kunzlik (eds), *Social and environmental policies in EC procurement law*, 381f., and T. Touminen, 'Green public procurement and eco-labels', see https://doria.fi/bitstream/handle/10024/76638/Tuominen.Tomi.pdf?sequence=1, 43.

23 See M. Cetik, 'Do Europe's product labels converge?', 11ff.

24 See also Recital 95 of Directive 2014/24/EU; see the discussion by S. Arrowsmith and P. Kunzlik, 'Public procurement and horizontal policies in EC law: general principles', in S. Arrowsmith and P. Kunzlik (eds), *Social and environmental policies in EC procurement law*, 37ff.

25 COM (2011) 15 final.

26 For arguments promoting a mandatory approach, see Chapter 4 of this volume by Anja Wiesbrock.

was thought better to leave it to sector-specific legislation to set mandatory objectives and targets, while at the same time promoting the development and use of European approaches to life-cycle costing.[27]

The main exception to this pattern is provided by the already recalled Regulation (EU) No 174/2013 amending Regulation (EC) No 106/2008 on a Community energy-efficiency labelling programme for office equipment. Under Article 6(1), central government authorities as defined under Directive 2004/18/EC shall specify energy-efficiency requirements not less demanding than the Common Specifications laid down following the procedure foreseen in the same regulation. Contracting authorities at regional and local level shall be encouraged by Member States to use those requirements.

The possibility to refer to labels was anticipated in Recital 29 of Directive 2004/18/EC, the old Public Sector Directive. The recital introduced the rules on technical specifications, the main concern being that public procurements are opened up to competition. In this framework, contracting authorities were expressly allowed to define environmental requirements for the technical specifications by referring to such characteristics as 'a given production method, and/or specific environmental effects of product groups or services'. The recital also made clear that contracting authorities were allowed (but not obliged) to use appropriate specifications 'defined in eco-labels, such as the European eco-label, (multi-)national eco-labels or any other eco-label'. In having an open-ended list, the recital bears witness to the large and varied nature of eco-labels available in Europe. At the same time, it anticipates the conditions under which label requirements were acceptable under EU law, namely they were drawn up and adopted on the basis of scientific information using a procedure in which stakeholders had the opportunity to participate; moreover, the label had to be accessible and available to all interested parties.

Article 23(6) of Directive 2004/18/EC did not do much to turn into rhyme what the recital had in prose. More specifically the provisions recalled the conditions making the reference to an 'other' eco-label appropriate. This can be considered as an example of regulatory overkill. Since, as it will be shown, contracting authorities were not empowered to refer to the eco-label directly, but rather to specific requirements covered in the label, it is doubtful whether its participatory nature or openness were

[27] Recital 95 of Directive 2014/24/EU and Recital 100 of Directive 2014/25/EU.

relevant.[28] What was indeed relevant was the need for the requirements for the label to be 'drawn up on the basis of scientific information'.[29] This was linked to the general EU law requirement of objectivity of the criteria spelt out by the contracting authority, which was reaffirmed – albeit with reference to award criteria – in the well-known *Concordia Bus* case.[30] The Court of Justice upheld *'objectively quantifiable environmental requirements' which do not 'confer an unrestricted freedom of choice on the contracting authority'*.[31]

The requirement of objectivity was elaborated upon in the EVN case which was about the supply of energy, preferably from renewable sources.[32] Here again the case concerned award criteria, but the Court of Justice made clear that 'the procedure for awarding a public contract must comply, *at every stage*, with both the principle of the equal treatment of potential tenderers and the principle of transparency so as to afford all parties equality of opportunity in formulating the terms of their tenders'.[33] Concerning specifically objectivity, the Court of Justice recalled that the principle of equal treatment of tenderers implies first of all that tenderers must be in a position of equality both when they formulate their tenders and when those tenders are being assessed by the contracting authority.[34] This means that 'when tenders are being assessed, the award criteria must be applied objectively and uniformly to all tenderers'.[35] The principle of equal treatment also implies 'an obligation of transparency in order to enable verification that it has been complied with, which consists in ensuring, *inter alia*, review of the impartiality of procurement procedures'.[36]

Article 23(6) of Directive 2004/18/EC also made clear that the label specifications referred to were to be 'appropriate to define the characteristics of the supplies or services that are the object of the contract'. This requirement was somewhat a rewording of another condition spelt out in *Concordia Bus*, namely that the criteria indicated in the contract

[28] D. Wilsher, 'Reconciling national autonomy and trade integration in the context of eco-labelling', pp. 423 and 429; this somewhat links to the specific EU approach to eco-labelling (ivi, 409).

[29] See, however, critically as to the adequacy of 'science', D. Wilsher, 'Reconciling national autonomy and trade integration in the context of eco-labelling', p. 427.

[30] Case C-513/99 *Concordia Bus [*2002] ECR I-7213.

[31] Para 66.

[32] Case C-448/01 *EVN and Wienstrom* [2003] ECR I-14527; see P. Kunzlik, 'The procurement of "green" energy', p. 369.

[33] Para 56, emphasis added.

[34] Para 47.

[35] Para 48.

[36] Para 50.

notice were 'linked to the subject matter of the contract'.[37] One might well doubt the pertinence of this requirement when laying down the technical specifications since it is at this moment that the contract is defined. In a way the provision was laying the ground for a chicken and egg problem, since the 'object of the contract' could not be defined *a priori* without first drafting the technical specifications.[38]

Finally Article 23(6) gave indications as to the value of the labels as evidence of the required qualities. Contracting authorities were empowered to stipulate that products and services bearing the eco-label would have been presumed to comply with the technical specifications. However, in line with the impossibility to require economic operators to have their products or services labelled, contracting authorities were under a duty to 'accept any other appropriate means of proof, such as a technical dossier of the manufacturer or a test report from a recognised body'.[39]

Article 23(6) was at the heart of the *Max Havelaar* case.[40] In the notice for the award of a public contract for the supply and management of automatic coffee machines, the province of North Holland inserted a condition requiring the Max Havelaar and EKO labels (a social and eco-label, respectively). Later, it specified that labels based on similar or the same criteria were acceptable. Advocate General Kokott opined that contracting authorities do not need to list separately in their contract documents every individual specification which forms part of an eco-label; rather, they are free to refer in the contract documents, by a simple reference to eco-labels, in general to all the specifications on which those labels are based.[41] In her opinion, a generic reference to all specifications on which an eco-label is based is compatible with the principle of transparency, 'since a reasonably well-informed tenderer of normal diligence can indeed be expected to be familiar with the eco-labels used on the

[37] Para 64; see also Case C-448/01 *EVN and Wienstrom* [2003] ECR I-14527, paras 66ff.; see Chapter 3 of this volume by Abby Semple.

[38] See R. Caranta, 'Award criteria under EU law (old and new)', in M. Comba and S. Treumer (eds), *Award of contracts in EU procurements* (DJØF Publishing, 2013), 23ff.

[39] This left the problem open in case of less than exact equivalence between the standards chosen by the contracting authority and those adhered to by an economic operator: D. Wilsher, 'Reconciling national autonomy and trade integration in the context of eco-labelling', p. 426.

[40] Case C–368/10 *Commission* v. *Netherlands* [2012] ECLI:EU:C:2012:284.

[41] Para 52.

relevant market or at least to obtain information on such labels from the bodies certifying them'.[42]

The Court of Justice stayed truer to the wording of Directive 2004/18/EC. It held that Article 23(6) allows contracting authorities to choose between using or not the detailed specifications of an eco-label, but not the option to refer to the eco-label as such. Moreover, the fact that Article 23(6) authorises the contracting authorities to indicate that the products bearing the eco-label are presumed to comply with the specifications concerned permits recourse to the eco-label itself only indirectly, as proof of compliance with the technical specifications.[43] The obligation of the contracting authority to mention expressly the detailed environmental characteristics it intends to impose even where it refers to the characteristics defined by an eco-label, is thought to be indispensable in order to allow potential tenderers to refer to a single official document.[44]

Allowing contracting authorities to refer directly to labels in the contract documents makes it easier for them to buy sustainably.[45] However, this may lead to a detrimental treatment for those economic operators having legitimately chosen not to have their products or services certified or to have them certified under a different label. As already recalled, there are many different types of labels, and a lot of them have limited diffusion, sometimes being limited to a single Member State or few Member States. Referring to them might amount to a technical barrier to trade, fragmenting the internal market.[46]

The Advocate General and the Court were instead on the same page in holding that the contracting authority should have mentioned already in the call for tenders that 'equivalent' labels would have been accepted and was too late in informing potential tenderers of the equivalence in a clarification issued six days before the deadline set for the receipt of tenders.[47]

[42] Para 56; she went on remarking that 'the administrative burden involved in laying down the requirements on contracting authorities cannot be overlooked. That burden should always be proportionate to the objectives pursued in public procurement law. If the environmental characteristics of a product can be described with sufficient precision from the point of view of a reasonably well informed tenderer solely by means of a general reference to the specifications underlying an eco-label, it would be excessively formalistic nevertheless to require the contracting authority to list all these specifications individually' (para 57).

[43] Para 64. [44] Paras 63ff. [45] See also R. Caranta, 'Sustainable procurement', 172f.

[46] M. Cetik, 'Do Europe's product labels converge?', 15.

[47] See paras 69f of the judgment and para 71 of the conclusions, respectively.

The case also raised some issue of classification with reference to social labels. The Max Havelaar label describes products of fair-trade origin purchased at a price and under conditions more favourable than those determined by market forces from organisations made up of small-scale producers in developing countries. More specifically, the price must cover all the costs and must contain a supplementary premium compared to the market price; production must be subject to pre-financing and the importer must have long-term trading relationships with the producers. Following the conclusions of Advocate General Kokott,[48] the Court of Justice held that such criteria do not correspond to the definition of the concept of technical specification 'given that that definition applies exclusively to the characteristics of the products themselves, their manufacture, packaging or use, and not to the conditions under which the supplier acquired them from the manufacturer'.[49] The Court concluded that those criteria fell under the concept of 'conditions for performance of contracts' within the meaning of Article 26 of Directive 2004/18/EC and consequently did not rule on the merits of the complaint of the Commission which was grounded on Article 23.[50]

In turn, contract performance conditions may translate in a certification scheme akin to labels such as eco-management and audit scheme (EMAS) thus further shifting the focus from technical specifications to qualifications requirements.[51] Under Article 48(2)(f) of Directive 2004/18/EC, evidence of the economic operators' technical abilities for public works contracts and public services contracts may be furnished, but only in appropriate cases, through an indication of 'the environmental management measures that the economic operator will be able to apply when performing the contract'. Under Article 50, should contracting authorities require the production of such certificates they should refer to the Community EMAS or to environmental management standards based on the relevant European or international standards. They shall anyway recognise equivalent certificates from bodies established in other Member States and accept other evidence of equivalent environmental management measures from economic operators, such 'a description of

[48] Paras 80ff. [49] Para 74. [50] Paras 75ff; see also paras 88ff of the conclusions.

[51] See also Case C–368/10 *Commission* v. *Netherlands* [2012] ECLI:EU:C:2012:284, paras 104f; the same requirements were read as a contract performance by Advocate General Kokott: see paras 128ff of the conclusions.

the measures implemented by the economic operator to ensure the same level of environmental protection'.[52]

In the end labels, and the certificates they represent, may be referred to in quite different phases of the procurement cycle, and proper qualification of the clauses in the contract documents issued by the contracting authority may be problematic as shown in *Max Havelaar*.

3. The 2014 reform

The rules concerning labels have been much reorganised and have been partially changed following the reform process. Article 2(1) of Directive 2014/24/EU includes now two definitions relevant for our topic. They were inserted at the eleventh hour during the trialogue. Under Article 2(1)(23) '"label" means any document, certificate or attestation confirming that the works, products, services, processes or procedures in question meet certain requirements'; under Article 2(1)(24) '"label requirements" means the requirements to be met by the works, products, services, processes or procedures in question in order to obtain the label concerned'. This is not rocket science, but in fact means that 'label' is quite a generic term to refer to different means to attest conformity to given standards.

The main provision on labels is Article 43 of Directive 2014/24/EU. The first main innovation in Article 43 of the new Public Sector Directive is that thanks to the changes proposed by the European Parliament labels have been freed from the close embrace of technical specifications.[53] Today, labels make the subject of a specific provision. Under Article 43(1):

> Where contracting authorities intend to purchase works, supplies or services with specific environmental, social or other characteristics they may, in the technical specifications, the award criteria or the contract performance conditions, require a specific label as means of proof that the works, services or supplies correspond to the required characteristics.

Max Havelaar attested to the challenges in exactly qualifying the requirements in the contract notice as either technical specifications or contract performance conditions. Article 43(1) makes the discussion moot, since the same set of rules will apply anyway. The problem will still be to distinguish labels under Article 43(1) from certification schemes like EMAS and environmental management standards more generally. The latter are now

[52] See also Recital 44; see A. Semple, *A Practical Guide*, 7.025.

[53] See amendment 154.

ruled under Article 62 which would probably have deserved to be better coordinated with Article 43 as it made evident by Recital 88 referring to eco-label certificates involving environmental management criteria.[54]

What makes the issues surrounding environmental management standards quite similar to those relating to labels is the existence of many standards, including European ones. Under Article 62(2), contracting authorities wishing to make sure that their contractors comply with certain environmental management systems or standards must refer to the EU EMAS set up in Regulation (EC) No 1221/2009 on the voluntary participation by organisations in a Community EMAS, or to other environmental management systems as recognised in accordance with Article 45 of the same regulation, or other environmental management standards based on the relevant European or international standards by accredited bodies.[55] Here again contracting authorities are required to recognise equivalent certificates from bodies established in other Member States.[56]

It is also important to stress that because of changes in the wording of the provision, environmental management standards may now also be required for supply contracts.[57]

The other significant change in the legislation on labels basically amounts to overturning the principle established in *Max Havelaar* that contracting authorities could not refer to specific labels when choosing the most economically advantageous tender. Contracting authorities are now empowered to refer directly to the label(s) defining the characteristics they have in mind. This will very much help contracting authorities in buying sustainably in line with one of the objectives of the reform process having led to the enactment of the 2014 Directives.[58] Concerns that competition might be limited or distorted through reference to specific labels have not all of the sudden disappeared, though. Under Article 43(1) contracting authorities requiring a specific label shall anyway accept any label based on equivalent requirements.[59] Moreover,

[54] And indeed amendment 154 proposed by the European Parliament proposed to expressly cover in the provision certificates and labels.

[55] See also recital 88.

[56] And again the European Parliament had taken a quite harsh attitude to those economic operators not seeking an environmental management standard: see amendment 183.

[57] See A. Semple, *A practical guide*, 7.026; see also Recital 88 referring in general terms to 'the performance of a public contract'.

[58] See, however, the discussion in B. Neamtu and D.C. Dragos, 'Sustainable public procurement', p. 98, and R. Caranta, 'The changes to the public contract directives and the story they tell about how EU law works', *Common Market Law Review* (2015), 394ff.

[59] A more general rule on the same lines is enacted in Art. 44(1) of Directive 2014/24/EU.

> Where an economic operator had demonstrably no possibility of obtaining the specific label indicated by the contracting authority or an equivalent label within the relevant time limits for reasons that are not attributable to that economic operator, the contracting authority shall accept other appropriate means of proof, which may include a technical dossier from the manufacturer.[60]

It is upon the economic operator to show that it could not get a label. This 'reflect(s) a shift in the burden of proof compared to the 2004 directives, under which operators were entitled to rely upon technical dossiers or other non-third-party evidence without special justification'.[61] However, in most cases the burden of proof will be easily discharged, since labels are normally awarded after an investigation and verification process taking longer time than an award procedure. This is especially so now that minimum deadlines have been considerably cut, answering the call for more flexibility in public procurement.[62]

Article 43(1) of the new Public Sector Directive also somewhat strengthens the traditional safeguards against abusive recourse to labels which were already spelt out in Article 23(6) of Directive 2004/18/EC. These safeguards are now referred to in respect of any label, rather than just 'other' labels. Direct reference to labels is allowed, provided that a number of conditions are all fulfilled. Again, the label requirements must base on objectively verifiable and non-discriminatory criteria; labels must be established in an open and transparent procedure in which all relevant stakeholders may participate by third parties over which no economic operator may exercise decisive influence.[63]

The LtSM of the contract is still required. The specific term of art is now employed, adding to the systematic coherence of EU law. Indeed, the label requirements must 'only concern criteria which are linked to the subject matter of the contract and are appropriate to define characteristics of the works, supplies or services that are the subject matter of the contract'. Article 43(2) provides that, where a label also sets out requirements not linked to the subject matter of the contract, contracting authorities may

[60] See also the last para of Recital 74; this rule as well is echoing Art. 44(2) and possibly the two set of rules might have been better coordinated.

[61] A. Semple, *A practical guide*, 7.033.

[62] Amendment 27 proposed by the Parliament to the recitals showed a clearer preference for those seeking certification by indicating that 'In order not to discriminate against tenderers who invest time and money for certificates or test reports, the burden to provide equivalence should be placed on the tenderer claiming equivalence'; discrimination was obviously not a pertinent reference here, and the text was dropped.

[63] See also Recital 75.

not require the label as such, but shall define the technical specification by reference to those of the detailed specifications or parts thereof which contain such a link. It is uncertain how picky contracting authorities must be in looking into the detailed specifications or parts thereof to decide what the relevant requirements are.[64]

On the one hand, for systematic reasons the LtSM must be understood here on the same lines drawn in Article 67(3) of Directive 2014/24/EU. Therefore, the condition must be considered to be met with reference to any requirement relating to the works, supplies or services to be provided under that contract in any respect and at any stage of their life cycle as defined in Article 68.[65] Contracting authorities should therefore be given a wide discretion in defining which aspects are relevant for them. Reference to the life cycle will call into operation the outer limit to discretion spelt out at the end of Recital 97. Accordingly, the condition of a link with the subject matter of the contract 'excludes criteria and conditions relating to general corporate policy, which cannot be considered as a factor characterising the specific process of production or provision of the purchased works, supplies or services'. In line with the conclusions rendered by Advocate General Kokott in *Max Havelaar*, contracting authorities are not allowed to require tenderers to have a certain corporate social or environmental responsibility policy in place.[66]

On the other hand, the quite general limit to the discretion of the contracting authorities laid down in the second sentence of Article 18(1) of Directive 2014/24/EU applies. Therefore, contracting authorities cannot refer to labels requirements with the intention of excluding a contract from the scope of the Directive or, and possibly more relevant here, of artificially narrowing competition, in particular by unduly favouring or disadvantaging certain economic operators. Moreover, according to Recital 75 *in fine*, 'References to labels should not have the effect of restricting innovation'.

4. Conclusions

The new rules on labels go some length in tidying up the regulatory landscape, including an *ad hoc* provision on labels to address something

[64] See also the discussion in A. Semple, *A practical guide*, 7.036.

[65] See also Recital 97.

[66] Case C–368/10 *Commission* v. *Netherlands* [2012] ECLI:EU:C:2012:284, para 88 of the conclusions; see also para 90 of the judgment; see again Recital 97. See further Chapter 3 of this volume by Abby Semple.

which previously sat rather uncomfortably within the rules on technical specifications.

More importantly, the new rules on labels and environmental management standards quite change the legal environment for sustainable public procurement, making it easier for contracting authorities to take environmental and or social considerations into account in their buying decisions. Contracting authorities may now directly refer to labels, greatly helping them to choose sustainable consumption patterns.[67]

One might lament that the EU law makers did not choose to go further down on the road of imposing mandatory requirements in this respect. And indeed the European Parliament seemed ready to push more strongly economic operators to seek labels and environmental management standards certificates.[68]

As already recalled Recital 95 of Directive 2014/24/EU makes it clear that the EU law makers thought it better to go on leaving it to sector-specific (or, more precisely, product-category specific) legislation 'to set mandatory objectives and targets in function of the particular policies and conditions prevailing in the relevant sector and to promote the development and use of European approaches to life-cycle costing as a further underpinning for the use of public procurement in support of sustainable growth'.[69]

The provisions on life-cycle costing analysis indeed play a pivotal rule in the new reform.[70] Concerns for the proper working of the internal market require objective, science-based methodologies to underpin the choices of contracting authorities. This means, as Recital 95 acknowledges, referring to life-cycle costing methodologies. Developing commonly accepted methodologies is indeed a major issue.[71] Assessments as to the progress

[67] See, however, A. Semple, *A practical guide*, 7.036; B. Neamtu and D.C. Dragos, 'Sustainable public procurement', 98.

[68] See amendments 27 and 183.

[69] The recital refers to Directive 2009/33/EC on the promotion of clean and energy-efficient road transport vehicles and to Regulation (EC) No. 106/2008 on a Community energy-efficiency labelling programme for office equipment as instances of sector-specific mandatory standards.

[70] This is discussed in Chapter 6 of this volume by Dacian C. Dragos and Bogdana Neamtu; see also A. Semple, *A practical guide*, 7.038. See also the Communication, *Integrated product policy – building on environmental life-cycle thinking*, COM (2003) 302 final; see also, with reference to the reform proposals, D.C. Dragos and B. Neamtu, 2013, 'Sustainable public procurement: life cycle costing (LCC) in the new EU directive proposal', *European Procurement & Public Private Partnership Law Review*, 1 (2013), 19.

[71] D.C. Dragos and B. Neamtu, 'Sustainable public procurement in the EU', 327ff; J.J. Czarnezki, 'The future of food eco-labelling', 42ff.

made so far vary greatly,[72] even if carbon footprint labelling seems to be taking root fast.[73]

As Recital 96 of the new Public Sector Directive puts it, 'Common methodologies should be developed at Union level for the calculation of life-cycle costs for specific categories of supplies or services'. The same recital goes on indicating that, once developed, their use might and 'should be made compulsory'.

The 'objectivisation' of social aspects of life-cycle costing analysis is even more difficult.[74] Again Recital 96 acknowledges that 'the feasibility of establishing a common methodology on social life-cycle costing should be examined, taking into account existing methodologies such as the Guidelines for Social Life-Cycle Assessment of Products adopted within the framework of the United Nations Environment Programme'.

Certainly guidance from the EU institutions, and the Commission first among them, on life-cycle costing methodologies and labels or certificates based on them, would much help the uptake of sustainable public procurement, at the same time making sure that this does not translate into artful or outright abusive distortions of competition in the internal market.[75] The existing green procurement criteria – GPP are themselves often based on eco-label,[76] but there is need for more.[77]

[72] See also M. Cetik, 'Do Europe's product labels converge?', 7.

[73] J.J. Czarnezki, 'The future of food eco-labelling', 18ff.

[74] See also T. Medina Arnaiz, 'Social considerations in Spanish public procurement law', *European Procurement & Public Private Partnership Law Review*, 2 (2011), 66.

[75] See in general terms stressing the transaction costs and complexity of devising sustainability criteria, D. Wilsher, 'Reconciling national autonomy and trade integration in the context of eco-labelling', 408f.

[76] See Commission guide, *Buying green! A handbook on green public procurement*, 2nd edn (2011), 13f.

[77] See R. Caranta, 'The changes to the public contract directives', 457.

6

Life-cycle costing for sustainable public procurement in the European Union

DACIAN C. DRAGOS AND BOGDANA NEAMTU

1. Introduction: life-cycle costing in the context of the modernisation of EU procurement

On 20 December 2011, the European Commission initiated the so-called public procurement modernisation package,[1] which resulted in the adoption by the Council on 11 February 2014 of two revised Directives – Directive 2014/24/EU (which replaces the 'Classical' Procurement Directive 2004/18/EC) and Directive 2014/25/EU (which replaces the 'Utilities' Procurement Directive 2004/17/EC), and of a new Directive 2014/23/EU on the award of concession contracts. One of the stated objectives of the reform was to facilitate strategic procurement taking account of environmental, social and innovation factors.[2] The three Directives, adopted following a complicated process necessitating significant compromises between the three actors involved in the process (the European Commission, the Parliament and the Council) introduce a number of novel provisions relating to the procurement of innovative and sustainable solutions, but do less in the way of clear mandates to apply these.[3] Along the same lines, it is argued that even after the adoption of the modernisation package, green procurement remains a rather technical effort.[4]

A sustainability-friendly approach is visible from the beginning in the new Directive 2014/24/EU: Recital 91 reminds us that Article 11 TFEU calls for environmental protection requirements to be integrated into

[1] H. Schebesta, 'EU green public procurement policy: modernisation package, eco-labelling and framing measures', in S. Schoenmaekers, W. Devroe and N. Philipsen (eds), *State aid and public procurement in the European Union* (Intersentia, 2014), p. 129.

[2] A. Semple, *New EU procurement directives and SPP: opening the floodgates?*, see www.sustainable-procurement.org/newsroom/special-features/new-eu-procurement-directives-and-spp-opening-the-floodgates/.

[3] Ibid. [4] Schebesta, 'EU green public procurement policy', p. 130.

the definition and implementation of all Union policies and activities, in particular with a view to promoting sustainable development. In this context, the aim of the new Directives is to clarify how the contracting authorities can contribute to the protection of the environment and the promotion of sustainable development, whilst ensuring that they can obtain the best value for money in their contracts.

The call for a green procurement policy framework at EU level emerged relatively late, around 2000, when it was enshrined in a number of documents such as the EU Sustainable Development Strategy (2001–11), the Sixth Environmental Action Programme (2002–12) and Lisbon strategy and Europe 2020.[5] One of the main reasons was that environmental and social considerations were not initially recognised by the Commission among the rationales underlying public procurement regulation, which showed 'a rather uncompromised dedication to the internal market logic'.[6] Traditionally, public procurement had to only be economically efficient, with little regard for other objectives than the purely economic ones. In the early stages it was the Court of Justice of the EU rather than the Commission which interpreted the Procurement Directives in force at that time as allowing under certain conditions the use of environmental and social criteria. From 'secondary considerations' in the 2004 Directives,[7] the need to include social and environmental considerations in public tendering procedures has led over time to the coining of new terms, much more powerful and all-encompassing, such as 'horizontal policies',[8] 'sustainable procurement'[9] or even 'strategic procurement'.[10] With the adoption of the new 2014 Directives, the sustainability paradigm is almost taking over the realm of public procurement (at least at a declaratory level), and it is marketed as a major 'selling point' of the new legislation.

[5] Ibid., p. 130. [6] Ibid.

[7] S. Arrowsmith and P. Kunzlik (eds), *Social and environmental policies in EC procurement law* (Cambridge University Press, 2009); J. Arnould, 'Secondary policies in public procurement: the innovations of the new directive', *Public Procurement Law Review*, 13 (2004), 187; R. Caranta and M. Trybus (eds), *The law of green and social procurement in Europe* (DJØF Publishing, 2010).

[8] S. Arrowsmith and P. Kunzlik, 'Public procurement and horizontal policies in EC law: general principles', in S. Arrowsmith and P. Kunzlik (eds), *Social and environmental policies in EC procurement law* (Cambridge University Press, 2009).

[9] R. Caranta, 'Sustainable procurement', in M. Trybus, R. Caranta and G. Edelstam (eds), *European union law of public contracts: public procurement and beyond* (Bruylant, 2014), pp. 165–7.

[10] J. Edler and L. Georghiou, 'Public procurement and innovation – resurrecting the demand side', *Research Policy*, 36 (2007), 953.

All these new concepts are the result of a paradigm change – public procurement legislation is to be used to correct market and system failures. Demand for certain technologies, products or services are encouraged via public procurement in order to stimulate the market. Of course, the traditional goals of public procurement regulation – transparency, best value for money, competition concerns and the creation of a strong internal market are still in place. The ultimate goal of the reform is to strike some sort of a balance between old (traditional) and new (strategic) objectives in public procurement. This is not an easy task, as evidenced by the complicated process of adopting the new Procurement Directives. Creating an umbrella framework to green and social public procurement is far more complicated than implementing specific buying requirements for contracting authorities. The modernisation package is predated by mandatory provisions for buying green: The 2008 Energy Star Regulation (obligation on central contracting authorities to buy energy-efficient IT office equipment); the 2009 Clean Vehicles Directive (obligation on all contracting authorities to buy environmentally friendly vehicles) and the 2010 Energy performance of buildings Directive (obligation for new buildings own or occupied by public authorities to be nearly zero energy by the end of 2018).[11]

While sustainable development is clearly the backbone of the modernisation reform of public procurement, life-cycle costing (LCC) is viewed as a novelty, one of the most fundamental modernisation challenges and one of the specific tools to be used in order to advance the goals of sustainable public procurement. According to the 2014 Directive, LCC is a cost-effectiveness approach used to evaluate cost. It is also a so-called horizontal provision with great application potential.[12] Article 68 of the Directive 2014/24/EU is dedicated entirely to this new concept, representing a useful clarification encouraging contracting authorities to move away from evaluating the lowest delivery cost/price towards consideration of the whole-life/long-term cost of the works, supplies or services procured.[13] The advantages of using LCC are mostly related to two different arguments:[14] First, the life-cycle costs over the life of an asset are

[11] Schebesta, 'EU green public procurement policy', p. 142. [12] Ibid.

[13] Bevan Brittan byte size procurement update, November 2014, see www.bevanbrittan.com/articles/Pages/BevanBrittanbytesizeprocurementupdate8Awardcriteriaandlife-cyclecosting.aspx.

[14] Davis Langdon Management Consulting, *Life cycle costing (LCC) as a contribution to sustainable construction: guidance on the use of the LCC methodology and its application*

widely acknowledged as a better indicator of value for money than the initial acquisition/construction costs alone. It is therefore clear that a greater focus on the maintenance and operating costs of assets rather than on capital costs alone, can deliver significant long-term financial and environmental benefits. Second, it provides a tool for the economic evaluation of alternative sustainability options exhibiting different capital, operating costs or resource usage. It also provides methods for evaluating the cost benefits of incorporating more sustainable options into different products/works/services. LCC should have a broad application in public procurement since the method was originally designed for procurement purposes in the US Department of Defence[15] and is still used most commonly in the military sector. However, it is difficult to analyse how often LCC is used. Some authors argue that the method is scarcely used[16] while other point out that in certain countries and for certain products it is relatively well used.[17]

Life-cycle costing was already a possibility under the old generation of Procurement Directives, as evidenced by the inclusion of this approach in the Clean Vehicles Directive (2009/33/EC).[18] The new Directives give greater prominence to LCC as a means of calculating costs, including the cost of environmental externalities such as greenhouse gas emissions, other pollutant emissions and climate change mitigation costs.[19]

This chapter explores the role of LCC in the context of sustainable public procurement. First, LCC is described and analysed in the context of other similar approaches which employ a life-cycle perspective (Section 2). Then, the chapter moves on towards analysing the implementation of the LCC in the context of the 2014 new Procurement Directives (Section 3). The following sections will emphasise how LCC can be a tool that can contribute at the same time to the objective of securing value for money and to promote non-economic goals. Section 4 concludes.

in public procurement, 2007, p. 3, see http://ec.europa.eu/DocsRoom/documents/5060/attachments/1/translations/en/renditions/native.

15 G.E. White and P.F. Ostwald, 'The life cycle cost of an item is the sum of all funds expended in support of the item from its conception and fabrication through its operation to the end of its useful life', *Management Accounting*, 57 (1976), 39–42.

16 O. Perera, B. Morton and T. Perfrement, *Life cycle costing in sustainable public procurement: a question of value* (IISD, 2009), p. 1.

17 US study argues that 40 per cent of city administrations use LCC analysis when assessing their building projects in D. Ardit and H.M. Messiha, 'Life cycle cost analysis (LCCA) in municipal organizations', *Journal of Infrastructure Systems*, 5 (1999), 1–10.

18 Semple, *New EU procurement directives.* 19 Ibid.

2. Assessment methods based on the life-cycle concept

Recently, there has been a significant increase in the number of concepts, models, tools and indicators related to sustainability in general and to the sustainability of industry and of the production-consumption system in our society. Life-cycle assessment (LCA) and life-cycle costing (LCC) are prominent among the plethora of these new approaches in the field of sustainability.[20] Their development is the direct reflection of new policy concerns derived from sustainability, where 'the assessment of costs and benefits has been expanded from private to societal; the economic assessment has been expanded to include environmental and social aspects as well; the realisation that every actor is embedded in a chain of activities has led to the development of notions such as supply chains, life cycle and extended producer responsibility'.[21] The significant number of somewhat similar concepts developed in this field has as a drawback, the lack of conceptual clarity and the difficulty of distinguishing the approach used in concrete situations. We therefore start with some conceptual clarifications regarding life cycle, LCA and LCC in the context of the sustainability goal. Building upon this foundation, we then analyse how LCC works in the framework of public procurement.

2.1. Life cycle

Before defining LCA and LCC, it is important to clarify the meaning of *life cycle.* Both LCA and LCC are generally described as life-cycle methods, meaning methods considering a product's life cycle.[22] However, the interpretation of life cycle under the two methods is quite different.

The concept of life cycle has existed outside the realm of the two methodologies discussed here, showing up in many disciplines and topics. It can be argued that organisms, businesses, technologies and products all have life cycles.[23] The International Organization for Standardization (ISO), for example, defines the life cycle as the consecutive and the

[20] R. Heijungs, G. Huppes and B. Guinée, 'Life cycle assessment and sustainability analysis of products, materials and technologies: toward a scientific framework for sustainability life cycle analysis', *Polimer Degradation and Stability*, 95, (2010), 422.

[21] Ibid.

[22] E. Hochschorner and G. Finnveden, 'Life cycle approach in the procurement process: the case of defence materiel', *International Journal of LCA*, 11 (2006), 203.

[23] Heijungs, Huppes and Guinée, 'Life cycle assessment', 424.

interlinked stages of a product system, from raw material acquisition or generation of natural resources to the final disposal.[24] A similar but more detailed definition is provided by the 2014 Public Procurement Directive which defines in Article 2(20) the life cycle as

> all consecutive and/or interlinked stages, including research and development to be carried out, production, trading and its conditions, transport, use and maintenance, throughout the existence of the product or the works or the provision of the services, from raw material acquisition or generation of resources to disposal, clearance and end of service or utilisation.

In public procurement, a distinction needs to be made between the life cycle of products and works on the one hand, and services on the other. The life cycle of a product or work covers all stages from raw material acquisition until the final disposal. This includes (amongst others) production, transport and maintenance. The life cycle of a service includes all stages from its preparation to the end of its provision.[25]

In LCA, the term life cycle includes the mining of raw materials, production, use and disposal of a product ('from cradle to grave'). LCC of a physical asset begins when its acquisition is first considered, and ends when it is finally taken out of service for disposal or redevelopment (where a new LCC begins).[26] Figure 6.1 shows what stages are included in the life cycle and the system's boundaries depending on the method used. The unbroken line describes typical system boundaries for LCC, the dashed line describes boundaries for LCA and the dotted line for life length. In most fields, LCC has the same boundaries as the life length of a product. There are fields, however, such as defence procurement, where research and development are also included as relevant stages in LCC.[27]

2.2. *Life-cycle assessment*

Life-cycle assessment (LCA) is a tool for evaluating the environmental effects of a product, process or activity throughout its life cycle or

[24] ISO, *Environmental management – life cycle assessment – Principles and framework (ISO 14040)* (Geneva: ISO, 2006).

[25] C. Jobse and N. Dimitri, *LCC-calculations and the principles of public procurement*, p. 1, see https://underpinn.portals.mbs.ac.uk/Portals/70/docs/2.1%20-%20Jobse%20&%20Dimitri%20-%20LCC%20calculations%20v1%200.pdf.

[26] Hochschorner and Finnveden, 'Life cycle approach', 203–4.

[27] Ibid., 203.

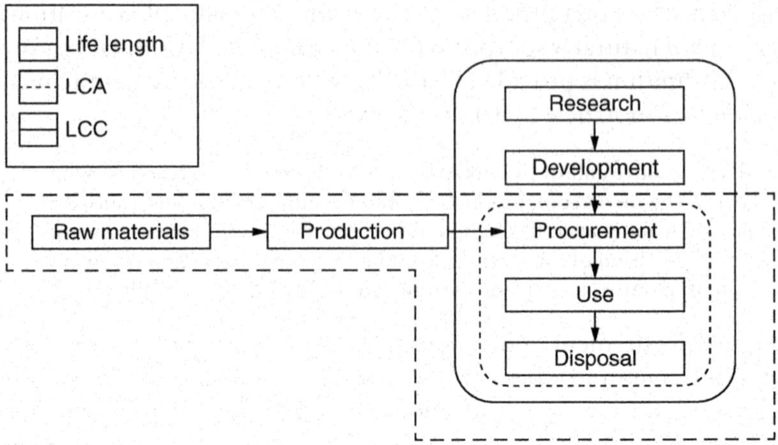

Figure 6.1 Life cycles and system boundaries.
Source: E. Hochschorner and G. Finnveden, 'Life cycle approach', p. 203.[28]

lifetime, which is known as 'from cradle to grave' analysis.[29] Also, social LCA (S-LCA) appears to be a coming issue, some of the social impacts considered including human rights, working conditions, health and safety, cultural heritage, etc.[30] A limited body of literature argues that the life cycle of a product can be broken down into labour units (hours) and calculate the income per unit; that income can then be used to approximate the well-being of people in different regions, which includes basic needs such as food and housing.[31] The ultimate goal of the S-LCA technique is to promote improvement of social conditions throughout the life cycle of a product.[32]

The purpose of LCA can be: comparison of alternative products, processes or services; comparison of alternative life cycles for a certain product or service and identification of parts of the life cycle where the greatest improvements can be made.[33]

LCA may also be seen as a multi-step procedure for calculating the lifetime environmental impact or footprint of a product or

[28] Figure reproduced with the permission of Springer.

[29] P. Roy, D, Nei, T. Orikasa, Q. Xu and H. Okadome, 'A review of life cycle assessment (LCA) on some food products, *Journal of Food Engineering*, 90 (2009), 2.

[30] UNEP, SETAC, Life Cycle Initiative, *Guidelines for social life cycle assessment of products*, see www.lifecycleinitiative.org/starting-life-cycle-thinking/life-cycle-approaches/social-lca/.

[31] D. Hunkeler, 'Societal LCA methodology and a Case Study', *International Journal of Life Cycle Assessment*, 11 (2006), 371–82.

[32] Ibid. [33] Roy, Nei, Orikasa, Xu and Okadome, 'A review of life cycle assessment', 2.

service.[34] While the concept of LCA evolved already in the 1960s and 1970s, it has drawn increasing attention since 1990s. LCA is also known as eco-balancing, environment profile analysis and cradle to grave assessment.[35] Since the 1990s, significant efforts towards harmonisation have taken place. Such efforts include the Life-Cycle Initiative of the United Nations Environmental Programme, the Society of Environmental Toxicology and Chemistry, the European Platform for LCA of the European Commission, and the emerging International Reference Life-Cycle Data.[36] As a result of these efforts, consensus has been achieved on an overall LCA framework/international standard.[37] This has without doubt increased the maturity and methodological robustness of LCA; however, the methodology continues to be under development.[38] LCA is currently the only internationally standardised environmental assessment method.[39]

There are four phases in an LCA study: goal and scope definition, life-cycle inventory analysis, life-cycle impact assessment (LCIA) and interpretation.[40] The goal and scope definition includes the reasons for carrying out the study, the intended application and the intended audience. It is also the place where the system boundaries of the study are described and the functional unit is defined. The functional unit is a quantitative measure of the functions that the goods (or service) provide. The result from the Life-Cycle Inventory is a compilation of the inputs (resources) and outputs (emissions) from the product over its life cycle in relation to the functional unit. The Life-Cycle Impact Assessment is aimed at understanding and evaluating the magnitude and the significance of the potential environmental impacts of the studied system. In the interpretation stage, the results from the previous phases are evaluated in relation to

[34] Athena Sustainable Materials Institute, see www.athenasmi.org/resources/about-lca/whats-the-difference/.

[35] Roy, Nei, Orikasa, Xu and Okadome, 'A review of life cycle assessment . . .', 2.

[36] G. Finvedden, M.Z. Huaschild, T. Ekval, J. Guinee, R. Heijungs, S. Hellweg, A. Koehler, D. Pennington and S. Suh, 'Recent development in life cycle assessment', *Journal of Environmental Management*, 91 (2009), 2.

[37] ISO, *Environmental management – life cycle assessment – principles and framework (ISO 14040)* (Geneva: ISO, 2006); ISO, *Environmental management – life cycle assessment – principles and requirements and guidelines (ISO 14044)* (Geneva: ISO, 2006).

[38] Finvedden, Huaschild, Ekval, Guinee, Heijungs, Hellweg, Koehler, Pennington and Suh, 'Recent development . . .', 2.

[39] W. Kloepffer, 'Life cycle sustainability assessment of products', *International Journal of LCA*, 13 (2008), 90.

[40] ISO, *Environmental management – life cycle assessment – principles and framework (ISO 14040)* (Geneva: ISO, 2006).

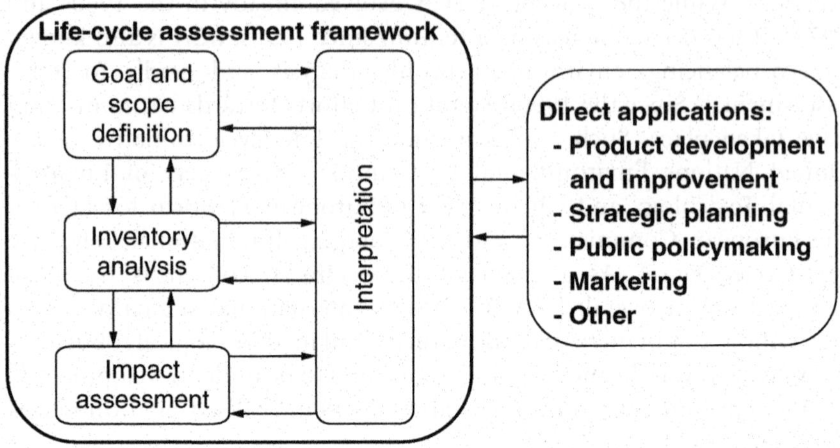

Figure 6.2 Stages of an LCA.
Source: *ISO, Environmental* management – life-cycle assessment – principles and framework (ISO 14040) (Geneva: ISO, 2006).[41]

the goal and scope in order to reach conclusions and recommendations.[42] Figure 6.2 illustrates these four stages and the linkages among them.

2.3. *Life-cycle costing*

The life-cycle cost of an item is the sum of all funds expended in support of the item from its conception and fabrication through its operation to the end of its useful life.[43] Another definition stresses that life-cycle costing (LCC) represents an assessment of all costs which are connected with a certain product, directly covered by one or several actors in the life cycle of this product.[44] According to Lindholm and Suomala,[45] LCC is not

[41] The figure taken from ISO 14040:2006, Environmental management–life-cycle assessment–principles and framework is reproduced with the permission of the International Organization for Standardization, ISO. This standard can be obtained from any ISO member at www.iso.org. Copyright remains with ISO.

[42] The description of the four phases is derived from ISO, *Environmental management – life-cycle assessment – principles and framework (ISO 14040)* (Geneva: ISO, 2006); see also Roy, Nei, Orikasa, Xu and Okadome, 'A review', 2–3.

[43] G. E. White and P.F. Ostwald, 'Life cycle costing', 40–42.

[44] D. Hunkeler, K. Lichtenvort, G. Rebitzer (Hg): A. Ciroth, D. Hunkeler, G. Huppes, K. Lichtenvort, G. Rebitzer, I. Rüdenauer and B. Stehen (Lead authors), *Environmental life cycle costing* (SETAC Publications, 2008); for similar definitions also see W.B. Taylor, 'The use of life cycle costing in acquiring physical assets', *Long Range Planning*, 14 (1981), 32–43.

[45] A. Lindholm and P. Suomala, 'The possibilities of life cycle costing in outsourcing decision making', *Frontiers of E-Business Research* (2004), 227, see http://citeseerx.ist.psu.edu/viewdoc/download?doi=10.1.1.457.8317&rep=rep1&type=pdf.

limited to the forecasting of future costs in the beginning of a life cycle; it also includes the monitoring of costs throughout the life cycle, with the goal of knowing the accrued cost of a particular product or service and the behaviour of different cost elements in different phases of the life cycle.

The costs usually covered under LCC include initial costs, installation and commissioning costs, energy costs, operation costs, maintenance and repair costs, down time costs, environmental costs and decommissioning and disposal costs.[46] More complex definitions also stress the inclusion of externalities among the relevant costs.[47] Externalities can be defined as value changes caused by a business transaction, though not included in its price or as side effects of economic activity. When these value changes are expressed in monetary terms, one speaks about external costs. By definition, these costs are not real cash flows for the directly involved actors and are usually borne by society in general.[48] As a consequence of negative externalities, the private costs of production tend to be lower than costs borne by the society at large. A growing focus on the polluter pays principle from the 1990s onwards[49] has given rise to the discussion of internalising the negative externalities, based on the goal that anyone causing a negative environmental impact should pay. In this context, LCC can be a vehicle for making visible and internalising such costs.[50] Despite significant progress reported in the literature, the most commonly used LCC methodologies by governments are based on a purely financial valuation of direct costs. This may be called an 'economic' LCC. In order for LCC to become an environmentally relevant methodology, it needs to include also the costs associated with the environmental externalities produced by works/services/products.

The life-cycle costs of a product can be many times the initial purchase or investment costs.[51] Life-cycle costing (in contrast to only focusing on

46 Hydraulic Institute, Europump, and the US Department of Energy's Office of Industrial Technologies (OIT), *Pump life cycle costs: a guide to LCC analysis for pumping systems*, see www1.eere.energy.gov/manufacturing/tech_assistance/pdfs/pumplcc_1001.pdf.

47 Definition by SETAC-Europe's working group on LCC, cited in D. Hunkeler and G. Rebitzar, 'The future of life cycle assessment, *International Journal of LCA*, 10 (2005), 306.

48 Öko-Institut e.V. and ICLEI, *Costs and benefits of green public procurement in Europe, part 1: comparison of the life cycle costs of green and non green products*, Final Report, 2007, p. 7.

49 *Glossary of environment statistics: studies in methods*, Series F, No. 67 (New York: United Nations, 1997).

50 B. Steen, 'Environmental costs and benefits in life cycle costing', *Management of Environmental Quality: An International Journal*, 16 (2005), 108.

51 D.G. Woodward, 'Life cycle costing: theory, information acquisition and application', *International Journal of Project Management*, 15 (1997), 335.

the purchase price) is especially useful if a relevant share of costs incurs during the use or end-of-life phase of the analysed products or services.[52] In spite of the obvious long-term benefits of life-cycle costing, the initial investment costs are most often used as the primary and sometimes the only criteria in purchase decisions.[53] Other benefits associated with using LCC include:[54] Transparency of future operational costs; ability to plan for future expenditure; improved awareness of total costs; ability to manipulate and optimise future costs at the design stages; evaluation of competing options, either for entire assets or parts thereof; performance trade-offs against cost (e.g. environmental performance).

Korpi and Ala-Risku[55] describe three methods of estimating costs: estimating by engineering procedures, estimating by analogy and parametric estimating models. In estimating by engineering procedures, costs are assigned to each element at the lowest level of design detail and then combined into a total for the product. In estimating by analogy, the cost estimator draws analogies between different products or their features. Parametric estimations use different statistical techniques and seek the factors on which the life-cycle costs depend.

The nature of life-cycle costs also depends on the specific product group. Depending on the product group and type, different cost elements can be taken into account. Also, depending on the perspective taken in an LCCA, the costs of the different stages can be calculated more or less detailed. In public procurement, the most relevant cost elements can be grouped into three main categories: purchase and installation, costs during use phase and costs for disposal.[56]

To calculate the life-cycle costs, next to the cost elements additional parameters regarding use patterns or the overall life time of the products have to be defined. Examples are the mileage per year for buses and bus services or passenger cars, time in on-/stand-by-/off mode and prints per year for IT devices, overall electricity demand, and so on.[57]

When calculating life-cycle costs other additional technical principles need to be taken into consideration: (a) An LCCA is always conducted for a certain function which has to be fulfilled by the analysed system. This

[52] Öko-Institut e.V. and ICLEI, *Costs and benefits*, p. 5.

[53] N.U. Ahmed, 'A design and implementation model for life cycle cost management system', *Information and Management*, 28 (1995), 261–9.

[54] Davis Langdon Management Consulting, *Life cycle costing*, p. 1.

[55] E. Korpi and T. Ala-Risku, 'Life cycle costing: a review of published case studies', *Managerial Auditing Journal*, 23 (2008), 243. For more details see also W.J. Fabrycky and B.S. Blanchard, *Life-cycle cost and economic analysis* (Prentice Hall, 1991).

[56] Öko-Institut e.V. and ICLEI, *Costs and benefits*, p. 4.

[57] Ibid., pp. 7–9.

function is quantified by the functional unit, which provides a reference to which all costs are related. The functional unit has to be equivalent for both versions (green and non-green) of the analysed product or service types. (b) An LCC has to be calculated on an actor-specific basis (in the case of public procurement, from the perspective of the procuring entity). (c) An LCC needs to be conducted based on clearly defined system boundaries which define for which geographic region the LCCA is conducted or which cost elements are included in the LCC – some costs are highly contextual/localised.[58]

2.4. LCA versus LCC

LCA and LCC are as a starting point quite different methods. LCA assesses environmental (also social) impacts while LCC focuses on the costs, both direct and generated by externalities, associated with a product.[59] The only connection in traditional approaches is the fact that both are based on a life-cycle approach to the product considered. The relationship between LCA and LCC was described for example by ISO which argues that LCA typically does not address the economic or social aspects of a product,[60] while LCC does. However, currently LCC seems to be developing in conjunction with LCA.[61] Reich distinguishes between financial and environmental LCCs and argues that the financial LCC is a tool for analysing the economic effects of an LCA system while the environmental LCC is the weighting of environmental impacts of an LCA system in monetary terms. In his view, financial LCC is to be performed in parallel to an LCA as they analyse the same problem but from a different perspective. LCA and LCC become consecutive tools, where the environmental LCC can be applied to the results of an LCA, aggregating the results.[62]

Such integrated approaches require a high level of sophistication and availability of data. While pilot studies are carried out in various policy fields, these endeavours remain mostly exploratory. Very often, producers

[58] Ibid.

[59] T.E. Swar, D. Hunkler, W. Kloppfer, H.-L. Pesone, A. Ciroth, A. Brent and R. Pagan, 'Environmental life cycle costing: a code of practice', *International Journal of LCA*, 16 (2011), 389–90.

[60] ISO, *Environmental management – life cycle assessment – life cycle interpretation (ISO 14043:2000)* (Geneva: ISO, 1997).

[61] M.C. Reich, 'Economic assessment of municipal waste management systems – case studies using a combination of life cycle assessment (LCA) and life cycle costing (LCC)', *Journal of Cleaner Production*, 13 (2005), 253–63.

[62] Ibid., 254–5.

rather than governments/contracting authorities are more likely to have the capacity to put forward such strategies. In public procurement, the concept of LCC itself is regarded as a novelty. Most of the discussions currently focus on how LCC can work together with the value for money principle; at the same time, the use of LCC is limited by the need to protect competition and to ensure fair treatment of all economic operators. It seems that it will take some time until the LCC methods and the technical strategies described in the general literature on this topic will become real concerns for contracting authorities in the Member States.

3. The application of LCC in the EU public procurement

3.1. Life-cycle costing in the Directive 2014/24/EU

Life-cycle costing is one of the new concepts or tools introduced by the 2014 Directive 2014/24/EU. According to Article 68(1), the list of costs covered includes both direct costs, borne by the contracting authority or other users, as well as costs resulting from the monetisation of the externalities linked to the product, service or work during its life cycle. The direct costs include costs relating to acquisition, costs of use, such as consumption of energy and other resources, maintenance costs and end of life costs, such as collection and recycling costs. Indirect costs, such as the cost of emissions of greenhouse gases and of other pollutant emissions, can be included only if their monetary value can be determined and verified.

In the final text of the Directive, common methodologies developed at the EU level for conducting LCC are mandatory for the contracting authorities from the Member States. Insofar, there is only one such methodology (Clean Vehicles Directive). In the absence of such common methodologies, national governments and contracting authorities are allowed to adopt their own LCC methodologies, provided that the methods used for the assessment of costs imputed to environmental externalities are based on objectively verifiable and non-discriminatory criteria. In situations where such methodologies have not been established for repeated or continuous application, the principle is that they should not favour or disadvantage certain economic operators. A transparency obligation requires that the method should be accessible to all interested parties, and data required by contracting authorities for calculating LCC should be provided with reasonable effort by normally diligent economic operators, including economic operators from third countries party to the GPA or other international agreements by which the Union is bound (Article 68 (2)).

We consider that the mandatory use of a common methodology adopted at EU level (or even at the national level) has the potential in the short term to encourage the use of LCC by contracting authorities. This can be achieved by limiting fragmentation and by increasing legal certainty in an already complicated field.[63] This is especially true for the newer Member States, whose institutions have low administrative capacities and less skilled procurement practitioners. However, in the long term and for governments that are more proactive in this area, a common methodology is likely to prevent a contracting authority from using state-of-the-art approaches that would allow it to be more ambitious than the EU or national methodology. The usefulness of common EU methodologies will ultimately depend upon their quality,[64] but this is hard to assess at this moment since only one such methodology exists.

In our view, the current regulation of LCC tries to balance the need to encourage the use of LCC and thus allows for flexibility in what regards the adoption of methodologies, while still observing the principles of transparency and non-discrimination. Theoretically, a common methodology is more transparent than methodologies developed by contracting authorities for specific purposes and subjected to continuous adaptation. However, the practice of LCC is difficult to predict, as a crucial role will be played by the interpretation of the concept of 'normally diligent economic operator', which is subject to the discretion of the contracting authorities. Schebesta argues that the LCC approach, especially with regard to possible methodologies, is rather unspecified and unstructured and seems to legitimise a certain degree of experimentation with regard to public procurement.[65]

Article 68 refers only to environmental externalities and provides examples of what they are. One question that arises in the context of LCC under the new Directive is whether there are other types of externalities that can be factored in, for instance social costs, which are harder to assess but still important. While the literature refers to Life-Cycle Assessment incorporating social criteria (labour conditions, equal opportunities and accessibility criteria), almost no reference is made to the monetisation of externalities pertaining to the social realm. One study refers to costs

[63] A. Semple, 'Mixed offerings for sustainability in a new European Union procurement Directive', *Public Procurement Law Review*, 21 (2012), 107.

[64] Ibid. [65] Schebesta, 'EU green public procurement policy', p. 135.

such as unemployment benefits the payment of which would have been necessary without the procurement of a given asset, or health care costs that would have been necessary if environmentally preferable alternatives would not have been procured and argues that they are difficult to forecast.[66]

The 2014/24/EU Directive does not go far enough on this. From Article 68, it could be inferred that social and employment criteria are excluded from LCC, which definitely represents in our view a weakening of the full potential of LCC. Recital 96 of the Directive 2014/24/EU, last paragraph declares that 'the feasibility of establishing a common methodology on social life-cycle costing should be examined, taking into account existing methodologies such as the Guidelines for Social Life-Cycle Assessment of Products adopted within the framework of the United Nations Environment Programme'. It is not clear whether this declaration of intention is addressed to the Member States, it relates to the future endeavours of the Commission or it is intended for the contracting authorities. At least in theory, contracting authorities may use the recital to justify the use of social LCC, and this would not be against the Directive.

3.2. LCC and award criteria

The use of LCC raises the question of its place in relation to award criteria. Can LCC be used when the lowest price criterion is chosen, or only as part of the most economically advantageous tender (MEAT)? In order to answer this question, a more in-depth discussion about which award criteria can be used under the new Directive, as opposed to the old legal regime, is required.

Under the 2004 Directive, a contract could be awarded based on the lowest price criterion or based on the MEAT. Criteria included in MEAT would be quality, price, technical merit, aesthetic and functional characteristics, environmental characteristics, running costs, cost-effectiveness, after-sales service and technical assistance, delivery date and delivery period or period of completion. Contracting authorities were responsible for creating the methodologies for assessing tenders under MEAT, on a contract by contract basis.

Under the new 2014 Directive, at a first glance price is no longer an option for awarding public contracts. Article 67(1) states that contracting

[66] Perera, Morton and Perfrement, *Life cycle costing*, p. 3.

authorities shall base the award of public contracts on the most economically advantageous tender. The wording of the Directive is however rather misleading on this topic. Abby Semple warns us that all that has been done was to expand the scope of the 'most economically advantageous tender' to include the award of contracts on price or cost only. She argues that while it is not allowed to exclude cost from the award decision altogether, there is no similar restriction on excluding quality considerations.[67] However, while price only is in principle still possible under the Directive, the Directive opens up the possibility for Member States to forbid the use of price only or cost only as the sole award criterion.

Under the new 2014 Directive, a distinction is made between price and costs, the latter requiring the use of a cost-effectiveness approach, such as life-cycle costing. The new Directive also introduces a new concept, the best price–quality ratio, which can include qualitative, environmental and social aspects. As opposed to the old Directive, currently the use of LCC is no longer restricted to tenders awarded on the price–quality ratio and it can be applied also to situations when the award is made exclusively on costs.

Resorting to LCC makes an award procedure based only on price as the sole award criterion a complex one. The difference from using the price–quality ratio will be that in case of an award based on the lowest price which in its turn is based on LCC, the price remains the only criterion for the award, so all the externalities have to be incorporated and monetised as elements of the price. In the case of an award on the basis of the best price–quality ratio, other criteria can be taken into account, but not as part of the costs. Externalities always have to be provided with a monetary value. Under the price–quality ratio, a weighting process needs to take place among the various criteria used.

3.3. LCC methodologies

Section 2.3 above discusses various possibilities for computing the life-cycle costs of a product within the framework of an LCC analysis. Most of them are highly technical, require a lot of data from the producers/industry, and imply a high degree of uncertainty (especially with regard to the monetisation of environmental and social externalities). The 2014 Procurement Directive encourages the use of LCC in public procurement

[67] Semple, *New EU procurement directives.*

but offers little guidance with respect to how this should be accomplished, especially at the level of the contracting authorities.

Perhaps this is the main reason why the most common LCC methodologies used by governments are based on a purely financial valuation, considering the types of direct costs already discussed in Section 2.3. Direct economic costs are easier to forecast and in most cases there is less uncertainty. In order to become an environmentally relevant methodology, LCC needs to include external costs associated with the work/service/product.[68]

The methodology best adapted to sustainable public procurement is the environmental life-cycle costing (ELCC). This approach, on top of financial assessments (the 'economic LCC'), takes into consideration the external impacts on the environment, which may be based on LCA.[69] Such an analysis may measure for example the external costs of global warming contribution associated with emissions of different greenhouse gases.[70] Environmental costs can be calculated also with respect to acidification (grams of SO2, NOX and NH3), eutrophication (grams of NOX and NH3), land use (m2*year) or other measurable impacts.[71] The Organisation for Economic Co-operation and Development (OECD) developed ten key environmental indicators derived from a larger set of major environmental issues.[72] The selection was made based on their political relevance, analytical soundness and measurability. The indicators include: climate change, ozone layer, air quality, waste generation, freshwater quality, freshwater resources, forest resources, fish resources, energy resources and biodiversity. These indicators can constitute a base for developing a common framework for the use of ELCC by contracting authorities throughout EU, taking into consideration the methodologies already developed at the national level.

Globally, there are various methodologies and software available for conducting LCCs, either for a fee or free of charge.[73] At the EU level, special attention is devoted to such methodologies and calculations because they

68 D. Dragos and B. Neamtu, 'Sustainable public procurement: life cycle costing (LCC) in the New EU directive proposal', *European Procurement & Public Private Partnership Law Review*, 1 (2013), 20.

69 Ibid. 70 For details, see http://ec.europa.eu/environment/gpp/lcc.htm.

71 The SMART-SPP project developed and tested a tool for public authorities to assess LCC and CO_2 emissions and to compare bids. It is available to download in four languages: see www.smart-spp.eu/index.php?id=7633.

72 OECD, *Key environmental indicators* (OECD, 2008).

73 The LCA resources directory for identifying such sources (in Europe and beyond), see http://eplca.jrc.ec.europa.eu/?page_id=137.

need to be in line with Treaty principles – not only non-discrimination and free movement, but also environmental integration according to Article 11 TFEU.

The European Commission has provided some guidance to public procurement authorities wishing to use LCC in the International Reference Life Cycle Data System (ICLD) Handbook – a handbook for businesses, life-cycle assessment experts and public authorities on how to conduct life-cycle assessments to calculate a product's total environmental impact.[74]

National contributions to the topic include the former Swedish Environmental Management Council (SEMCO), which has developed several Excel Tools for calculating life-cycle costs in public procurement. In addition to a general tool, specialised ones are available for professional kitchens (fridges and freezers), indoor and outdoor lighting and vending machines.[75]

The most important question regarding LCC deals with the entire process of drafting the methodology underlying LCC. Some important questions that had to be considered by the European legislator (and which required compromises among the stakeholders involved) while drafting the 2014 Directive included: Who should be responsible for drafting the methodology? Can methodologies be developed for individual tenders? What tests/principles will be used to determine if a methodology violates the principles of equal treatment or non-discrimination? Are economic operators allowed to submit their own methodology?

In the initial proposal by the Commission,[76] economic operators were allowed to submit their own LCC methodology, when such methodology was not provided for by the contracting authority. The final text of the new Directive removed such possibility, but Article 68 does require that data requested for LCC could be provided with reasonable effort by normally diligent economic operators, including operators from third countries

[74] See http://eplca.jrc.ec.europa.eu/uploads/JRC-Reference-Report-ILCD-Handbook-Towards-more-sustainable-production-and-consumption-for-a-resource-efficient-Europe.pdf.

[75] Swedish Competition Authority, *Sustainable procurement criteria*, see www.konkurrensverket.se/en/publicprocurement/sustainable-public-procurement/use-sustainable-criteria/sustainable-procurement-criteria/.

[76] European Commission, *Proposal for a directive of the European Parliament and of the council on public procurement*, COM (2011) 896 final, Brussels, 20 December 2011, see http://ec.europa.eu/internal_market/publicprocurement/docs/modernising_rules/COM2011_896_en.pdf.

party to the Agreement or other international agreements by which the Union is bound.

This enables the adoption of national requirements for the formats or types of data that can be provided in such circumstances. In the event such requirements are not in compliance with the standards set by the Directive, the courts can then review the decisions of the contracting authorities, by resorting to the principle of proportionality. The yardstick against which the LLC requirements will be measured is the 'diligent economic operator' concept. This will involve a high degree of expertise. In cases where national legislation does not complement the Directives with the adequate methodologies or characteristics of data to be provided by bidders, the courts will have again the difficult task of assessing whether the data requested by the contracting authorities was within the reach of a 'diligent economic operator'.

Article 68 of the new Public Sector Directive has not maintained the position from the Commission's draft that LCC methodologies must be 'established for repeated or continuous application' – meaning that tailor-made methodologies developed for the purpose of an individual contract would not be allowed. The adopted text only forbids methodologies which would favour a particular undertaking in the context of a specific contract. This is a welcomed provision which is clearly linked to corruption concerns in public procurement.

For certain contracts, an off-the-shelf LCC methodology, which adequately captures all internal and external costs, may not be available (either at EU or another level). Under the existing provisions, it seems that contracting authorities can modify an existing methodology, and must strictly apply a pre-existing methodology only when it was adopted at EU level. This means that contracting authorities may adopt their own methodologies as along as the European Commission (or the Member State, which can supplement this absence internally) has not adopted one for a specific product or service. These methodologies may then be modified for the specific purpose of other tendering procedures, as they are not for repeated or continuous application.

A first conclusion is that this approach gives flexibility to contracting authorities, which is necessary in specific circumstances, but also may lead to abuses. The line between a methodology that is adapted to the needs of a specific procedure and one that is intended to favour a particular undertaking is a quite fine one. Such forbidden practices are hard to trace and remedy, because the right of undertakings to challenge the tender documentation is limited in time and the only option left for tenderers that did not challenge the methodology in due time is to play according to the rules already established. Moreover, it is difficult to state that a contracting authority has adopted a methodology that would favour one undertaking or another as long as this decision making process is well within its discretion. The review performed by courts over this discretion will be not only technically challenging, but also a tough mission from a legal point of view.

For some contracts, the methodologies referred to above can be used as best practices or even incorporated into contracting's authorities operating manuals.

3.4. *The future of LCC in public procurement*

In the context of sustainable public procurement, LCC has the potential to become a very important element in the enterprise of shifting the paradigm beyond the confinement of the sole purchase price of a product. However, such an approach may be contested as representing an interference with the 'good old reliable' judgment of value for money, especially during economic crises, or even as a venue for discriminatory practices, a way of ensuring that local or preferred suppliers can compete on grounds other than costs. Such deterrents in the way of LCC and sustainable procurement are most likely to be present in countries where environmental concerns rank low on the public agenda, where the transparency of the procurement process is limited and corrupt practices are the norm rather than the exception. Some of the newly Member States of the EU, such as Romania and Bulgaria fall into this category, while even more robust Western democracies, such as Spain, encounter numerous integrity-related challenges.[77]

While advocating the use of LCC in public procurement, one should keep in mind that the science behind LCC is far from perfect. Until now, LCC has been scarcely used in public procurement and studies show that it is not yet considered to be a critical component of sustainable public procurement worldwide.[78] Moreover, procurement professionals may lack the skills and knowledge necessary to successfully implement

[77] B. Neamtu and D. Dragos, 'Fighting corruption in public procurement: the case of Romania', in G.M. Racca and C.R. Yukins (eds), *Integrity and efficiency in sustainable public contracts. balancing concerns corruption in public procurement internationally* (Bruylant, 2014), pp. 89–116.

[78] Perera, Morton and Perfrement, *Life cycle costing*, p. 3.

sustainable procurement, LCC included. A recent survey found that 83 per cent of purchasing professionals considered themselves ill equipped to deliver sustainability through procurement.[79] Other studies, although not that new, have shown that purchasing managers are unsure of how to incorporate ethical and social issues in their buying.[80] In this context, the success of LCC in the future will heavily depend on the availability of methodologies prepared at EU or national levels for certain types of products. Among the EU Member States there is a clear divide based on the experience with green procurement and LCC and the existing administrative capacity in general. While those countries that are at the fore of the sustainability movement can more quickly develop the capacity to incorporate LCC into their public procurement and further experiment with more sophisticated methodologies, other countries will be at least on the short and medium term confined to implementing the minimum mandatory requirements in specific policy areas (such as clean vehicles and energy efficient computers).

The success of LCC will also depend on its scope (meaning the inclusion of environmental externalities or/and other externalities) and the methodology used (which in many cases is incomplete[81] and based on experts' perceptions, not on hard scientific evidence).[82] One of the recurring deterrents in the application of LCC in public procurement is the fact that data in the public domain is often aggregated and incomplete, presented in different formats, thus making comparison and extrapolation difficult.[83] In addition to the lack of data, procurers in the public sector may also be confronted with high levels of uncertainty – for example, due to fluctuations in commodity and electricity prices.

One of the most critical challenges in the case of LCC has to do with the accounting technicalities involved. When using LCC one should consider the method based on which future costs are perceived and forecasted, the discounting rates which are applied and the stages within the asset's life cycle which are included in the analysis. The public sector is often reluctant to embrace the multi-year accounting and budget frameworks that allow temporal flexibility to carryover or borrow-against-the-future.

[79] P. Snell, 'Struggle with sustainability', *Supply Management*, 11(23) (2006).

[80] R.W. Cooper, G. Frank and R. Kemp, 'A multinational comparison of key ethical issues, helps and challenges in the purchasing & supply management profession: the key implications for business and the professions', *Journal of Business Ethics*, 23 (2000), 83–100.

[81] E. Hochschorner and M. Noring, 'Practitioners' use of life cycle costing with environmental costs – a Swedish study', *International Journal of Life Cycle Assessment*, 16 (2011), 897–902.

[82] Korpi and Ala-Risku, 'Life cycle costing', 240–61.

[83] Perera, Morton and Perfrement, *Life cycle costing*, p. 3.

Also, in many instances the procuring agency is not the same with the agency that will operate/use the product/service.[84] Additional uncertainties arise when quantifying the lowered risks, avoided environmental damage, avoided clean-up costs and non-financial benefits such as the contributions to social cohesion through the creation of jobs, livelihoods and new industries. Forecasting such costs and benefits with an acceptable degree of certainty is very challenging[85] although there are solutions envisaged in the literature.[86]

One significant problem arising when considering sustainable public procurement is that procuring goods, services or works on the basis of life-cycle costing may mean paying more in the beginning.[87] It has been argued that in developing countries, the production of sustainable and LCC-efficient goods and services is still emergent, which means that the only way to acquire sustainable alternatives will be through expensive imports or paying a very high cost premium to stimulate infant local industries. In lower income economies, this difference can be higher, as much as 10 to 50 per cent.[88] Perera, Morton and Perfrement believe that over time, however, the large volumes demanded by public procurement contracts can make economies of scale more feasible, and the prices of these products can be expected to decrease as more producers enter the market. Also, public procurers can begin to use their strong market positioning to negotiate bulk discounts as the market begins to mature. In times of economic crisis, due to budget constraints, LCC may prove hard to be implemented effectively due to the existence of 'buy national' policies (often 'regular' public procurement gives pre-eminence to local companies over foreign suppliers).

4. Final considerations

It is quite evident that LCC was intended to be one of the pivotal elements of the new reform.[89] Buying green can save money, particularly when

[84] Ibid., p. 1. [85] C. Jobse and N. Dimitri, 'LCC-calculations', p. 3.

[86] A. Bala, M. Raugei, G. Benveniste, C. Gazulla and P. Fullana-i-Palmer, 'Simplified tools for global warming potential evaluation: when "Good Enough" is best', *International Journal of Life Cycle Assessment*, 15 (2010), pp. 489–98.

[87] H. Min and W.P. Galle, 'Green purchasing practices of US firms', *International Journal of Operations & Production Management*, 21 (2001), pp. 1222–38.

[88] Perera, Morton and Perfrement, *Life cycle costing*, p. 3.

[89] See also D. Dragos and B. Neamtu, 'Sustainable public procurement in the EU – experience and prospects', in F. Lichere, R. Caranta and S. Treumer (eds), *Modernising public procurement: the new directive* (DJØF Publishing, 2014), pp. 301–37.

an LCC approach is taken during the procurement process. The new Procurement Directives are encouraging national governments to foster the use of sustainable public procurement and of LCC but they still rely in numerous situations on voluntary compliance. Due to legal uncertainties, especially in countries not used to the techniques of green procurement, contracting authorities may choose not to implement LCC.

A famous quote attributed to Einstein warns us that 'not everything that can be counted counts and not everything that counts can be counted'.[90] This summarises in a way the opportunities and challenges of LCC as a sustainability tool: There are numerous costs associated with a product throughout its life cycle but contracting authorities need to include into their LCC analyses only those costs which are relevant. On the other hand, costs resulting from the internalisation of environmental and social externalities, which are highly relevant, might be difficult to be assigned a monetary value. Monetising all costs of environmental and social externalities are difficult, but that does not mean that they should not be part of the tendering offer. A purely monetary offer does not encompass all the costs of a product or service.

Even though LLC is an important new mechanism, it is not always suitable and must be used in combination with the other mechanisms provided for in the Directive. There are many sustainability considerations which can and should be reflected in technical specifications and award criteria that are not easily monetised.[91]

In times of economic crisis, LCC may prove hard to be implemented effectively due to the existence of 'buy national' policies, given the fact that 'regular' public procurement gives preference to local companies over foreign suppliers.[92]

Generally speaking, the often ambitious objectives of the EU with regard to sustainable development are in practice limited by more pragmatic considerations related to economic development. In the field of public procurement, sustainability is becoming more important but cost concerns are the most serious obstacle for taking environmental factors into account in the purchasing process. Public authorities will be more inclined to pursue sustainable procurement in contexts where they

90 See http://quoteinvestigator.com/2010/05/26/everything-counts-einstein/.

91 As discussed further in other chapters of this volume, for example, Chapter 3 by Abby Semple and Chapter 5 by Roberto Caranta.

92 M. Brulhart and F. Trionfetti, 'Public expenditure, international specialisation and agglomeration', *European Economic Review*, 48 (2004), 851–81.

perceive win-win situations.[93] It will be much harder to resort to the use of LCC and other sustainability tools when the outcomes are not very clear or documented properly or fair competition concerns arise.

The Directive is a clear step forward towards advancing sustainability goals, at least in declaratory terms, albeit it remains to be seen whether the tools envisaged by the new legal framework are effective enough or whether more decisive measures are necessary.

[93] P. Rao and D. Holt, 'Do green supply chains lead to competitiveness and economic performance?', *International Journal of Operations & Production Management*, 25 (2005), 898–916.

7

Sustainable public procurement under framework agreements

MARTA ANDRECKA

1. Introduction

This chapter considers what challenges and opportunities framework agreements pose when considering sustainable procurement under the new Public Sector Directive 2014/24/EU.[1] It is interesting, valuable and relevant to analyse the linkage between sustainable public procurement, innovation and framework agreements for several reasons: on the one hand, the aims of the EURO 2020 strategy for sustainable and inclusive growth to develop an economy based on knowledge and innovation,[2] to promote a low-carbon, resource-efficient and competitive economy, and to foster a high-employment economy delivering social and territorial cohesion. Indeed the newly introduced package on Public Procurement Directives from 2014[3] has as one of its goals to make public procurement more 'strategic' to spur innovation.[4] On the other hand, in recent years

[1] Directive 2014/24/EU of the European Parliament and of the Council of 26 February 2014 on public procurement and repealing Directive 2004/18/EC (further: Public Sector Directive 2014/24/EU).

[2] Communication from the Commission Europe 2020 on a strategy for smart, sustainable and inclusive growth, Brussels, 3 March 2010, COM (2010) 2020 final (further: The Commission, Europe 2020 on a strategy for smart, sustainable and inclusive growth).

[3] Public Sector Directive 2014/24/EU; Directive 2014/25/EU of the European Parliament and of the Council of 26 February 2014, respectively, on procurement by entities operating in the water, energy, transport and postal service sectors and replacing Directive 2004/17/EC (further: Directive 2014/25/EU); Directive 2014/23/EU of the European Parliament and of the Council of 26 February 2014 on the award of concession contracts.

[4] The goal of spurring innovation is relevant as buying '*innovative products, works and services plays a key role in improving the efficiency and quality of public services while addressing major societal challenges. It contributes to achieving best value for public money as well as wider economic, environmental and societal benefits in terms of generating new ideas, translating them into innovative products and services and thus promoting sustainable economic growth*'. See Recital 47 of the Public Sector Directive 2014/24/EU.

framework agreements have become a 'hot topic' in Europe owing not only to their strong political support and their frequent application (for example, one third of public procurement in Denmark is conducted in the form of framework agreements),[5] but also the controversies and lack of clear rules regarding their use.[6] In this chapter, the author argues that framework agreements, as tools for aggregated procurement, can be effective to implement sustainable public procurement under the new Public Sector Directive 2014/24/EU, but face particular challenges due to their scale, broader scope and issues of control in an aggregated procurement.

Sustainability is commonly understood as a synonym for progress and a long-term maintenance of well-being, which has environmental, economic and social elements and intergenerational justice in mind.[7] In the context of public procurement, sustainable development most often means that contracting authorities will apply socially and environmentally responsible practices when contracting for public works, services or supplies.[8] Incorporation of sustainable development in the procurement law started with the Court of Justice of the European Union's (CJEU) judgments in the *Beentjes* case[9] and *Concordia* case.[10] They confirmed that social and environmental criteria may be taken into consideration

[5] S. Poulsen, P. Jakobsen and S. Kalsmose-Hjelmborg, *Public procurement law – the EU directive on public contracts* (DJØF Publishing, 2012), p. 400; PwC, London Economics and Ecorys. 'Public procurement in Europe: cost and effectiveness', a study on procurement regulation prepared for the European Commission (London, 2011), see http://ec.europa.eu/internal_market/publicprocurement/docs/modernising_rules/cost-effectiveness_en.pdf.

[6] The EU rules on framework agreements are often differently interpreted, amongst other in countries like Denmark, Sweden and the UK (the conclusion of the Conference on Framework Agreements and Public Procurement Law in the European Perspective, Aarhus University, 26 January 2015); also, see www.business.dk/oekonomi/chefen-for-statens-indkoeb-fyret-0; Danish Complaints Board for Public Procurement: Decision of 15 March 2013, *Cowi A/S* v. *SKI A/S*; Decision of 1 February 2013, *Abena A/S* v. *SKI A/S*; Decision of 11 December 2012, *Dafolo A/S* v. *SKI A/S*; Decision of 16 May 2012, *EKJ Rådgivende Ingeniører A/S* v. *SKI A/S*; Decision of 23 January 2012, *Proffice A/S* v. *SKI A/S*.

[7] U. Steger, W. Achterberg, K. Blok, H. Bode, W. Frenz, C. Gather, G. Hanekamp, D. Imboden, M. Jahnke, M. Kost, R. Kurz, H.G. Nutzinger and T. Ziesemer, *Sustainable development and innovation in the energy sector* (Springer, 2010), p. 27; see J. Agyeman, *Sustainable communities and the challenge of environmental justice* (New York University Press, 2005), p. 2.

[8] See Anja Wiesbrock and Beate Sjåfjell in Chapter 1 of this volume.

[9] Case C-31/87 *Gebroeders Beentjes BV* v. *the Netherlands* [1988] ECLI:EU:C:1988:422.

[10] Case C-513/99, *Concordia Bus Finland* v. *Helsingin kapunki and HKL-Bussiliikenne* [2002] ECLI:EU:C:2002:495.

when awarding public contracts, and the establishment of a Public Sector Directive 2004/18/EC,[11] which introduced the availability of the 'secondary' environmental and social considerations during the procurement process into procurement legislation.[12] This initiative was followed by the Europe 2020 strategy for smart, sustainable and inclusive growth, which recognised that in realisation of its aims public procurement plays a key role.[13] However, the legal framework needed to be modernised if public procurement should contribute to the Europe 2020 strategy. Therefore, at the beginning of 2014, the European Parliament and the Council adopted the new Public Sector Directive 2014/24/EU, which has links directly to sustainable development both in its recitals and provisions.[14]

The concept of linking public procurement to other government policy objectives, such as sustainable development, is not new, but concerns about protectionism and lack of transparency for a long time impeded the use and development of sustainable public procurement in practice. It seems, however, that trade-related objections to sustainable public procurement have largely been overcome. Debates generally no longer focus on whether to use sustainable public procurement, but rather on how to use them in practice. Among others issues, sustainable public procurement poses challenges of how to identify and define environmental or social considerations in a manner that will be possible to include in the procurement conditions as these needs to be linked to the subject matter of the contract.[15] For life-cycle costing, a challenge also lies in determining and verifying the monetary value of environmental or social clauses that should be used. In practice this may be a difficult task, particularly in cases of social clauses, as these may not have a monetary value as such. The Public Sector Directive 2014/24/EU maintains the possibility to have

[11] Directive 2004/18/EC on the co-ordination of procedures for the award of public works contracts, public supply contracts and public service contracts, OJ 2004 (L134/114).

[12] See Recital 5 of the Directive 2004/18/EC: '*Under Article 6 of the Treaty [now Article 11 TFEU], environmental protection requirements are to be integrated into the definition and implementation of the Community policies and activities referred to in Article 3 of that Treaty, in particular with a view to promoting sustainable development. This Directive therefore clarifies how the contracting authorities may contribute to the protection of the environment and the promotion of sustainable development, whilst ensuring the possibility of obtaining the best value for money for their contracts*'; see also Arts. 27 and 50 of Public Sector Directive 2004/18/EC.

[13] The Commission, Europe 2020 on a strategy for smart, sustainable and inclusive growth.

[14] Amongst others: Recitals 2, 41, 47, 91, 93, 95, 96, 123; and Arts. 2(22), 18(2), 42(3)(a), 43, 62, 68, 70 of Public Sector Directive 2004/24/EU.

[15] See Abby Semple in Chapter 3 of this volume.

qualitative environmental/social award criteria or contract clauses as well as those monetised for inclusion in life-cycle costing calculations.[16]

Taking as a starting point the importance of sustainable public procurement, which has been underlined by EU acts[17] and policies,[18] as well as by many authors,[19] Section 2 will provide further conceptual background for the analysis in this chapter, considering the concept of framework agreements. In Section 3, opportunities and challenges of procuring a sustainable manner under framework agreements will be discussed. In particular, the capacity of framework agreements, established through central purchasing bodies, to promote innovation and sustainable solutions is analysed. Also discussed are the opportunities and risks in framework agreements, in regard to control of supply chains, in the context of compliance with environmental and social law, from a 'bottom-up' and 'top-down' perspective. Section 4 concludes the chapter, arguing that even though the sustainable procurement of framework agreements is

[16] See Dacian C. Dragos and B. Neamtu in Chapter 6 of this volume.

[17] Directive 2009/33/EC of the European Parliament and of the Council of 23 April 2009 on the promotion of clean and energy-efficient road transport vehicles; Regulation (EC) No. 106/2008 on a community energy-efficiency labelling programme for office equipment; Directive 2010/31/EU on the energy performance of buildings; Directive 2006/32/EC on energy end-use efficiency and energy services; Directive 2010/30/EU on the indication by labelling and standard product information of the consumption of energy and other resources by energy-related products.

[18] Interpretative Communication of the Commission on the Community law applicable to public procurement and the possibilities for integrating social considerations into public procurement (2001/C 333/08) COM (2001) 566 final; Communication from the Commission to the European Parliament, the Council, the European Economic and Social Committee and the Committee of the Regions Public procurement for a better environment, SEC(2008) 2124, SEC(2008) 2125, SEC(2008) 2126, see http://eur-lex.europa.eu/legal-content/EN/TXT/?qid=1398255660927&uri=CELEX:52008DC0400; *Buying social – a guide to taking account of social considerations in public procurement*, see http://ec.europa.eu/social/BlobServlet?docId=6457&langId=en; *Buying green! – a handbook on green public procurement*, see http://ec.europa.eu/environment/gpp/pdf/handbook.pdf.

[19] A. Semple, *A practical guide to public procurement* (Oxford University Press, 2015); S. Arrowsmith and P. Kunzlik (eds), *Social and environmental policies in EC procurement law* (Cambridge University Press, 2009); A. Semple 'Reform of the EU procurement directives and WTO GPA: forward steps for sustainability?', see http://ssrn.com/abstract=2089357; C. McCrudden, *Buying social justice: equality, government procurement & legal change* (Oxford University Press, 2007); J. Arnould, 'Secondary policies in public procurement: the innovations of the new directive', *Public Procurement Law Review*, 13 (2004), 187; R. Caranta and M. Trybus (eds), *The law of green and social procurement in Europe* (DJØF Publishing, 2010); R. Caranta, 'Sustainable procurement', in M. Trybus, R. Caranta and G. Edelstam (eds), *European union law of public contracts: public procurement and beyond* (Bruylant, 2014).

promoted by the new Directive, the practical effect of the relevant provisions depends to a great extent on national discretion.

2. Framework agreements

A framework agreement is a type of 'umbrella agreement' for the provision of goods, works or services for which the contracting authority has a repeated need.[20] Article 33 of the Public Sector Directive 2014/24/EU defines framework agreements as

> an agreement between one or more contracting authorities and one or more economic operators, the purpose of which is to establish the terms governing contracts [call-offs] to be awarded during a given period, in particular with regard to price and, where appropriate, the quantity envisaged.[21]

In this definition, the wording 'in particular' and 'where appropriate' needs to be emphasised. These phrases are significant from a sustainability perspective, as they mean that (i) price and quantity are not the only terms which may be established by framework agreements and (ii) it is not always necessary to establish quantity in the framework's terms. Also, the reference to a framework agreement being 'an agreement' suggests that it is different from a public contract.

Since the introduction of framework agreements as procurement instruments in the Directive 2004/18/EU, they have gained popularity and importance on the public tender market due to their perceived efficiency. It is claimed that framework agreements are more efficient than traditional procurement as they save both the purchaser and the supplier the time, resources and costs associated with agreeing to the terms and conditions every time an individual contract is made.[22]

An example of a typical framework agreement may be an office supplies order when the contracting authority knows it will need paper, toner,

[20] On framework agreement, see M. Andrecka, 'Framework agreements, EU procurement law and the practice', *Upphandlingsrättslig Tidskrifts*, 2 (2015); P. Arden 'Legal regulation of multi-provider framework agreements and the potential for bid rigging: a perspective from the UK local government construction sector', *Public Procurement Law Review*, 17 (2008); C. Nicholas, 'Framework agreements and the UNCITRAL model law on procurement', *Public Procurement Law Review*, 17 (2008), 20; S. Arrowsmith, 'Framework agreements under the UK procurement regulations: the Denfleet case', *Public Procurement Law Review*, 14 (2005), 86–91.

[21] In Directive 2014/25/EU, the definition may be found in Art. 51.

[22] S. Arrowsmith, 'Framework purchasing and qualification lists under the European procurement directives: Part 1', *Public Procurement Law Review*, 3 (1993), 115.

pens, etc. But at the moment of awarding the framework agreement, it is not able to provide specific time, place or quantities of the orders. Therefore, framework agreements are often characterised as 'incomplete agreements',[23] which usually establish general terms and conditions applicable to multiple orders, and more specific issues will be agreed upon when orders are placed.[24]

Depending on the contracting authority's needs, different types of framework agreements may be established. Where a framework agreement is concluded with just one provider (a single provider framework), call-offs under the agreement should be awarded within the terms laid down in the framework agreement.[25] The provider may be asked in writing to supplement its tender if necessary. Where a framework agreement is concluded with more than one provider (multi-provider framework), contracts may be awarded by: (a) direct award of call-offs, following the terms and conditions of the framework agreement without reopening competition, where all the terms and conditions for awarding the call-offs are set, or by (b) mini-competitions, where the framework agreement sets out the terms and conditions for reopening of competition amongst the providers of the framework agreement for the award of call-offs.[26]

In regard to the multi-provider framework agreements the Public Sector Directive 2014/24/EU introduces an important clarification, establishing that this type of framework agreements may include more than one type of procedure to award the call-offs. This means that part of the framework agreement orders may be directly awarded and other parts may be granted on the basis of a mini-competition. The only requirement imposed by the Directive 2014/24/EU is that it needs to be possible to choose between the two mentioned methods of the call-offs award on the basis of objective criteria, which must be set out in the procurement documents for the framework agreement.[27] Such objective criteria may relate to the quantity, value or characteristics of the works, supplies or services contracted, including the need for a higher degree of service or

[23] Framework agreements will not always be incomplete, in the case of framework contracts they will establish all terms and conditions for the subsequent award of call-offs, see European Commission Explanatory Note 'Framework agreements – classic directive', (CC2005/03 rev/ of 14 July 2005), p. 3.

[24] S. Mouzas and D. Ford, 'Leveraging knowledge-based resources: the role of contracts', *Journal of Business Research*, 2 (2012), 155.

[25] Art. 33(3) of Public Sector Directive 2014/24/EU.

[26] Art. 33(4) of Public Sector Directive 2014/24/EU.

[27] Art. 33(4) (b) of Public Sector Directive 2014/24/EU.

an increased security level, or to developments in price levels compared to a predetermined price index.[28]

3. Opportunities and challenges

In the following subsections, the opportunities and challenges of promoting sustainable solutions in framework agreements' procurement will be considered. It is argued that the possibilities and potential success of including sustainability considerations in framework agreements largely depend on their capacity as well as on the control down the supply chain, while opportunities to control up the supply chain (parent company) are limited.

3.1. Capacity of framework agreements

Framework agreements may be concluded by one or more contracting authorities or by central purchasing bodies in the name of the contracting authorities.[29] If a framework is established by a coalition of contracting authorities or by a central purchasing body, its capacity will usually be larger than in case of a framework agreement concluded by a single contracting authority. In the former scenario the framework agreement will usually include a larger basket of products understood as a larger quantity and variety of products. Moreover, there will be more users involved in such a framework agreement as there will be more than one addressee of the framework agreement, and the value of the framework agreement will be higher than in the scenario of a framework agreement concluded just for one contracting authority. Finally, there will usually be a higher level of professionalism in carrying out the procurement. All these elements create situations in which there are chances to promote innovation and other sustainable solutions.[30]

It is a general perception (often a misconception) that the inclusion of sustainability considerations in the procurement process is difficult and costly. From this perspective, it could be argued that in framework agreements with a large volume and value of the contract, the suppliers will be more willing to invest in new, innovative solutions, as the potential profits

[28] Recital 61 of Public Sector Directive 2014/24/EU.

[29] See Arts. 2(16) and 33 of Public Sector Directive 2014/24/EU.

[30] M. Andrecka, 'Innovation partnership in the new public procurement regime – a shift of focus from procedural to contractual issues?', *Public Procurement Law Review*, 2 (2015), 18–31.

will be larger. The counterargument could be that such solutions hinder participation of SMEs, and suppliers will not be willing to participate in a long costly tender procedure, as there will be no guarantee of winning the tender.[31]

As mentioned in Section 2, in practice many framework agreements are delivered by central purchasing bodies, which act as agents for several contracting authorities and usually conclude framework agreements of extended volume and value.[32] Public Sector Directive 2014/24/EU defines central purchasing bodies as contracting authorities, which conduct purchasing activities on a permanent basis in one of the following forms: (a) the acquisition of supplies and/or services intended for contracting authorities, (b) the award of public contracts or the conclusion of framework agreements for works, supplies or services intended for contracting authorities.[33]

Using framework agreements established by central purchasing bodies may be very beneficial for contracting authorities. Thanks to aggregation of procurement, the central purchasing bodies are able to achieve the best price for products, services and works on a market.[34] Also, it reduces the procedural burden for individual contracting authorities as they do not need to deal with the formalities of setting up the EU approved tender for the establishment of a framework agreement. This may be particularly advantageous in case of more complex procurement such as those which include sustainability considerations. A small contracting authority may lack in competencies, skills or appropriately trained staff to deal with such a task.

However, central purchasing brings several challenges and risks that need to be considered when a contracting authority is deciding whether to use such a framework agreement. For example, central purchasing

[31] Ibid.

[32] In 2009, over 25,000 framework contracts amounted to about one seventh of the value of all the contracts published in the OJEU. In the same year, 6.8 per cent of all contracts were awarded by contracting authorities purchasing on behalf of other authorities. Over 40 per cent of the value of contracts published by central or joint purchasing bodies was through framework agreement contracts. European Commission Internal Market and Services, 'EU public procurement legislation: delivering results Summary of evaluation report', p. 10, see http://ec.europa.eu/internal_market/publicprocurement/docs/modernising_rules/executive-summary_en.pdf.

[33] See Art. 2 (14–16) of Public Sector Directive 2004/24/EU.

[34] G.L. Albano, A. Ballarin and M. Sparro, 'Framework agreements and repeated purchases: the basic economics and a case study on the acquisition of it services', *Quaderni Consip*, 4 (2010), 5.

bodies' frameworks have been identified as less transparent, less fair and more bureaucratic than other public procurements.[35] This may be due to the scale and volume of central purchasing. Quite often they will limit the accessibility to the framework agreements for small- and medium-sized enterprises (SMEs), as they will often lack in capacity to compete for participation in such framework agreements.[36] It is often argued that most innovations originate from SMEs,[37] and thus it could be said that central framework agreements may potentially hinder the introduction of new innovative and sustainable solutions to the public markets.[38]

Also, central framework agreements are designed to include a vast amount of services, supplies or work under one agreement. From the sustainability perspective, this characteristic has both advantages and disadvantages. On the upside, it permits the inclusion of environmental and social considerations in a large amount of public contracts all at once. It allows for faster standardisation of sustainability clauses – in particular environmental ones – in the public procurement tenders. On the downside, a central purchaser's framework agreement includes a vast amount of services products of a different type and characteristics and one sustainability clause may not fit them all. Therefore, it may require a large range and amount of sustainability clauses to such frameworks, which may increase their costs, time and complexity, or in the worst case distorts these frameworks' core features.

Central framework agreements not only cover a lot of services, supplies or works, but also a lot of users, and thus they will not always fully respond to the particular needs of the individual contracting authorities. For example, a central purchaser concludes a framework agreement for stationary PCs or phones. However, due to specifics of its day-to-day work, municipality X needs laptops and mobile phones, which will allow the staff members to be mobile. Similar situations are present in cases of operating systems for computers; if municipality Y has iPads and Mac

[35] Europe Economic Market 2004/10/D, Evaluation of Public Procurement Directives §§ 5.7–5.28, (2006), see http://ec.europa.eu/internal_market/publicprocurement/studies_en.htm.

[36] C. Risvig-Hammer, 'Regular purchases and aggregated procurement: the changes in the new Public Procurement Directive regarding framework agreements, dynamic purchasing systems and central purchasing bodies', *Public Procurement Law Review*, 4 (2012), 207.

[37] See A. Cepilovs, *Public procurement of innovation and small and medium-sized enterprises*, Semester Project, Aalborg University, 2012, p. 3, see www.academia.edu/1649133/public_procurement_of_innovation_and_SMEs; J.A. Schumpeter, *The theory of economic development: an inquiry into profits, capital, credit, interest, and the business cycle* (Harvard University Press, 2008 (1934)).

[38] See Sarah Schoenmaekers in Chapter 7 of this volume.

computers, they may not be interested in the central purchasing body's framework agreement for a Microsoft operating system, as they will rather want to buy iOS.

Finally, from a sustainability perspective it is relevant to consider the consequences of central framework agreements having many addresses. Where certain general policies may be more easily implemented, for example, environmental standards, policy of waste disposal, sustainable production methodology (environmental considerations), other, more specific needs may be difficult to facilitate in such a general framework agreement (social considerations). For example, the contracting authority may wish to implement local policies, such as to activate the unemployed, to provide training of local youth entering into the job market and so on. These local policies will usually not be included in the central framework agreements as these frameworks need to stay generic to a large extent for two reasons: (a) to be able to gain the best economic outcome – meaning get the best price–quality ratio[39] and (b) to be able to include many contracting authorities as users in the framework agreements. The second reason is particularly relevant as the central purchasing bodies often are driven by self-interest to establish contracts with the highest amount of users as they often charge fees for using their framework agreements from their users.[40] Such a situation also poses the risk of central purchasing bodies´ overuse of framework agreements in practice, that is, in situations where they are not the most efficient procurement tools, but where the central purchasing bodies have an economic incentive in promoting the usage of framework agreements. Therefore, their approach may not always be an objective one.

3.2. *Control under framework agreements*

Sustainable public procurement under framework agreements also gives rise to the question of whether the contracting authority has the possibility to control the framework agreement or the subsequent call-off is handled

[39] Inclusions of more specific and/or local considerations in central framework agreements make it more difficult to achieve the best economic outcome. That is because the inclusion of such considerations would increase the price of the framework agreement and could potentially limit the scope of users wanting to become part of such a framework as particular social (local) considerations may not be relevant to all the potential users of the framework. Consequences could be seen in a smaller scale of framework agreements in which the central purchaser would not be able to achieve as large rebates or as good prices.

[40] C. Yukis, 'Are IDIQs inefficient? Sharing lessons with European framework contracting', *Public Contract Law Journal*, 3 (2008), 566.

in a sustainability-promoting manner during the procurement process or during the implementation phase of the framework agreement. In other words, can the contracting authority control the suppliers, their parent companies or subcontractors respect environmental and social laws or sustainability terms and conditions established in the procurement process?

In the context of framework agreements, the issue of control may at times be particularly complex, for example, in cases involving a framework agreement with many suppliers and an elaborate basket of products or services. In this situation, it may be especially difficult to follow the suppliers' supply chains. An example would be a multi-provider framework agreement conducted by a central purchasing body for IT supplies (computers, laptops, docking stations, keyboards, etc.), of which the biggest suppliers are situated in China. Factory X violates environmental or social law (methods of production; waste disposal and child labour), and the information breaks into the news. In such a situation, the central purchasing body needs to control all their frameworks with the mentioned products and control all of the suppliers in the frameworks to find out whether factory X was involved in any of the supplies provided. Also, finding out whether a production factory in China is breaking environmental and/or social laws while producing supplies, which the contracting authority buys at the end of the day, is extremely difficult. Control in framework agreements can pose not only legal uncertainties and difficulties, but also practical challenges.

Two major questions arise with respect to the issue of control under framework agreements from a sustainability perspective. First, it is important to consider to what extent the contracting authority may control the supply chain – that is the subcontractors of the winning bidder ('the top to bottom approach') in regard to compliance with environmental and social law and sustainability clauses. The second question concerns the possibility of controlling the compliance with environmental and social laws and sustainability clauses by the parent company of the bidder participating in the tender ('the bottom up approach').[41]

3.2.1. Control over the supply chain

Until recently, the EU Procurement Law Directives focused mainly on the relationship between the contracting authority conducting the procurement and the winner of the tender. The Directives did not focus

[41] More on social considerations in public procurement, see Anja Wiesbrock in Chapter 4 of this volume.

on the relationship with subcontractors. Therefore, in the procurement process it could only be ensured that, for example, the winning bidder[42] would comply with environmental and social law.[43] There were no legal tools in procurement law to control whether the subcontractors of the winning bidder respected these laws. A subcontracting relationship with its purely contractual character has until now – as a general rule – fallen outside the scope of the procurement situation and thereby procurement law regulation.[44]

The EU legislator recognised that it was necessary to ensure some transparency in the subcontracting chain.[45] This would make it possible to ensure that the contracting authorities have control of who is present at building sites on which works are being performed for them, or on which undertakings are providing services in or at buildings, infrastructure or areas, such as town halls, municipal schools, sports facilities, ports or motorways, for which the contracting authorities are responsible or over which they have a direct oversight.

The EU institutions thus introduced a new provision in the Public Sector Directive 2014/24/EU, for the first time regulating subcontracting in EU procurement law.[46] The new provisions give the contracting authority a right to ask – or the contracting authority may be required by a Member State to ask – the bidder to indicate in its tender any share of the contract it may intend to subcontract to third parties and any proposed subcontractors.[47] Member States may provide that at the request of the subcontractor and where the nature of the framework or subsequent call-off so allows, the contracting authority shall transfer due payments directly to the subcontractor for services, supplies or works provided to the economic operator to whom the framework agreements' call-off

[42] Also other bidders, if the violation fell under one of the exclusion grounds or selection criteria.

[43] On issues regarding secondary considerations (social and environmental) as well as the issue of linkage to the subject matter of the contract see Chapter 3 of this volume by Abby Semple; Also see P. Kunzlik, 'From suspect practice to market-based instrument: policy alignment and the evolution of EU law's approach to 'green' public procurement', *Public Procurement Law Review*, 3 (2013), 97–115; R. Caranta and M. Trybus (eds), *The law of green and social procurement in Europe*, European Procurement Law Series (DJØF Publishing, 2010), vol. II.

[44] There are some exceptions where the CJEU discussed the issue of subcontracting in the context of the procurement process, see Case C-91/08 *Wall AG v. Stadt Frankfurt am Main* [2010] ECLI:EU:C:2010:182.

[45] Recital 105 and Art. 71(1) of Public Sector Directive 2014/24/EU.

[46] It is necessary to underline that most of the provisions on subcontracting are actually voluntary for the Member States to implement.

[47] Art. 71(2) of Public Sector Directive 2014/24/EU.

have been awarded (the main contractor).[48] Such measures may include appropriate mechanisms permitting the main contractor to object to undue payments. The arrangements concerning that mode of payment shall be set out in the procurement documents.

However, the rules mentioned in the previous paragraph are without prejudice to the question of the main procurement contractor's liability.[49] Further, article 71(5) states that in the case of works contracts and in respect of services to be provided at a facility under the direct oversight of the contracting authority, after the award of the contract and at the latest when the performance of the contract commences, the contracting authority shall require the main contractor to indicate to the contracting authority the name, contact details and legal representatives of its subcontractors involved in such works or services, as far as is known at this point in time (the identification information).[50] In the context of framework agreements, the information will most likely be required at the stage of awarding call-offs or implementing them. It is doubtful that this information would need to be provided at the time of establishing the framework agreement, particularly if the framework is a multi-provider one, as bidders still compete for the call-offs, unless the direct award mode is being used. Therefore, a contracting authority requiring provision of the identification information at this stage would, most likely, be disproportionate, as it would also require bidders who may not receive any public contract in the end to provide this information, and that may be associated with additional time and costs. Also, the bidders will often not know who their subcontractors are, as they have not been given a specific contract.

It is conceivable that the identification information could be required at the stage of establishing a framework agreement, when the framework agreement is conducted with a single provider. However, it appears to be more appropriate to require such information at the time of placing an order rather than when setting up the framework because a substantial amount of time may pass between the establishment of the framework agreement and the time of placing the order. During this period circumstances may change, and the supplier may be in a situation where different subcontractors will be better fitted for the job or a change of a subcontractor will be necessary due to for example external circumstances (bankruptcy, liquidation, etc.).

[48] Art. 71(3) of Public Sector Directive 2014/24/EU.

[49] Art. 71(4) of Public Sector Directive 2014/24/EU.

[50] Ibid.

The contracting authority must require that the main contractor notifies the contracting authority of any changes to the identification information during the course of the contract as well as of the required information in connection with any new subcontractors subsequently involved in such works or services.[51] Notwithstanding what has already been said, Member States may impose the obligation to deliver the required information directly on the main contractor.

However, the discussed first subparagraph of Article 71(5) is not applicable to suppliers, which is especially important for framework agreements as the majority of those concern supplies. Framework agreements will rarely be established for work contracts.[52] However, contracting authorities may extend or may be required by Member States to extend the obligations provided for in the first subparagraph of Article 71(5) to for instance:

(a) supply contracts, to services contracts other than those concerning services to be provided at the facilities under the direct oversight of the contracting authority or to suppliers involved in works or services contracts;
(b) subcontractors of the main contractor's subcontractors or further down the subcontracting chain.

Further, in Recital 105 of the Public Sector Directive 2014/24/EU, it is underlined that it is important that observance by subcontractors of applicable obligations in the fields of environmental, social and labour law, established by Union law,[53] be ensured through appropriate actions by the competent national authorities (within the scope of their responsibilities and remit, such as labour inspection agencies or environmental protection agencies).[54] Those obligations contained in Article 18(2) are referred to in the provisions regarding selection of the bidders,[55] exclusion grounds,[56]

51 Art. 71(5) of Public Sector Directive 2014/24/EU.
52 Framework Agreements are used very rarely for works contract especially in Denmark, they occur more often in the United Kingdom; see www.ted.europa.eu.
53 Also, by national law, collective agreements or by the international environmental, social and labour law provisions listed in the Directive provided that such rules, and their application, comply with Union law.
54 Recital 105 of Public Sector Directive 2014/24/EU.
55 Art. 56 of Public Sector Directive 2014/24/EU.
56 Art. 57 of Public Sector Directive 2014/24/EU.

abnormally low tenders[57] and subcontracting.[58] We see for the first time this type of regulation in the Procurement Directives.

With the aim of avoiding breaches of the obligations referred to in Article 18(2), appropriate measures may be taken, such as: (a) Where the national law of a Member State provides for a mechanism of joint liability between subcontractors and the main contractor, the Member State concerned shall ensure that the relevant rules are applied in compliance with the conditions set out in Article 18(2);[59] (b) Contracting authorities may, in accordance with Articles 59 (European Single Procurement Document), 60 (means of proof) and 61(e-Certis), verify or may be required by Member States to verify, whether there are grounds for exclusion of subcontractors pursuant to Article 57 (selection of bidders).[60] In such cases, the contracting authority shall require that the economic operator replaces a subcontractor in respect of which the verification has shown that there are compulsory grounds for exclusion.[61] The contracting authority may require or may be required by a Member State to require that the economic operator replaces a subcontractor in respect of which the verification has shown that there are non-compulsory grounds for exclusion.[62]

If Member States choose to provide for these measures, they shall, by law, regulation or administrative provisions and having regard for Union law, specify the implementing conditions for those measures.[63] In doing so, Member States may limit their applicability, for instance in respect of certain types of contracts, certain categories of contacting authorities or economic operators or as of certain amounts.[64]

Inclusion of subcontracting rules in the Public Sector Directive 2014/24/EU introduces not only a level of legal certainty, but it also extends the scope of promoting EU sustainable market of public contracting. It is done by emphasising that procurement relationships must be understood more broadly and where applicable include subcontractors. In framework agreements often a specific subcontractor may provide services, supplies or works for more than one member of a framework agreement. Under such circumstances, the subcontractor may in fact become more involved in the delivery of a public contract than an

[57] Art. 69 of Public Sector Directive 2014/24/EU.
[58] Art. 71 of Public Sector Directive 2014/24/EU.
[59] Art. 71(6)(a) of Public Sector Directive 2014/24/EU.
[60] Art. 71(6)(b) of Public Sector Directive 2014/24/EU. [61] Ibid. [62] Ibid.
[63] Art. 71(7) of Public Sector Directive 2014/24/EU. [64] Ibid.

individual member of the framework. Therefore, ensuring that subcontractors respect environmental, social and labour laws under framework agreements is undisputable.

In case of framework agreements with a vast amount of orders and suppliers, and subsequently many subcontractors, it is easy to loose control of the supply chain. This is an issue as the public responsibility for the public contract delivery always stays with the contracting authority. The subcontracting rules provide help in control of often very broad and long supply chains regarding sustainable considerations as it is confirmed that contracting authorities may require subcontractors to respect environmental, social and labour law.

3.2.2. Control over the parent company

It follows from Section 3.2.1 that under the newly introduced Public Sector Directive 2014/24/EU, contracting authorities are able to control the supply chain 'down' the ladder ('the top-to-bottom approach') when it comes to obedience of environmental and social laws. Another interesting and relevant question is whether contracting authorities may control 'up' the supply chain ('the bottom-up approach'). In other words, if a company X that is well known worldwide for breaches of environmental law sets up a subsidiary Y, which then competes in framework agreement procurement, is a contracting authority able to require that parent company X respects environmental and social law in the procurement process? Or is it possible to disqualify subsidiary Y from participation in the tender because its parent company X breaches environmental or social law? One viewpoint in this discussion may be that the answer to the above question will depend on whether (a) we want to focus just on having a good framework agreement in general; or (b) we want to have sustainable companies and a sustainable EU internal market in general. The latter seems to be the right answer, based not only on policy goals of more sustainable procurement,[65]

[65] See Recital 2 of Public Sector Directive 2014/24/EU pointing out that the Directive should enable procurers to make better use of public procurement in support of common societal goals; see also European Commission, *Green Paper on the modernisation of EU public procurement policy: towards a more efficient European Procurement Market*, COM (2011) 15; The Commission, *Europe 2020 on a strategy for smart, sustainable and inclusive growth*; Communication from the Commission to the European Parliament, the Council, The European Economic and social Committee and the Committee of the Regions on pre-commercial procurement: *Driving innovation to ensure sustainable high quality public services in Europe*, COM (2007) 799 final (Brussels, 14 December 2007); Commission, *Green Paper on public procurement in the European Union: exploring the way forward*, COM (1996) 583; Anja Wiesbrock in Chapter 4 of this volume.

but also from the Treaty objectives of sustainable development[66] and the codification of the principle of sustainable development in Article 11 TFEU,[67] which states:

> Environmental protection requirements must be integrated into the definition and implementation of the Union's policies and activities, in particular with a view to promoting sustainable development.

It seems that on the basis of this Treaty Article and Recital 41 of the Public Sector Directive 2014/24/EU, it should be possible to impose measures controlling that subsidiary Y would be excluded from the public tender if the parent company X breaches environmental law.[68]

However, as Sjåfjell and Wiesbrock point out, in spite of the importance of the environmental integration principle codified in Article 11 TFEU in the strive to reach the long-term environmental objectives of the EU, this principle has been remarkably undervalued in the EU policy making, case law and secondary legislation, if present at all.[69] Article 11 TFEU is not only improperly implemented, it is to a large extent simply ignored by the EU legislator and judiciary.[70]

Public procurement law is one of the relatively rare areas where Article 11 TFEU is expressly referred to, in Recital 91:

> Article 11 TFEU requires that environmental protection requirements be integrated into the definition and implementation of the Union policies and activities, in particular with a view to promoting sustainable development. This Directive clarifies how the contracting authorities can contribute to the protection of the environment and the promotion of sustainable development, whilst ensuring that they can obtain the best value for money for their contracts.

However, this does not mean that it is possible on a general basis to exclude subsidiary Y from the procurement process solely because its parent company breaches the environmental laws, or to force parent company X to respect environmental and societal law referring to Article 11

[66] See Arts. 3(3) and 3(5) TEU.

[67] See B. Sjåfjell and A. Wiesbrock (eds), *The greening of European business under EU law: taking Article 11 TFEU seriously* (Routledge, 2015).

[68] Recital 41 of Public Sector Directive 2014/24/EU underlines that nothing in the Directive should prevent the imposition or enforcement of measures necessary to protect public policy interest as well as societal and environmental measures, in particular with a view to sustainable development, provided that those measures are in conformity with the TFEU.

[69] A. Wiesbrock and B. Sjåfjell, 'Jigsaw puzzle of sustainability', in B. Sjåfjell and A. Wiesbrock (eds), *The greening of European business under EU law: taking Article 11 TFEU seriously* (Routledge, 2015), Chapter 10.

[70] Ibid.

TFEU. Such a practice would be disproportional because procurement law regulates the procurement relationship (public contract or framework agreement), in other words, the parties involved in this relationship: the winning bidder, or the participant of the framework agreement, and the contracting authority or authorities. On this basis, the subcontracting is also regulated in procurement law, as subcontractors are also involved in the procurement relationship. They are involved in implementing the particular framework agreement that is the subject matter of the tender. Although procurement law enables the contracting authority to apply sustainable considerations, its primary concern and focus is on economic efficiency of a framework agreement.[71] The parent company will not be involved in the procurement relationship solely by being the parent company; as such it stands outside the procurement relationship. However, there are circumstances (elaborated below) in which the parent company–subsidiary relationship may give the basis for the exclusion of the subsidiary from the public tender.

It is thus under certain circumstances possible to control 'up' the supply chain in the procurement process, since the procurement law provides provisions that allow the contracting authority to exclude a subsidiary from the tender process when a parent company breaches environmental or social law.

When it comes to the bidders' selection stage in the procurement process,[72] the tenders must comply with terms, conditions and requirements of the procurement and candidates must meet the selection criteria contracting authorities must furthermore verify that the tenderers are not excluded from participation in the procurement procedure on grounds of Article 57 of the Public Sector Directive 2014/24/EU. In addition, a contracting authority *may* decide not to award a contract to the tenderer submitting the most economically advantageous tender, where it has established that the tender does not comply with the environmental, social and labour law referred to in Article 18(2).[73] Even though this is merely formulated as a right, rather than an obligation of the contracting authority concerned, it is important to note that the Member State must otherwise provide for other appropriate measures to ensure that operators comply with such legislation.

[71] There has to be a link to the subject matter of the contract to be able to use environmental or social considerations. See Art. 67(2) and Art. 70 of Public Sector Directive 2014/24/EU.

[72] Art. 56 of Public Sector Directive 2014/24/EU.

[73] Art. 18(2) also creates the basis for facultative exclusion from the procurement process in Art. 57(4)(a) of Public Sector Directive 2014/24/EU.

Further, Article 57(1) provides grounds for exclusion, which may potentially create the basis for tying the bidder – the subsidiary – to the parent company in the procurement scenario, at least to some extent. That is when the contracting authority is obliged to exclude a bidder where the member of the administrative, management or supervisory body of that bidder or a person who has powers of representation, decision or control therein is convicted by the final judgment in circumstances enumerated in Article 57. Amongst others, corruption, terrorism, money laundering and child labour are mentioned in the Article.[74]

Consequently, when the parent company's board members (with the final conviction) are also board members of the subsidiary and have a representation or control powers, etc., the subsidiary will be excluded from the tender process – something which takes place quite often in practice.[75] There is no requirement for the conviction to be linked to someone's current role, position or employment, so the violation of law could occur in different or prior capacities than the one that the person holds currently. What is crucial though is that none of the enumerated circumstances in Article 57(1) where the final judgment gives the basis for exclusion refers to environmental breaches. The reference in Article 57(1) is only made to child labour, which is a form of social law breach. Protection of the environment may be, though, one of the reasons that Member States may provide in exceptional cases for derogation from the mandatory exclusion.[76]

In addition to the mandatory exclusions, there are facultative grounds for exclusion where contracting authorities have a right of exclusion but not an obligation. In regard to environmental or social breaches it seems that particularly two reasons could be used for exclusion. First, where the economic operator has shown significant or persistent deficiencies in the performance of a substantive requirement under a prior framework agreement, a prior contract with a contracting entity or a prior concession contract, which led to early termination of that prior contract, damages or other comparable sanctions.[77] Such significant deficiencies may include not respecting the agreed environmental standards, or other societal/environmental contract performance clauses. Second, where the

[74] Art. 57(1) of Public Sector Directive 2014/24/EU.

[75] However, the reason is not that the member is involved in the parent company, but that he/she has a final conviction and is involved in the subsidiary – is a bidder in the procurement process.

[76] Art. 57(3) of Public Sector Directive 2014/24/EU.

[77] Art. 57(4)(g) of Public Sector Directive 2014/24/EU.

economic operator has been found guilty of serious misrepresentation in supplying the information required for the verification of the absence of grounds for exclusion or the fulfilment of the selection criteria, has withheld such information or is not able to submit the supporting documents required pursuant to Article 59.[78] These may include information claiming that the bidder fulfils the obligations stated in Article 18(2) regarding compliance with social and environmental laws when that is untrue.

However, Article 63 of the Public Sector Directive 2014/24/EU gives the contracting authority the power to look deeper into the behaviour of the parent company. It regulates reliance on the capacities of other entities. In regard to the selection criteria regulated in Article 58, bidders may, where it is appropriate and for a particular contract or framework agreement, rely on the capacities of other entities, regardless of the legal nature of the links, which they have with them.[79] In practice, this means that when a subsidiary wants to compete for a framework agreement, but does not have a sufficiently large yearly turnover, or does not own particularly needed professional capacities such as certificates or experience, which its parent company poses, the subsidiary may rely on the capacities of its parent company in the procurement process. In such a situation, the bidder shall prove to the contracting authority that it will have the necessary resources at its disposal, for example, by producing a commitment by the parent company to that effect.

The contracting authority shall verify whether the parent company on whose capacity the bidder-subsidiary intends to rely fulfils the relevant selection criteria, and whether there are grounds for exclusion pursuant to Article 57.[80] Further, the contracting authority shall require that the bidder replaces a parent company – as the institution on which capacities the bidder-subsidiary relies in the procurement process – if it does not meet a relevant selection criterion, or in respect of which there are compulsory grounds for exclusion. At the same time the contracting authority may require, or may be required by the Member State legislator to require – under specific circumstances – that the bidder-subsidiary substitutes a

[78] Art. 57(4)(h) of Public Sector Directive 2014/24/EU.

[79] However, with regard to criteria relating to the educational and professional qualifications, as set out in point (f) of Annex XII Part II, or to the relevant professional experience, bidders may, however, only rely on the capacities of other entities, where the latter will perform the works or services for which these capacities are required; See Art. 63 of Public Sector Directive 2014/24/EU.

[80] In accordance with Arts. 59–61 of Public Sector Directive 2014/24/EU.

parent company even if in respect of that parent company there are only facultative grounds for exclusion.

Consequently, if environmental or social considerations linked to the subject matter of the framework agreement are mentioned in the selection criteria, the parent company must fulfil these if the bidder is to rely on the capacities of the parent company. If environmental or social conditions are not fulfilled by the parent company, the bidder may replace it – as the institution providing the bidder-subsidiary the necessary capacities – for another entity that can fulfil these requirements. If that is impossible, the tender will be rejected.

In regard to the compliance with environmental and social laws by the parent company, the contracting authority may require a replacement of this parent company if it does not fulfil obligations referred to in Article 18(2). In this way, Article 63 provides provisions that allow to control 'up' the supply chain if the parent company becomes involved in the procurement relationship with a bidder-subsidiary wanting to rely on its parent company capacities.

Even if limited, the possibility to control 'up' the supply chain in framework agreement procurement should be accounted positively from the sustainability perspective. First, it makes it permissible to ensure that everyone involved in the framework agreement respects environmental, social and labour laws. Second, it permits bidders to depend on other bodies, such as parent companies, to provide capacity-support in fulfilling the required social or environmental requirements, during the procurement process, which the bidders lack on their own.

4. Conclusion

This chapter highlights the characteristics of a framework agreement, which may be described as possessing a high capacity in the context of a great economic value of the agreement due to the large volume of products and large amount of potential users as they are usually concluded by central purchasing bodies. These characteristics bring with them advantages as well as disadvantages related to the inclusion of sustainability consideration in public procurement procedures. On the one hand, framework agreements allow the promotion of a wide standardisation of general policies such as environmental considerations. They allow inclusion of sustainable considerations to a vast amount of public contracts all at once under one agreement. On the other hand, they may limit the possibilities of promoting local more individual initiatives such as social considerations because to a large extend the characteristics of framework agreements, particularly the central ones, are generic. That enables the body setting up the framework agreement to gain the best deal by including a vast amount of products or services of different type under the agreement as well as many users. However, the generic character of frameworks may pose challenges or even hinder the possibility of including more specific sustainable considerations.

Also, the structure of framework agreements is particularly adaptable to the division into lots, which in Public Sector Directive 2014/24/EU is one of the tools to promote SMEs' participation in the public procurement. Keeping that in mind that SMEs are to a large extent responsible for the delivery of new innovations, it could be argued that if framework agreements are divided into smaller orders, they have potential to be means to promote new improved (innovative) sustainable delivery of public contracts in the EU market.

It can be concluded that sustainable procurement of framework agreements is not only possible under the new Public Procurement Directive 2014/24/EU – it is also promoted. Whether it will be applied, however, depends on the contracting authorities, as the majority of environmental and social provisions have a facultative character. The only mandatory provision on sustainability concerns rejection of the abnormally low tender in cases where the tender is abnormally low because it does not comply with environmental, social laws and obligations. Nevertheless, the new provisions, which provide a possibility of controlling the supply chain 'up' (reliance on capacities of other entities) and 'down' (subcontracting), the ladder of connections in the procurement process should be seen as a major improvement. These provisions promote the sustainable public market in a broad sense.

8

The role of SMEs in promoting sustainable procurement

SARAH SCHOENMAEKERS

1. Introduction

The most important recent development in the field of public procurement is undoubtedly the new procurement package that entered into force on 17 April 2014. The package, of which most provisions have to be transposed by Member States by April 2016, consists of Directive 2014/24/EU on public procurement,[1] Directive 2014/25/EU[2] and Directive 2014/23/EU.[3] An important reason for the development of this new procurement package is that public procurement has increasingly been seen as an attractive instrument for achieving not only economic, but also non-economic policy objectives. With public authorities in Europe spending around 18 per cent of GDP on supplies, works and services every year,[4] public procurement is an important tool for opening up markets to international trade and obtaining better value-for-money. Moreover, procurement is increasingly used as a tool to contribute to the Union's and Member States' social and environmental policies. This is confirmed by two key objectives of the new public procurement package: encouraging the access to public procurement for small- and medium-sized enterprises (SMEs) and ensuring a better use of public procurement in support of common societal goals. The new Public Sector Directive

[1] Directive 2014/24/EU of the European Parliament and of the Council of 26 February 2014 on public procurement and repealing Directive 2004/18/EC, OJ 2014 (L 94/65–242).

[2] Directive 2014/25/EU of the European Parliament and of the Council of 26 February 2014 on procurement by entities operating in the water, energy, transport and postal services sectors and repealing Directive 2004/17/EC, OJ 2014 (L 94/243–374).

[3] Directive 2014/23/EU of the European Parliament and of the Council of 26 February 2014 on the award of concession contracts, OJ 2014 (L 94/1–64).

[4] PwC, London Economics and Ecorys, 'Public procurement in Europe: cost and effectiveness', a study on procurement regulation prepared for the European Commission (2011), p. 13.

2014/24/EU contains a number of mechanisms that are aimed at improving the involvement of SMEs in the public procurement market, such as the division of contracts into lots, the reduction of administrative burdens, direct payments to subcontractors and the prohibition to solicit overly demanding requirements concerning the economic and financial capacity of economic operators. At the same time, the Directive contains several methods to take sustainability into account in public procurement procedures. Reference can be made to the possibility to submit tenders that are based on the sustainability of the production process of the works, supplies and services and the fact that contracting authorities can determine the most economically advantageous tender and the lowest cost using a life-cycle costing approach.

This chapter discusses the mutually beneficial relationship between SMEs and sustainability criteria in public procurement: SMEs can benefit economically from a greater focus on sustainability in public procurement, whilst subjecting SMEs to sustainability criteria can have a great impact on key environmental objectives. Even though these objectives have often been considered to be contradictory (with a perception that stringent sustainability requirements are a barrier to SMEs), we will see that they are in fact complementary: while SMEs have a great potential to boost the use of sustainable public procurement if they are provided with the right tools, sustainability criteria can be an advantage to increase SMEs' participation in public tendering.

Section 2 of this chapter discusses innovation and sustainability as key objectives in the most recent procurement strategy of the EU and reflects on their synergies. Sections 3 and 4 focus on the potential of SMEs to contribute to green public procurement objectives. The potential of sustainable public procurement to improve the economic performance of SMEs will be discussed in Section 5, while Section 6 concludes.

2. Innovation and sustainability in public procurement

The concept 'Sustainable Public Procurement' refers to public authorities seeking to achieve the appropriate balance between the three pillars of sustainable development (economic, social and environmental) when procuring goods, services or works at all stages of a project.[5] It includes Green Public Procurement, which entails that public authorities seek to

[5] European Commission, Green and sustainable public procurement, see http://ec.europa.eu/environment/gpp/versus_en.htm.

procure goods, services and works with a reduced environmental impact throughout their lifecycle compared to goods, services and works with the same primary function that would otherwise be procured.[6] Sustainable public procurement is considered to be a policy instrument to obtain value for money for contracting authorities while at the same time reaching sustainable goals, efficiency and innovation. Sustainable public procurement can thus contribute to innovation since it may trigger economic operators to develop new ideas or technologies to reach a sustainable outcome for a particular work, supply or service.

Conversely, innovation can be considered as a tool contributing to more sustainability and efficiency and hence to sustainable public procurement. This is confirmed by the OECD, which considers innovation as one of the essential tools to achieve smart, sustainable and inclusive growth.[7,8] Indeed, by putting innovation at the core of public procurement practices, it is possible to leverage the substantial investment that has been made in R&D and to create better value for money in public services, through achieving efficiencies, improved productivity, quality, faster response times and reduced whole life costs.[9] The synergies between innovation on the one hand and sustainability on the other hand are also captured by the EU in its Europe 2020 flagship initiative 'Innovation Union' in which it indicates that Member States should set aside budgets for the procurement of *innovative* products and services to improve the efficiency and quality of public services, while addressing the major *societal* challenges. In the new public procurement package, innovation and sustainability are indicated as key objectives for future growth. According to recital 47 of Directive 2014/24/EU, buying innovative products plays a key role in improving the efficiency and quality of public services while addressing major societal challenges and contributing to achieving best value for public money.

Concerns have been raised, however, that sustainability criteria in public procurement procedures may hamper innovation and economic growth. The reasoning is that if additional (environmental or social) requirements are imposed, costs increase so that business is less willing

[6] European Commission, Green and sustainable public procurement, see http://ec.europa.eu/environment/gpp/versus_en.htm.

[7] Recital 124 of Directive 2014/24/EU.

[8] OECD, *The OECD innovation strategy: getting a head start on tomorrow* (OECD, 2010).

[9] Procurement Innovation Group, *Using public procurement to stimulate innovation and SME access to public contracts*, Report of July 2009, p. 6.

to invest in new or better techniques. Furthermore, sustainability criteria may be considered as scientific and non-economic and may offset economic operators on grounds of fears that they will not be able to live up to sustainability standards. Sustainability requirements may also impose constraints on operators and may discourage the use of certain production processes or materials, so that they are not willing to take part in a procurement procedure and refrain from thinking about innovative solutions for a particular problem. Innovation may also be hampered if business fears that it will be closely scrutinised and judged upon if it does not manage to live up to the sustainability criteria. New innovations may also bring about new sustainability issues which may in turn need new and more investments that economic operators are not willing to do.

Nevertheless, even though sustainability criteria in public procurement procedures have often been seen as hampering innovation and economic growth, there are many arguments as to why sustainable public procurement can equally be seen as a policy instrument to foster innovation and obtain value for money. First, contracting authorities are increasingly looking for tenders with the lowest cost, rather than the lowest price. Cost-effectiveness approaches such as life-cycle costing, which includes all costs over the life cycle of a work, supply or service, are gaining importance and generally bring about that tenderers have to pay attention to environmental, and to a certain degree, social aspects.[10] According to Article 68 of Directive 2014/24/EU, life-cycle costing covers not only acquisition costs but also costs of energy use, maintenance costs and end-of-life costs such as collection and recycling costs. It can also include costs imputed to environmental externalities linked to the product, service or works during its life cycle. In this regard it can be noted that although there might be a short-term gain for companies by cutting corners from a social or environmental perspective, markets and consumers may punish companies whose brand let them down.[11] Institutional investors are increasingly considering sustainable procurement factors as part of their assessments of a company's medium to long-term prospects for return on equity. For this reason, a growing number of global investment funds are including

[10] On life-cycle costing, see Chapter 6 of this volume by Dacian Dragos and Bogdana Neamtu.

[11] Accenture, *The sustainable organisation: the chief procurement officer's perspective*, part of Accenture's 'Lessons from leaders' series (Accenture, 2012). Also see B. Berthon, G. Hanifan, K. Timmermans and A. Williams, *Sustainable organizations? Start with sustainable procurement* (Accenture, 2013), p. 1.

specific sustainability-related metrics in their portfolio allocations and publish sustainability indices.

For consumers (natural person), buying sustainable products is mostly not an economic but an ethical choice. In recent years, consumers' preferences have evolved and green products such as organic food and fair trade products are becoming increasingly popular. Through green public procurement, green products will become more easily accepted and known on the market and a direct increase of demand can be achieved. It is thus not surprising that whilst sustainable procurement in 2003 was a top ten priority among just 40 per cent of firms, in 2011, it was a top five priority at more than 90 per cent of firms, according to a biennial benchmark fHEC-EcoVadis.[12] Sustainability is thus not only an important issue on the agenda of European policymakers, but also on the agenda of contracting authorities, companies (specifically SMEs) and (certain) private consumers.

The EU and its Member States have in recent years increasingly identified SMEs as a vehicle for more sustainable business practices. SMEs can contribute to a green and social economy due to their specialisation and know-how. In this regard reference can be made to the 2008 Small Business Act (SBA),[13] a self-commitment from the Member States to improve the business environment for small enterprises, which highlights that the EU and its Member States should enable SMEs to turn environmental challenges into opportunities. The SBA was followed in 2013 by the EU programme for the Competitiveness of Enterprises and SMEs (COSME) in the framework of the Horizon 2020 Programme.[14] The programme has a planned budget of 2.3 billion Euros to contribute to the reinforcement and sustainability of Union enterprises and SMEs by encouraging enterprises to adapt to a low-emission, climate-resilient, resource- and energy-efficient economy.[15] The COSME programme includes a number of financial instruments meant to facilitate access to finance for

[12] B. Berthon, G. Hanifan, K. Timmermans and A. Williams, *Sustainable organizations? Start with sustainable procurement* (Accenture, 2013), p. 1. This does not mean however that all these companies are also actively bidding for public procurement contracts including environmental requirements.

[13] A review of the Small Business Act was published in February 2011.

[14] Regulation (EU) No. 1287/2013 of the European Parliament and of the Council of 11 December 2013 establishing a Programme for the Competitiveness of Enterprises and small and medium-sized enterprises (COSME) (2014 – 2020) and repealing Decision No. 1639/2006/EC, OJ 2013 (L 347/33–49), 20 December 2013.

[15] Art. 4(2) Regulation 1287/2013.

SMEs in their start-up, growth and transfer phases.[16] Moreover, it aims to promote a business environment and culture favourable to sustainable enterprises[17] and to support the Enterprise Europe Network (EEN), which promotes partnership between public and private organisations and SME associations to raise SMEs' awareness of their environmental impact, existing and new environmental legislation and the benefits of environmental management systems.[18]

Raising awareness of SMEs regarding the positive effects of sustainability can also be achieved by emphasising the economic benefits of sustainable policies. In particular, the use of energy labels, eco-labels and the certification of products may give smaller companies a market advantage whilst at the same time reducing their environmental impact. For example, the EU Ecolabel Scheme, a pan-European labelling scheme allows companies to promote their products and services as eco-friendly with the well-known flower logo and grants preferential treatment to SMEs.[19] SME participation in such initiatives is reinforced by Small Business Standards (SBS), a European non-profit association established with the support of the European Commission that aims to raise awareness about the benefits of standards and to encourage SMEs to get involved in the standardisation process.

Furthermore, on 2 July 2014, the European Commission adopted a 'Green Action Plan for SMEs'.[20] The Action Plan presents a series of SME-oriented actions proposed at European level to help exploit the business opportunities that the transition to a green economy offers, by improving resource efficiency of European SMEs, supporting green

[16] Art. 17(1) Regulation 1287/2013. [17] Art. 12(1) Regulation 1287/2013.

[18] OECD, Working Party on Integrating Environmental and Economic Policies, *Green transformation of small businesses: achieving and going beyond environmental requirements*, ENV/epOC/WPIeep(2012)1/FINAL, (2012), p. 38; A.N. Miller and A. Varma, *First assessment of the environmental assistance programme for SMEs (ECAP)*, Final Report, prepared by AEA Technology Plc. for the European Commission, DG Environmental and Climate Action (London, 2011).

[19] According to the 2013 Eurobarometer, 75 per cent of SMEs consider the role of environmental labels in facilitating access to market for green products and/or services to be important.

[20] European Commission, Green action plan (GAP) for SMEs: enabling SMEs to turn environmental challenges into business opportunities, COM (2014) 440 final. This Action plan was made a few months after the meeting of the European Council in March 2014 which called for sustained efforts to moderate the energy costs borne by energy end-users, in particular through sustained investment in energy efficiency and demand-side management all along the value chain and at the R&D stage.

entrepreneurship, exploiting the opportunities of greener value chains and facilitating market access for green SMEs.

It follows that since the focus on sustainability has increased, the importance of sustainable procurement has increased as well. This is strengthened by the increasing occurrence of price volatility in most markets and the pressure from consumers and regulators to achieve more supply chain transparency.[21] Sustainable public procurement can thus be seen as a policy instrument to obtain value for money. SMEs are an important actor for contributing to sustainable policies and innovation and can be seen as a tool that links these two objectives.

3. The potential of SMEs to contribute to green public procurement objectives

On account of their specific characteristic and market position, SMEs hold great potential to contribute to sustainability objectives in public procurement processes, in spite of the fact that their current 'green record' is far from as good as it could be. Even though the individual environmental footprint of SMEs may be low, their aggregate can, in some respects, exceed that of large businesses. In fact, SMEs account for approximately 64 per cent of industrial pollution in Europe.[22] While 40–45 per cent of SMEs have a high impact on the environment,[23] only up to 24 per cent of SMEs actively engaged in reducing their environmental impact (energy use, CO2, waste, etc.) in 2010.[24] Moreover, only one quarter (26 per cent) of SMEs in the EU actually offer green products or services and the majority do not have plans to provide such products or services in

[21] B. Berthon, G. Hanifan, K. Timmermans and A. Williams, *Sustainable organizations? Start with sustainable procurement* (Accenture, 2013), p. 2.

[22] K. Miller, A. Neubauer and A. Varma, *First assessment of the environmental assistance programme for SMEs (ECAP)*, Final Report, prepared by AEA Technology Plc. for the European Commission, DG Environmental and Climate Action (London, 2011); OECD, Working Party on Integrating Environmental and Economic Policies, *Green transformation of small businesses: achieving and going beyond environmental requirements*, ENV/epOC/WPIeep(2012)1/FINAL, (2012), p. 8.

[23] C. Constantinos, S.Y. Sørensen, P.B. Larsen, S. Alexopoulou et al., *SMEs and the environment in the European Union* (PLANET SA and Danish Technological Institute, Published by European Commission, DG Enterprise and Industry, 2010), p. vii, see http://ec.europa.eu/enterprise/policies/sme/business-environment/files/main_report_en.pdf.

[24] The increase takes place mostly in SMEs not offering green products due to rising costs of energy and materials. While 93 per cent of SMEs are taking at least one action to be more resource efficient, only 0.4 per cent of SMEs use a certified Environmental Management System. See ibid, p. viii.

the future.[25] According to a 2012 Eurobarometer survey, the likelihood of having an environmental policy increases with the size of the business.[26] Environmental legislation is often considered too general to take into account the specificities of SMEs' operations. Furthermore, even though the specialisation and know-how of SMEs allows for the development of green products, SMEs may have a limited capacity to obtain information, absorb regulatory requirements and comply with them.[27]

It follows that the transition of SMEs to sustainable practices is key to the successful adoption of the green growth model. This is increasingly recognised by EU and national policymakers, including in the area of public procurement. In particular after the entry into force of the new EU Public Procurement package, SMEs have emerged as important potential counterparts of contracting authorities in making procurement sustainable. In the past, there has been a growing trend towards strategic procurement in the public sector through developing key supplier relationships with larger suppliers, supplier reduction and consolidation, which had a negative impact on SME involvement in the public sector.[28] In recent years, however, the specific potential of SMEs has been recognised and sustainable procurement actors are focusing more on increasing SME participation in procurement procedures and the potential of public procurement to increase the growth and sophistication of SMEs.

Even though falling short of meeting sustainability objectives to date, SMEs have great potential to boosting the use of sustainable public procurement if provided with the right tools. As indicated above, SMEs can contribute to a green and social economy due to their specialisation and know-how. Consequently, most contracting authorities and entities have developed rather favourable views on SMEs when working with them on public contracts.[29] Due to the fact that they have less personnel,

[25] Eurobarometer 2013.

[26] OECD, Working Party on Integrating Environmental and Economic Policies, *Green transformation of small businesses: achieving and going beyond environmental requirements*, ENV/epOC/WPIeep(2012)1/FINAL, (2012), p. 23.

[27] OECD, Working Party on Integrating Environmental and Economic Policies, *Green transformation of small businesses: achieving and going beyond environmental requirements*, ENV/epOC/WPIeep(2012)1/FINAL, (2012), p. 8.

[28] J. Zheng, H. Walker and C. Harland, *The role of SMEs in public procurement: a review of literature and research agenda*, p. 7, see www.ipsera.com/assets/documents/57.pdf; P. Smith and A. Hobbs, *SMES and public sector procurement, Shreeveport Management Consultancy, 704/V07*, (2001), pp. 1–36.

[29] See http://microsites.lincolnshire.gov.uk/procurementdeleted/buyer/sustainable-procurement/what-small-and-medium-sized-enterprises-can-do-for-us/.

SMEs often have short management chains and thus lower management costs, shorter approval routes and lower administrative overheads so that they can respond quickly to changing circumstances. Flexible and more customised solutions can be offered at a much shorter timescale. Their simpler organisational structure makes them more accessible so that they are able to develop sound long-lasting relationships with their customers and can offer a more personalised level of service. Due to their specialism in niche markets, SMEs fill the gaps in markets which large companies do not enter due to the absence of large economies of scale. By concentrating on specific markets, SMEs can retain skills, originality and commitment to their specialist field and focus on quality and innovation. Since they are often locally based, they have better knowledge and understanding of the local context and specific needs of a client. Being located closer to their customers speeds up (face-to-face) communication and allows them to develop bespoke products and services or tailor existing ones to their customers' needs. Since on average 89 per cent of their employees are local, SMEs contribute to local employment, regeneration of the local economy and overcoming social exclusion.[30] This also entails a reduction of transportation costs and a lower carbon footprint.

It can be concluded that SMEs are generally more innovative, more flexible, can offer higher levels of customer service and can contribute to their client's wider organisational objectives in relation to sustainability.[31] Hence, procurement that involves local SMEs fits well with sustainability objectives. The small-scale production methods and proximity of the entire supply chains of SMEs tend to overcome the problems and unsustainable developments related to large-scale or long-distance procurements. Instead, SMEs tend to create opportunities for innovative business, protect local employment and encourage cleaner production in the local economy.[32]

4. Facilitating sustainable SME participation through the new EU Procurement Directives

The new EU Procurement package contains several provisions that, whilst primarily aimed at increasing the participation of SMEs in public

[30] European Commission, *Flash Eurobarometer: observatory of European SMEs*, (2007). See also J. Zheng, H. Walker and C. Harland, *The role of SMEs in public procurement: a review of literature and research agenda*, p. 4, see www.ipsera.com/assets/documents/57.pdf.

[31] Institute for Sustainability, *Best practice guidance for successful SME engagement* (2012), p. 8.

[32] EPROC, *Adopting sustainable e-procurement practices*, p. 14.

procurement procedures and fostering innovation, may at the same time contribute to reaching the Directives' sustainability objectives. The European Code of Best Practices, which was developed in 2008, provides guidance on how contracting authorities can apply the public procurement framework in a way that facilitates SME participation.[33] It provides general guidance on how to apply the EU legal framework in a way that enables SMEs to participate in contract award procedures, and highlights a number of national rules and practices that facilitate access to public contracts by SMEs.

A first important mechanism to reach the goal of greater SME involvement is the requirement that contracting authorities should be encouraged to divide large contracts into lots, so that the size of the individual contracts better corresponds to the capacity of SMEs, or is better in accordance with the different trades and specialisations involved. In this way, the content of the individual contracts can be adapted more closely to the specialised sectors of SMEs or in accordance with different subsequent project phases. A subdivision into lots also allows contracting authorities to spread risks. According to Article 46(1) of the Directive, contracting authorities have to provide an indication of the main reasons for their decision not to subdivide into lots. Even though the possibility to divide contracts into lots is not new, this provision entails that it now has become more or less mandatory so that it can be qualified as a comply-or-explain mechanism.

The splitting up of contracts into lots enables a multiplication of the amount of contracts that SMEs will be able to tender for and allows contractors to bid for more manageable pieces of business.[34] It addresses SMEs' potentially more restricted skills bases, technical capacities or action radius.[35] As held by Article 46(2), contracting authorities may even limit the number of lots that may be awarded to one tender. Even though large contracts can bring benefits (economy of scale savings), sometimes not only in terms of better value, but also in terms of reduced procurement and contract management costs, they can hurt the supply base and therefore the potential for competition in the future.[36] It is therefore important that larger bidders for contracts engage more SMEs,

[33] See recital 78 of Directive 2014/24/EU.

[34] Department of Enterprise, Trade and Employment of Ireland, *Buying innovation: the 10 step guide to smart procurement and SME access to public contracts*, p. 13.

[35] European Commission, DG Enterprise and Industry, *Evaluation of SMEs' access to public procurement markets in the EU*, Final Report (September 2010), p. 114.

[36] Procurement Advice and Support Service, *A Guide to . . . Helping SMEs*, Version 2:290109, p. 6, see www.bipsolutions.com/pass.

for example, as subcontractors. This can even be made a requirement in the procurement documents.[37] If contracting authorities openly advertise details of their prime contractors via their website, they can assist SMEs to find subcontracting opportunities. They can also include in the contract an obligation for the prime contractor to advertise their subcontracting opportunities.[38] Furthermore, according to Article 71(3), Member States may provide that at the request of the subcontractor and where the nature of the contract so allows, the contracting authority shall transfer due payments directly to the subcontractor for services, supplies or works provided to the economic operator to whom the public contract has been awarded (the main contractor). This will give SMEs more incentives to be involved in a procurement project.

The subdivision of contracts into lots may also be advantageous from a sustainability perspective. If more SMEs are able to bid for certain parts of contracts, more use can be made of their expertise and specialisation. Contracts can be divided into product-specific lots, for example, bread, eggs, milk, fruits and vegetables in the food industry[39] or in geographic lots to ensure accessibility for smaller, local or regional suppliers. This can bring about a reduction of food miles and packaging waste and thus lower the ecological footprint of suppliers which has a positive impact on natural resources and ecosystems. Innovative SMEs may also invest in low impact production methods with reduced carbon inputs and greenhouse gas emissions or new production and consumption approaches to reduce environmental externalities and improve the quality of natural resources.

Another provision in the Directive that benefits SMEs whilst at the same time contributing to the objective of more sustainable procurement is the prominent role of electronic procurement. Even though electronic procurement already existed before the publication of the new procurement package, Directive 2014/24/EU now explicitly foresees that the new

[37] In the UK, there is an increasing amount of legislation encouraging the public and private sector down this route. Bidders for contracts have to submit information about supplier diversity at both the pre-qualification questionnaire and invitation to tender stage and this features in the scoring mechanism. Successful bidders together with their supply chains then have to implement supplier diversity plans and monitor and report on the participation of different categories of supplier. See Institute for Sustainability, *Best practice guidance for successful SME engagement* (2012), p. 6.

[38] Framework agreements also help SMEs that do not have the necessary capacities to satisfy the full demand in case a framework contract would be chosen.

[39] See, for example, European Commission, *Revaluing public sector food procurement in Europe: an action plan for sustainability*, www.foodlinkscommunity.net/fileadmin/documents_organicresearch/foodlinks/publications/Foodlinks_report_low.pdf.

rules on e-procurement have to be transposed by Member States by 18 October 2018 so that Member States no longer have a choice with regard to their application.[40] According to recital 52 and Article 22 of Directive 2014/24/EU, electronic means should become the standard means of communication and information exchange in procurement procedures, as they greatly enhance the possibilities of economic operators to participate in procurement procedures across the internal market.[41] E-certis, an electronic system managed by the Commission, which facilitates the exchange of certificates and other documentary evidence frequently required by contracting authorities, will be made mandatory at a later stage. However, e-procurement allows the pooling of contracts and supports outsourcing of procurement to centralised procurement agencies. Larger contracts may exceed the technical or financial capabilities of SMEs and over-aggregation may stifle competition as it can wipe out smaller SMEs resulting in higher prices.[42] Due to increased competition, there will also be a pressure to reduce prices, which may be problematic for SMEs but which is advantageous for the contracting authority involved.

The European Single Procurement Document (ESPD) is an updated self-declaration as preliminary evidence in replacement of certificates issued by public authorities or third parties confirming that the relevant economic operator fulfils certain conditions. Companies can only provide it in electronic form at the time of submission of requests to participate or of tenders.[43] This will result in considerable simplification and less administrative burdens for the benefit of both contracting authorities and economic operators.[44]

Contracting authorities using an e-procurement system are applying a more sustainable way of procuring services, works or supplies. E-procurement is automated and paperless and hence more efficient and less expensive to the benefit of economic operators in general and SMEs in particular. It reduces not only the amount of paper to be used but also the

[40] Art. 90(2) Directive 2014/24/EU.

[41] In 2010, 73 per cent of the surveyed contracting authorities and 82 per cent of the companies indicated to use e-procurement. However, electronic submission was only done by less than 50 per cent of the procurers surveyed. See European Commission, DG Enterprise and Industry, *Evaluation of SMEs' access to public procurement markets in the EU* (2010), p. 91.

[42] European Commission, DG Enterprise and Industry, *Evaluation of SMEs' access to public procurement markets in the EU* (2010), pp. 71 and 85.

[43] Certain conditions have to be fulfilled. See Art. 59(1) of Directive 2014/24/EU.

[44] Recital 84 of Directive 2014/24/EU.

manual work involved. If specific parameters are set up, automated systems can easily monitor compliance with sustainable procurement policies. Furthermore, in the light of centralised procurement governance, e-procurement can provide a central hub for disseminating information and maintaining visibility and control over the whole supply chain.[45] Supplier information can be actively managed and past purchasing patterns and sustainable requirements can be easily communicated which is specifically important with regard to sustainable products.

Other aspects that benefit SMEs in public procurement procedures are the use of variants which stimulate innovation and gives SMEs the opportunity to distinguish themselves,[46] the joint fulfilment of technical or financial capacities by groups of economic operators which allows them to submit a tender for bigger contracts[47] and the use of technical specifications in terms of performance or functional requirements which allows for more innovative solutions.[48] Article 58(3) and Recital 83 indicate that requirements concerning economic and financial capacity should be proportionate to the subject matter of the contract and may normally not exceed at the most twice the estimated contract value. Furthermore, an increased use of procurement procedures that involve negotiation can help SMEs to convince the procurer of their capabilities, the quality of the good or service offered and their strong client focus.[49] For each award, contracting authorities have to indicate in the contract award notice whether the successful tenderer is a SME.[50]

It can be concluded that SMEs can significantly contribute to the development of sustainable public procurement. Due to their specialism and potential for innovation, SMEs can develop sustainable products and their

[45] Dimension data, Building sustainability into your supply chain through e-procurement, see www.dimensiondata.com/Global/Downloadable%20Documents/Building%20Sustainability%20into%20Your%20Supply%20Chain%20Through%20e-Procurement%20Whitepaper.pdf.

[46] Art. 45 and Recital 48 of Directive 2014/24/EU.

[47] Recital 15 and Art. 19(2) of Directive 2014/24/EU. This is the most popular option used by contracting authorities to engage more SMEs. See European Commission, DG Enterprise and Industry, *Evaluation of SMEs' access to public procurement markets in the EU*, Final Report (September 2010), p. 59.

[48] Art. 42 and Recital 74 of Directive 2014/24/EU.

[49] European Commission, DG Enterprise and Industry, *Evaluation of SMEs' access to public procurement markets in the EU* (September 2010), p. 63.

[50] See Art. 50 and Annex Part D of Directive 2014/24/EU. With regard to contests, contracting authorities also have to publish the number of participants who are SMEs (Art. 79(2) and Annex Part F of Directive 2014/24/EU).

shorter approval routes allow for more flexibility and customised solutions. SMEs can also bring about social benefits since they often contribute to local employment, regeneration of the local economy and overcoming social exclusion, which in turn leads to a lower carbon footprint. The new procurement package contains several mechanisms that aim at greater SME involvement in public purchasing such as the division of contracts into lots, e-procurement and the use of variants. These mechanisms serve sustainability objectives at the same time.

5. Sustainable public procurement's potential for improving SMEs' economic performance

Whilst the promotion of SME involvement in the Directive is likely to contribute to reaching sustainability objectives, sustainable public procurement policies can at the same time have a positive impact on the economic performance of SMEs. Currently, SMEs in the EU face a number of challenges related to their economic performance and specifically their participation in public contracting.

SMEs[51] account for 99 per cent of enterprises in the Union, provide two out of three existing jobs in the private sector and 80 per cent of newly created jobs and contribute to more than half of the total added value created by enterprises in the Union. Nevertheless, the limited internationalisation of SMEs affects their competitiveness: 25 per cent of Union SMEs export or have exported at some point over the last three years while only 13 per cent export outside the Union on a regular basis.[52] Only 2 per cent have invested outside their home country.[53]

[51] The main factors determining whether a company is a SME are the number of employees and the turnover or balance sheet total. The category SMEs is made up of enterprises which employ fewer than 250 persons and which have an annual turnover not exceeding 50 million Euros and/or an annual balance sheet total not exceeding 43 million Euros. Member States, the EIB and the EIF may fix lower ceilings. See Art. 2 of Annex 2 Commission Recommendation 2003/361/EC as published in OJ (L 124/36), 20 May 2003.

[52] Regulation (EU) No. 1287/2013 of the European Parliament and of the Council of 11 December 2013 establishing a Programme for the Competitiveness of Enterprises and small and medium-sized enterprises (COSME) (2014–20) and repealing Decision No. 1639/2006/EC, recital 19.

[53] This may be related to the fact that there is a relatively weaker entrepreneurial spirit in the Union: only 45 per cent of Union citizens would to be self-employed as compared to 55 per cent of the population in the US and 71 per cent in China. See 2009 Eurobarometer survey on entrepreneurship.

Moreover, when it comes to public contracting, SMEs secure 42 per cent of the value and 60 per cent of the number of contracts above the thresholds fixed by the Procurement Directives.[54] This is less than their overall weight in the economy would warrant: their share in total turnover or gross premium written was 52–58 per cent and indicates that SMEs are, on average, underrepresented in public procurement above EU-thresholds.[55] This is due to a several reasons.

According to a study funded by the European Commission,[56] SMEs face difficulties in obtaining information on procurement opportunities. They complain about the shortage of opportunities to ask questions, the lack of feedback, the short time span to prepare the proposal and the lack of transparency. This is often related to the fact that they do not have tender specialists. Furthermore, SMEs hold that the costs of preparing a proposal are very high. Since many costs are fixed, it is true that these costs are often disproportionately high for SMEs in comparison with larger enterprises.

Another problem that SMEs encounter is that contracting authorities often demand high qualifications levels, a substantial amount of information and burdensome turnover requirements which represent higher transaction costs. The large size of contracts can also be a problem for SMEs. If contracting authorities do not allow the joint fulfilment of requirements by members of a consortium, they are often not able to perform high value contracts.[57] Since their geographical coverage is generally more limited, it is not easy for them to find collaboration partners abroad. Due to their fear to be discriminated against foreign tenderers, they often decline from participating in a foreign procurement procedure.

[54] See http://ec.europa.eu/enterprise/policies/sme/business-environment/public-procurement/index_en.htm; European Commission, DG Enterprise and Industry, *Evaluation of SMEs' access to public procurement markets in the EU*, Final Report (September 2010), p. 21; OECD, Working Party on Integrating Environmental and Economic Policies, *Green transformation of small businesses: achieving and going beyond environmental requirements*, ENV/epOC/WPIeep(2012)1/FINAL (2012), p. 5.

[55] European Commission, DG Enterprise and Industry, *Evaluation of SMEs' access to public procurement markets in the EU*, Final Report (September 2010), pp. 26, 29 and 114. The involvement of SMEs tends to be higher in local than in central government: at the local/regional level public procurement can easily represent 30 to 40 per cent of public expenditure.

[56] Ibid.

[57] The share of public contracts secured by SMEs is only 21–29 per cent for contracts worth more than 5 million Euro, but more than 60 per cent in contracts of below 300,000 euro. European Commission, DG Enterprise and Industry, *Evaluation of SMEs' access to public procurement markets in the EU*, Final Report (September 2010), p. 32.

An overemphasis on price rather than on quality and flexibility can also be identified as a barrier for SMEs to engage in public procurement.[58]

Furthermore, SMEs are more vulnerable to key personnel leaving. The lack of reserve capacities and additional expertise, specifically if the scope of a project is amended, entails that SMEs are not always as flexible as they would like to. A danger is that they may overstretch themselves and take on huge risks.[59] Furthermore, SMEs can often not afford complex and costly external and internal audit systems or certification measures, often have no sustainable, equality and diversity policies, may be less e-enabled than their larger competitors and have lower levels of insurance so that they are perceived as a higher risk option.

It is thus not surprising that buyers may think that SMEs represent more risk and that they cannot be relied upon since they have no suitable track record or seem to be too small for the type of contract on offer. Contracting authorities therefore sometimes feel that SMEs should not climb up the learning curve at taxpayers' expense and may be risk averse when it comes to engaging with SMEs.[60] This negative perception may be increased by SME's narrower range of products and the lower productivity levels in comparison with large firms.[61]

At the same time, SMEs are often not interested in public contracts since they find private contracts easier and faster to win and prefer to engage only with contractors they trust. Their weakness to build up and maintain contacts with contracting authorities inevitably results in less direct notifications by contracting authorities. Another reason not to engage in public contracts is the fear of payment delays.[62] Since SMEs generally are risk averse, they do not like uncertainty with regard to payment periods.

This section argues that focusing on sustainable procurement mechanisms can improve SMEs' participation in public contracting as well as their overall economic performance. Currently, only one out of ten EU SMEs bid for public procurement contracts that include environmental requirements versus 16 per cent of large companies.[63] Nevertheless, it has

[58] European Commission, DG Enterprise and Industry, *Evaluation of SMEs' access to public procurement markets in the EU*, Final Report (September 2010), p. 66.

[59] Ibid., p. 59. [60] Ibid., p. 65.

[61] European Commission, Impact Assessment, *Think small first – small business act.*

[62] This is the second biggest barrier. See European Commission, DG Enterprise and Industry, *Evaluation of SMEs' access to public procurement markets in the EU* (2010), p. 49.

[63] SMEs account for 99 per cent of enterprises in the Union, provide two out of three existing jobs in the private sector and 80 per cent of newly created jobs and contribute

been established that sustainable policies may bring about reduced operating costs for business in the long run, improved image and increased sales. By using sustainable public procurement, a process whereby public authorities take into consideration in their procurement activities the environmental, social and economic impacts of products, services or works throughout their life cycle, contracting authorities can foster a market for the commercial introduction of new sustainable products and technologies. Since contracting authorities are major consumers, they can act as strategic tools for the creation and development of sustainable policies and can stimulate a migration towards green growth models that cover economic, environmental, innovative and social aspects.

If SMEs are required to take into account sustainability concerns, they will be better adapted to subsist in markets that require higher environmental standards. Furthermore, by investing in sustainable procurement, SMEs can demonstrate their capabilities, establish their credibility in international markets, prove the viability of new products or services and gain authoritative and essential reference contacts from the public sector.[64] In this way, SMEs can create more jobs for themselves in upcoming green markets.

Sustainable or innovative elements that may benefit SMEs can be found in all phases of the procurement process. In the pre-procurement phase, emphasis can already be put on sustainable or social requirements through a preliminary market consultation.[65] By collecting and analysing data about the specific market, contracting authorities can establish beforehand what is important for them and can open a dialogue with potential suppliers to develop a more realistic picture of the specific market. Moreover, for all types of contacts, technical specifications may include references to the production process or any other stage of the life cycle for all types of contract.[66] Since technical specifications can be defined in terms of performance of functional requirements, including environmental characteristics, there is more scope for innovative solutions and green offers, which is beneficial for SMEs.[67] Contracting authorities can even refer to specific environmental or social labels in the technical

to more than half of the total added value created by enterprises in the Union. See European Commission, Commission Staff Working Paper, Executive Summary of the Impact Assessment, SEC(2011), 1586 final.

[64] Procurement Innovation Group, *Using public procurement to stimulate innovation and SME access to public contracts*, Report of July 2009, p. 6.

[65] Art. 40 of Directive 2014/24/EU. [66] Art. 42(1) of Directive 2014/24/EU.

[67] Art. 42(3) and Recital 73 of Directive 2014/24/EU.

specifications[68] and can allow for green variants so that bidders can offer different green solutions.

In the tendering phase, contracting authorities can invoke non-compliance with EU, international or national social and environmental law as grounds for refusal to award a contract to a tenderer.[69] At the selection stage, they can thus look at the environmental and social record of tenderers and request evidence of environmental management measures. The Directive contains an increased scope for contracts to be reserved for enterprises employing disabled or disadvantaged workers.[70] According to Article 62(2) of the Directive, where contracting authorities require the production of certificates drawn up by independent bodies attesting that the economic operator complies with certain environmental management systems or standards, they shall refer to the Eco-Management and Audit Scheme (EMAS) of the Union or to other environmental management systems (EMS) that are based on the relevant European or international standards by accredited bodies. Such schemes can demonstrate that the economic operator has the technical capability to perform the contract.[71]

Sustainable production practices can also be important at the award stage since life-cycle costs can be used as an award criterion. As held by Article 67 of the Directive, contracting authorities have to base the award of public contracts on the most economically advantageous tender which has to be identified on the basis of the price or cost, using a cost-effectiveness approach, such as life-cycle costing, and may include the best price–quality ratio, which shall be assessed on the basis of criteria, including qualitative, environmental and/or social aspects, linked to the subject matter of the public contract in question. Article 68 contains a definition of life-cycle costs. These are internal costs, such as research to be carried out, development, production, transport, use, maintenance and

[68] Art. 43(1) and Recital 75 of Directive 2014/24/EU.

[69] Art. 57(4) of Directive 2014/24/EU.

[70] They may also provide for such contracts to be performed in the context of sheltered employment programmes, provided that at least 30 per cent of the employees of those workshops, economic operators or programmes are disabled or disadvantaged workers. Art. 20(1) of Directive 2014/24/EU.

[71] Art. 62(2) and Recital 88 of Directive 2014/24/EU. Where an economic operator has no access to such environmental management registration schemes or no possibility of obtaining them within the relevant time limits, it should be allowed to submit a description of the environmental management measures implemented, provided that the economic operator concerned demonstrates that those measures ensure the same level of environmental protection as the measures required under the environmental management.

end-of-life disposal costs but also include costs imputed to environmental externalities, such as pollution caused by extraction of the raw materials used in the product or caused by the product itself or its manufacturing.[72] Specific environmental or social labels can be demanded as award criteria as well.[73]

The choice of the appropriate procurement procedure is important since it may allow SMEs and other companies to engage in a dialogue or in negotiations on green and innovative aspects with the contracting authority. The competitive dialogue, the competitive procedure with negotiation and the innovation partnership are often very suitable to exchange views.[74] This last procedure, which takes place in successive stages, was introduced by Directive 2014/24/EU and allows contracting authorities to establish a long-term partnership for the development and subsequent purchase of a new, innovative product, service or work without the need for a separate procurement procedure for the purchase. It should provide the necessary market-pull to incentivise the development of an innovative solution without foreclosing the market.[75]

With regard to the contract execution phase, contracting authorities can include a best available technology clause under which the supplier is required to migrate to better technologies, especially under longer-term contracts.[76] By offering the sharing of gains from future cost savings under a longer-term contract or by giving suppliers intellectual property rights companies may invest more in innovation which may result in additional cost savings for the procurer.[77] Such agreements may lie at the heart of certain public–private partnerships investments. Contracting authorities can also lay down innovation-related or environmental conditions relating to the performance of a contract or ask for specific environmental or social labels in the contract performance conditions.[78]

In addition to the phases of the traditional procurement process, reference should also be made to pre-commercial procurement clauses. The Commission Communication of 14 December 2007 entitled 'Pre-commercial procurement: driving innovation to ensure sustainable high quality public services in Europe', deals with the procurement of those research and development (R&D) services not falling within the scope

[72] Recital 96 of Directive 2014/24/EU.
[73] Art. 43(1) and Recital 75 of Directive 2014/24/EU.
[74] Arts. 29–31 of Directive 2014/24/EU. [75] Recital 49 of Directive 2014/24/EU.
[76] European Commission, DG Enterprise and Industry, *Evaluation of SMEs' access to public procurement markets in the EU* (2010), p. 93.
[77] Ibid. [78] Arts. 43(1) and 70 and recitals 75 and 98 of Directive 2014/24/EU.

of Directive 2014/24/EU.[79] Pre-commercial procurement (PCP) enables public authorities to challenge industry to develop solutions for public sector problems that are technologically demanding and for which either no commercially suitable solution exists on the market, or existing solutions exhibit shortcomings which require new R&D. It concerns the R&D phase before a product or service is commercialised. Contracting authorities procure R&D services and share the risks and benefits at market conditions, whilst several companies propose and develop innovative solutions that address the needs of the public sector in a competitive environment. PCP is thus a way for contracting authorities to promote innovation and for undertakings to bring innovative ideas to the market more quickly and demonstrate their capacities. It has a market-pull approach. PCP initiatives are mostly awarded to SMEs, hence underlining their enormous potential.[80] It allows them to develop and provide innovative solutions without the necessity to provide developed products or services on a commercial scale. The development of products would mainly benefit large enterprises which can exercise economies of scale in production or delivery of products or services.[81] The advantage for contracting authorities is that since the products will be newly developed and will not be commercialised, they can obtain them at lower prices. Furthermore, through the staged approach and the input from SMEs that is applied in PCP, contracting authorities face lower risks (less adverse effects) and lower costs of failure. PCP increases thus the overall potential and competitiveness of the European economy.

Currently, there are already many public procurement networks, projects and programmes focusing on sustainability and SMEs. Many of them are referred to above. With regard to sustainability in particular, reference should be made to the European Commission's 'Buying green! Handbook' and its 'Guide on dealing with innovative solutions in public procurement – 10 elements of good practice' and the Procura+ Manual 'A guide to cost effective SPP'. All these initiatives indicate the importance of sustainability and innovation in public procurement and the key role of SMEs to contribute to this aim.

[79] Recital 47 of Directive 2014/24/EU.

[80] European Commission, DG Enterprise and Industry, Evaluation of SMEs' access to public procurement markets in the EU (September 2010), p. 106.

[81] A. Cepilovs, *Public procurement of innovation and small and medium-sized enterprises* (Aalborg University, 2012), p. 36, see www.academia.edu/1649133/public_procurement_of_innovation_and_SMEs; J. Sylvest, *Opportunities for public technology procurement in the ICT-related sectors in Europe* (2008), pp. 48–9.

6. Conclusion

As held by Porter and Vanderlinden, increased environmental performance will lead to increased competitiveness of both nations and industries.[82] For this reason, SMEs should invest more in sustainable practices. The 2014 public procurement modernisation package contains several methods to take sustainability concerns into account, such as the sustainability of the production process of the works, supplies and services and the possibility to determine the most economically advantageous tender by using a life-cycle costing approach. At the same time, the Directive aims to increase the level of success of SMEs in public procurement procedures, that is, the share of SMEs in the total value of contracts awarded. Directive 2014/24/EU contains several mechanisms to reach this goal, such as the division of contracts into lots, the use of e-procurement, the possibility to allow for variants and the prohibition to solicit overly demanding requirements concerning the economic and financial capacity of economic operators.

If SMEs take sustainability concerns into account, they will be better adapted to markets that require higher environmental standards. The transition of SMEs to sustainable practices is thus beneficial for SMEs and is the key to the successful adoption of the green growth model. Indeed, due to their specialisation and know-how, sustainable public procurement practices will allow SMEs to unlock their growth and innovation potential with a positive impact on the European economy and will allow them to contribute to a green and social economy. For contracting authorities, diversifying the supply chain and offering opportunities to SMEs, will entail that they can pursue wider organisational objectives such as equality, diversity and inclusion, economic and community development, a better range of solutions, more competition and thus keener prices, a

[82] M.E. Porter and C. Vanderlinden, 'Towards a new conception of the environment-competitiveness relationship', *The Journal of Economic Perspectives* 9(4), (1995), 97–118. As held by Lu and Faure, it should be noted however that there is no conclusive empirical evidence indicating that firms with good social/environmental performance will necessarily also perform better in financial aspects than those with bad social/environmental performance. Nevertheless, the majority of research proves that good social/environmental performance does in any case not lead to poor financial performance. See M. Lu and M. Faure, 'The regulation of corporate environmental responsibility', in N.J. Philipsen, S.E. Weishaar and G. Xu (eds), *Market integration: the EU experience and implications for regulatory reform in China* (Springer, 2014), p. 23.

culturally diverse market place, a possible reduction in transport and logistic costs and more innovation and sustainability.[83]

While sustainable public procurement can contribute to innovation, since it may trigger economic operators to develop new ideas or technologies to reach a sustainable outcome for a particular work, supply or service, innovation can likewise be considered as a tool contributing to more sustainability and efficiency and hence to sustainable public procurement. It follows that the use of sustainability criteria in public procurement allows for greening the business of SMEs, whilst at the same time giving them an opportunity to distinguish themselves and potentially boosting their performance. Even though these objectives have often been considered to be contradictory, they are indeed complementary: while SMEs have a great potential to boost the use of sustainable public procurement if they are provided with the right tools, sustainability criteria can be an advantage to increase SMEs' participation in public tendering.

As held by United Nations' Secretary General Ban Ki-moon: 'Through investment in new technology and research, the promotion of domestic manufacturing, increased transparency and accountability in public fund management, and support for small- and medium-sized enterprises (SMEs), procurement systems can help develop national capacity and attain sustainable development goals'.[84] Even though a focus on sustainability aspects in public procurement may possibly exclude some SMEs that do not meet the required environmental or social requirements, it also brings about many benefits. It follows that SMEs should use public procurement strategically: by investing in sustainable procurement, SMEs can demonstrate their capabilities, establish their credibility in international markets, prove the viability of new products or services and gain authoritative and essential reference contacts from the public sector.[85] In this way, they can strengthen their competitiveness and create more jobs for themselves in upcoming markets whilst at the same time contributing to the greening of the European economy.

[83] Institute for Sustainability, *Best practice guidance for successful SME engagement* (2012), pp. 7–8.

[84] United Nations, *2013 Annual Statistical Report on United Nations Procurement*, foreword.

[85] Procurement Innovation Group, *Using public procurement to stimulate innovation and SME access to public contracts*, Report of July 2009, p. 6.

9

Sustainable public procurement as a driver for sustainable companies?

The interface between company law and public procurement law

BEATE SJÅFJELL

1. Public procurement through the lens of international company law

This chapter discusses the relationship between public procurement and company law within the context of the overarching EU objective of sustainable development.[1] The EU recognises the importance of business to achieve sustainability and the relevance of public procurement law as a policy strategy instrument in this context, but it does not yet recognise the importance of company law.[2] Reform of public procurement law is seen as an essential part of the EU's 2020 Strategy,[3] with public procurement being mentioned several times: as a potential driver to stimulate innovation[4] and resource-efficiency,[5] and as an integral part of an industrial policy for a global, low-carbon economy.[6] While

[1] Set out in Art. 3(3) and 3(5) TEU; see Beate Sjåfjell and Anja Wiesbrock in Chapter 1 of this volume for a further discussion.

[2] Concentrating rather on reporting to promote awareness of sustainability issues, and even that limited to the largest businesses, in spite of the EU Commission's revised definition of corporate social responsiblity as 'the responsibility of enterprises for their impact on society' (COM (2011) 681, *A renewed EU strategy 2011–14 for corporate social responsibility*, s. 3.1. This paradigm shift of the new CSR definition is not followed up in company law, see B. Sjåfjell and L. Anker-Sørensen, 'Directors' duties and corporate social responsibility (CSR)', in H. Birkmose, M. Neville and K. Engsig Sørensen (eds), *Boards of directors in European companies – reshaping and harmonising their organisation and duties* (Kluwer Law International, 2013).

[3] See, for example, in Recital 2 of Directive 2014/24/EU.

[4] Communication from the Commission, *Europe 2020: a strategy for smart, sustainable and inclusive growth*, COM (2010) 2010 final, p. 12.

[5] Ibid., p. 15. [6] Ibid., p. 16.

public procurement is also mentioned as a tool to ensure efficient use of public funds,[7] company law is only regarded in the economic context, as something to be simplified to facilitate single-market access for SMEs and encourage entrepreneurship.[8] However, company law does have a crucial role to play in the transformation towards sustainability because it provides the legal framework for the internal workings of the company, including its decision-making.[9] Indeed, the argument can be made that without a reform of the legal infrastructure for the internal decision-making in companies, sustainability is very difficult, if not impossible, to achieve.[10]

This chapter draws on a research-based reform proposal for EU company law and corporate governance.[11] Section 2 proceeds with a brief presentation of the reform proposal for sustainable companies and discusses the potential role of public procurement in that context. On this basis, Section 3 considers whether ideas from the reform proposal can be promoted by public procurement as a potential front-runner and a driver for the necessary transformation of business. As we will see, there are some possibilities but also significant limitations. Section 4 discusses whether there are any lessons to be learned for public procurement from the insights derived from international company law research on how to internalise environmental and social externalities in the decision-making in companies. Section 5 conversely questions whether innovative approaches in the new Public Procurement Directives can inspire a further development of the reform ideas for company law itself. Section 6 concludes with some reflections on the interaction between public procurement law and company law.

[7] Ibid., p. 26, and also in Recital 2 of Directive 2014/24/EU.

[8] Ibid., p. 20 – the only mention of company law in the whole document. Improving business legislation is mentioned on p. 17 as something Member States need to do, together with reducing administrative burdens on companies – clearly along the same simplification and deregulation path.

[9] B. Sjåfjell, A. Johnston, L. Anker-Sørensen and D. Millon, 'Shareholder primacy: the main barrier to sustainable companies', in B. Sjåfjell and B.J. Richardson, *Company law and sustainability: legal barriers and opportunities* (Cambridge University Press, 2015), pp. 79–147.

[10] Not as fix-it-all, but as a vital piece in the jigsaw puzzle of sustainability, see B. Sjåfjell and B.J. Richardson, *Company law and sustainability: legal barriers and opportunities* (Cambridge University Press, 2015).

[11] B. Sjåfjell, 'Corporate governance for sustainability', in B. Sjåfjell and A. Wiesbrock, *The greening of European business under EU law: taking Article 11 TFEU seriously* (Routledge, 2015), pp. 97–117.

2. A company law reform for sustainable companies

The reform proposal summarised here springs out of a research project that has had the deeper integration of environmental concerns into the decision-making of companies as its aim: the Sustainable Companies Project.[12] The first formulation of the reform proposal, as a tentative Nordic suggestion, concentrated on integrating the environmental dimension of sustainability.[13] Envisaged as the basis for a proposal for a new EU Directive, and in recognition of the inextricable interconnectedness of environmental, social and economic aspects of business, the reform proposal this chapter summarises presents ideas for a reform that is holistic in the sense that it covers all three dimensions of sustainable development, as does the concept of sustainable public procurement.[14]

The reform proposal is based on three premises: First, sustainable development cannot be achieved without the contribution of business.[15] Second, business can with existing knowledge and technology shift away from business as usual and onto a sustainable path. This entails that we should not be content with waiting for technological innovation.[16] Third, business is not doing enough on a voluntary basis. Therefore legal reform is necessary.[17] This section first very briefly presents the research-based findings as regards company law, then the reform proposal itself, before

[12] See more about this Oslo-led international research project at www.jus.uio.no/companies under Projects.

[13] See B. Sjåfjell and J. Mähönen, 'Upgrading the Nordic corporate governance model for sustainable companies', *European Company Law*, 11 (2014), 58–62.

[14] The reform proposal was first presented in B. Sjåfjell, 'Corporate governance for sustainability'.

[15] As the European Commission also states: 'enterprises can significantly contribute to the European Union's treaty objectives of sustainable development and a highly competitive social market economy', COM (2011) 681 final, s. 1.2.

[16] Although that does of course not mean that we do not need innovation – just that a lot can be done with existing technology. As stated already in an IPCC report from 2005, there is a great potential for business to reduce greenhouse gas emissions already with existing technology, but there are barriers that prevent this from being put into use; see B. Metz, O.R. Davidson, P.R. Bosch, R. Dave and L.A. Meyer (eds), Climate Change 2007: Mitigation of Climate Change, Contribution of Working Group III to the Fourth Assessment Report of the Intergovernmental Panel on Climate Change (2007), see http://ipcc.ch/publications_and_data/ar4/wg3/en/contents.html.

[17] That legal reform is necessary has been substantiated through the research done in the Sustainable Companies Project, see B. Sjåfjell and B.J. Richardson, *Company law and sustainability*.

discussing the potential role of public procurement in such an envisaged new regime.[18]

2.1. *Possibilities and barriers for sustainable companies*

The pervasive myth that maximisation of returns to shareholders is the sole purpose of companies is debunked through a proper analysis of law and exposed to be incorrect.[19] This is analysed both on the level of what company law regulates and in the more overarching perspective of what is society's purpose with companies in aggregate.[20] Although there are variations as to the extent of focus on shareholder value and the explicit or implicit inclusion of a broader set of interests, no company law system insists on boards focusing only on returns for shareholders.[21] All jurisdictions we investigated expect boards to ensure environmental legal compliance. Generally company law across jurisdictions also allow boards to internalise environmental and social externalities beyond legal compliance,[22] at least as far as the business case argument allows – that is, as far as the case can be made that this is profitable for the company in the long run. Our comparative analysis shows that company law provides perhaps surprising latitude to the board and by extension the management to shape business in a sustainable manner.[23]

However, boards generally do not choose environmentally and socially sustainable options within the realm of the business case, let alone challenge the outer boundaries of the scope to pursue profit in a sustainable manner. This is because of the overriding social norm of shareholder primacy, which, supported by management remuneration incentives and other drivers, leads to an extremely narrow, short-term, profit maximisation focus.[24] The resulting practice of companies in aggregate is

[18] The focus is here on companies, as a dominant business form and where shareholder primacy, especially for the listed companies, is prevalent. In a possible implementation of the reform, also other business forms need to be encompassed and SMEs especially considered.

[19] See B. Sjåfjell, A. Johnston, L. Anker-Sørensen and D. Millon, 'Shareholder primacy: the main barrier to sustainable companies'.

[20] Ibid. [21] Ibid.

[22] Ibid. – while this analysis focuses on environmental concerns, much of the same arguments may be made for social impacts of the company's business.

[23] Ibid.

[24] Ibid. Short-termism has been identified by the EU Commission as a problem but not adequately acted on; see B. Sjåfjell and L. Anker-Sørensen, 'Directors' duties and corporate social responsibility (CSR)'.

detrimental to those affected by climate change and environmental degradation today and to the possibility for future generations to fulfil their own needs. It is also damaging to any shareholder with more than a very short-term perspective on their investment, including institutional investors such as pension funds or sovereign wealth funds, as well as to the companies themselves.[25]

This social norm of shareholder primacy and its pervasive myth of maximising returns being the overarching objective, has been allowed to develop because of what company law generally does not speak about: the societal purpose of companies and the role and duty of the board in that context. This indicates the direction for reform.

2.2. Reforming EU company law

Based on the research findings briefly set out above, reforming company law on an EU level to achieve sustainable companies should address two main points: a redefinition of the purpose of the company as a matter of law and of the role and the duties of the board. Combating shareholder primacy requires more than permitting a sustainability approach – as we saw above, company law already gives boards a perhaps surprisingly large room to shift away from the path of business as usual and onto a sustainable path. We therefore need firmer rules that set out the direction that boards must seek to shift the companies towards, providing thereby a redefined space for the creation of value. Legal reform on the EU level is necessary to codify sustainable business as the norm, so that the competitive advantage is given to companies that wish to contribute to sustainable development and taken away from those who do not. As we are far off track from sustainable development,[26] we need to go beyond stipulating long-term, inclusive concepts of the purpose of the company and the interests of the company. What urgently needs to be done is to clarify that while companies in the aggregate may and should have profit

[25] While the preamble of the proposal for an amendment of the Shareholder Rights' Directive claims in Recital 2 that the financial crisis has 'revealed that shareholders in many cases supported managers' excessive short-term risk taking', an at least as valid concern is that shareholders have pressurized directors and managers to focus on short-term returns only.

[26] Notably, the fifth assessment report of climate change by the Intergovernmental Panel on Climate Change (IPCC) published in April 2014, reiterates its message from the fourth assessment report in 2007, namely that it is urgent to begin reducing emissions, otherwise we will not be able to stay below the agreed upon limit of two degree temperature rise; see O. Edenhofer et al., *Final Draft Summary for Policymakers*, IPCC WGIII AR5, 8. This is but one of several pressing issues as a case in point for sustainable development.

as an integrated part of their purpose this should be achieved within the overarching societal goal of sustainable development.[27]

In the long run, economic sustainability presupposes that business is conducted within these ecological limits. As the impacts of climate change and other environmental degradation take effect, the economy will also be affected. And as the negative impacts of transgression of the ecological limits become more apparent, legislators will at some point, probably too late, require greater internalisation of environmental externalities through stricter environmental regulation, higher taxes on emissions, and so on. Businesses that today are allowed to ignore these issues will find themselves forced to change. We can also expect more cases where victims of climate change and other environmental harm sue businesses whose operations have contributed to their loss. Conversely, the rise of socially responsible investment, green procurement policies and also a shift in private consumer choice towards environmentally friendly products and services, may over time lead to more demand for responsible businesses – although these drivers today appear to be insufficient.[28] However, the main issue in the long term is that the very basis of our societies and thereby also our economies is threatened – making it in everybody's interest, including that of today's business leaders, to participate in the shift away from 'business as usual' and onto a sustainable path. If we are to achieve a safe operating space for humanity and its businesses, incremental improvements are blatantly insufficient. The concept of planetary boundaries,[29] based on state-of-the-art natural science, embodies this fundamental recognition and should form the space within which all economic and social development is to take place. This concept should

[27] See also B. Willard, 'Better is not good enough: toward true corporate sustainability' (June, 2014), see http://greattransition.org/document/better-is-not-good-enough-toward-true-corporate-sustainability.

[28] See for example concerning responsible investment, B.J. Richardson, 'Financial markets and socially responsible investing', in B. Sjåfjell and B.J. Richardson (eds), *Company law and sustainability*.

[29] Introduced by J. Rockström, W. Steffen, K. Noone, Å. Persson, F.S. III Chapin, E. Lambin, T.M. Lenton, M. Scheffer, C. Folke, H.J. Schellnhuber, B. Nykvist, C.A. de Wit, T. Hughes, S. van der Leeuw, H. Rodhe, S. Sörlin, P.K. Snyder, R. Costanza, U. Svedin, M. Falkenmark, L. Karlberg, R.W. Corell, V.J. Fabry, J. Hansen, B. Walker, D. Liverman, K. Richardson, P. Crutzen and J. Foley, 'Planetary boundaries: exploring the safe operating space for humanity', *Ecology and Society*, 14(2) (2009), see www.ecologyandsociety.org/vol14/iss2/art32/; updated in W. Steffen et al., 'Planetary boundaries: guiding human development on a changing planet', *Science* (January 2015), see www.sciencemag.org/content/347/6223/1259855.abstract.

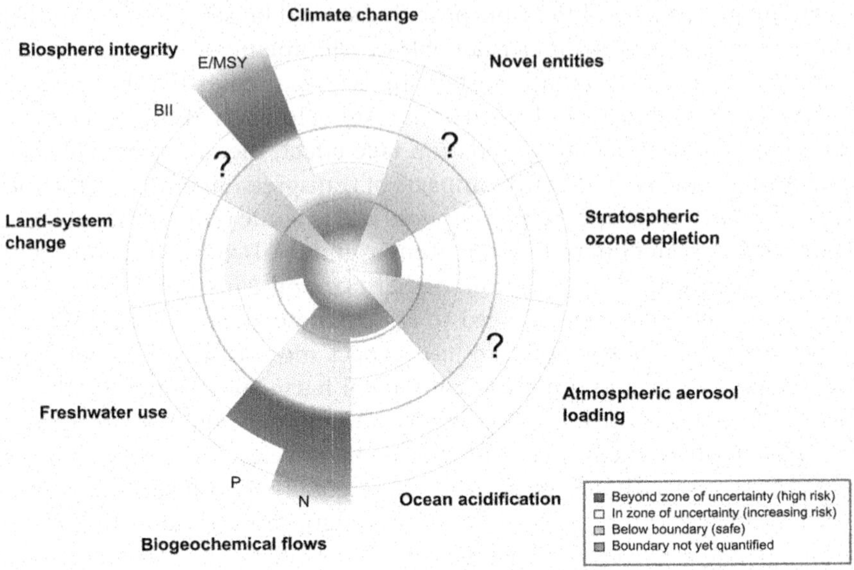

Figure 9.1 Planetary boundaries.

therefore be a key issue in a redefined purpose of companies as a matter of company law.

It is estimated that humanity has already transgressed four of these nine planetary boundaries shown in Figure 9.1: climate change, biosphere integrity, biogeochemical flows and land-system integrity.[30] The environmental precautionary principle is of essence.[31]

The proposal suggests redefining the purpose of companies in an EU Company Law Directive like this:

> The purpose of a company is to create sustainable value within the planetary boundaries while respecting the interests of its investors and other involved parties.

The fundamental key issues here are the purpose of creating *sustainable value* and the space within which value can be created: *within the*

[30] The other five being global freshwater use, ocean acidification, atmospheric aerosol loading, stratospheric ozone depletion and cycling of phosphorus and nitrogen. W. Steffen et al., 'Planetary boundaries: guiding human development on a changing planet, 2015'.

[31] Indeed, the conceptual framework for planetary boundaries itself proposes a strongly precautionary approach, by 'setting the discrete boundary value at the lower and more conservative bound of the uncertainty range', J. Rockström et al., 'Planetary boundaries'.

planetary boundaries. The formulation *within the planetary boundaries* is used to signal clearly that these are non-negotiable boundaries, where the room for trade-offs is limited.[32] A further development of this idea into a proper legislative proposal would require explanatory notes where the concept of *sustainable value* was given content. The basic idea is that *sustainable value* is long term and inclusive, as opposed to short-term pursuit of shareholder returns. Protection and promotion of the interest of the shareholders, other investors and other involved parties, including employees, creditors and other contractual parties, is encompassed through the formulation that sustainable value is to be sought *while respecting the interest of its investors and other involved parties.*[33] Broader societal impact can also be included in *sustainable value* and *other involved parties* depending on how this is defined in explanatory notes and implemented, interpreted and put into practice. The ultimate goal is to achieve not only a safe operating space for humanity but a safe and *just* space for humanity.[34]

The key components to operationalise this redefined purpose are to integrate the purpose into the duties of the board[35] and require that each company draws up a long-term, life-cycle-based *sustainable business plan.* Boards have a 'vital part to play in the development of responsible companies' as the European Commission has pointed out,[36] also stating that the '. . . enterprises should have in place a process to integrate social, environmental, ethical, human rights and consumer concerns into

[32] This distinguishes the proposal from the much debated 'enlightened shareholder value' in the UK Companies Act, see, for example, A. Johnston, 'Reforming English company law to promote sustainable companies', *European Company Law*, 11 (2014), 63–6, and emphasises the non-negotiable ecological limits as opposed to what is done in the traditional pluralistic approach of Continental-European law, see, for example, T. Lambooy, *Corporate social responsibility: legal and semi-legal frameworks supporting CSR: developments 2000–2010 and case studies* (Kluwer Law International 2010), pp. 107–46.

[33] Using 'investors' rather than 'shareholders' recognises the complex structures of finance through debt, equity or grants.

[34] See K. Raworth, *A safe and just space for humanity: can we live within the doughnut* (Oxfam International, 2012), see www.oxfam.org/sites/www.oxfam.org/files/dp-a-safe-and-just-space-for-humanity-130212-en.pdf.

[35] The duties of the board are arguably the best place in the regulatory ecology of the companies. On the significance of boards, see, for example, B. Sjåfjell and L. Anker-Sørensen, 'Directors' duties and corporate social responsibility (CSR)'. On the concept of regulatory ecology, see B. Sjåfjell and M. Taylor, 'Planetary boundaries and company law: towards a regulatory ecology of corporate sustainability' (26 May 2015), University of Oslo Faculty of Law Research Paper No. 2015–11, http://ssrn.com/abstract=2610583'.

[36] COM (2011) 164 final.

their business operations and core strategy in close collaboration with their stakeholders, with the aim of: maximising the creation of shared value for their owners/shareholders and for their other stakeholders and society at large; and identifying, preventing and mitigating their possible adverse impacts'.[37] The OECD Guidelines for Multinational Enterprises also support the formulation of such duties.[38]

The proposal suggests redefining the directors' duties like this:

> The board of the company is to ensure the life-cycle-based creation of sustainable value. To this end, the board shall adopt and regularly revise a long-term business plan for the company, based on a life-cycle assessment of the company's main areas of business.

A mandatory table of contents of the business plan should be drawn up as an annex to the Directive, to encourage proper compliance and comparability between companies. Guidelines endorsed by the European Commission should set out how the relevant and sufficient key performance indicators (KPIs) are to be selected according to the sector and concrete business plan of the company.

The operationalisation of the board's duty to ensure *life-cycle-based creation of sustainable value* is the *sustainable business plan*, which shall contain the long-term plan for the company.[39] The sustainable business plan will outline how the company is to achieve life-cycle-based value creation within the planetary boundaries. A requirement for such a business plan, designed thoughtfully, would involve a standardisation of a process that companies wishing to achieve long-term sustainable value would need to do anyway. The standardisation would contribute to lowering costs and establishing a level playing field.

This proposal, with its life-cycle focus on the products and services businesses offer, fits well together with the integrated product policy of the EU where the life-cycle perspective is identified as the leading principle[40] as it does with the public procurement reform, where

[37] COM (2011) 681 final, s. 3.1.

[38] See, for example, Chapter VI Environment, see www.oecd.org/corporate/mne/48004323.pdf.

[39] A tentative indication is that long-term here would be 15–30 years (or the full time span of the company, if it has a shorter time horizon).

[40] See E.M. Ekern, 'Towards an integrated product regulatory framework based on life cycle thinking', in B. Sjåfjell and A. Wiesbrock (eds), *The greening of European business under EU law* (Routledge, 2015), pp. 144–62. See also the Joint Research Centre's establishment of the European Platform on Life Cycle Assessment (EPLCA), see http://eplca.jrc.ec.europa.eu/, and the identification already in the Commission Communication of 2003 of

life-cycle costing is an important approach to including broader concerns.[41] A full life-cycle analysis to identify and mitigate negative environmental and social impacts, would have to be undertaken for any products the company sells or services it offers, either by the company itself, or by the manufacturer/supplier.[42] This would be a way of dealing with the pulverisation of responsibility for environmental and social impacts that we see today through multinational groups of companies and international supply chains. Any European company would need to draw up its own life-cycle-based business plan or substantiate that this was included for example by a parent company's business plan.[43]

The sustainable business plan is envisaged to include milestones or objectives to be achieved along the way, and KPIs in as far as the impacts can be quantified, relevant to the specific plan of the company, which the company can report on annually. The proposal bridges the gap between the internal decision-making in the company and reporting, giving a clear duty on which to report, and content to the recently adopted non-financial reporting requirement on the EU level.[44] The long-term plan should be broken down into shorter time segments,[45] entailing that the company at these regular intervals must undertake a full assessment of its business plan and consider necessary revisions.

2.3. *The potential role of public procurement in a sustainable companies regime*

Envisaging the implementation of the reform proposal summarised above, effective enforcement of these duties would be necessary to ensure

life-cycle assessment as the 'best framework for assessing the potential environmental impacts of products', *Integrated product policy*, COM (2003) 302.

41 See Chapter 6 of this volume by Dacian C. Dragos and Bogdana Neamtu.

42 This would entail a cradle-to-cradle perspective of, for example, a product, including every phase from the sourcing of the materials used in the production through the production, marketing and selling of the product, to the user phase and finally to the recycling or waste management of the product, to identify all environmental and social impacts.

43 An issue for further research will be how to ensure that such a reform is not circumvented through companies in third countries selling their products to European purchasers.

44 Proposal for a Directive of the European Parliament and of the Council amending Council Directives 78/660/EEC and 83/349/EEC as regards disclosure of non-financial and diversity information by certain large companies and groups, COM (2013) 207 final – 2013/0110 (COD), adopted by the European Parliament April 2014; see C. Villiers and J. Mähönen, 'Article 11: integrated reporting or non-financial reporting?', in B. Sjåfjell and A. Wiesbrock, *The greening of European business under EU law*, pp. 118–43.

45 For example, 15 years broken down into three- or five-year segments.

that the requirements become more than words on paper and that they are not used as a basis for greenwashing. The drawing up of the business plan itself should be made into an enforceable duty. The qualitative control of the business plan should probably be limited to the selection of KPIs to ensure that these core indicators against which the company is to report are relevant and sufficient. With guidelines or standards endorsed by the European Commission to identify the relevant and sufficient indicators, such a check, which only needs to be undertaken when the business plan is drawn up or fundamentally revised, should not be too burdensome to require.[46]

In such a new regime, public procurement would be a useful enforcement mechanism. A verified sustainable business plan could be a prerequisite to be allowed to submit a tender, and audited reporting against the verified KPIs requirements throughout the procurement contract period.[47] This would, for the businesses interested in being considered in public procurement bidding rounds, be an efficient way of ensuring that the new regime is complied with.

3. Can sustainable public procurement be a front-runner?

Business does not have to wait for a new EU Company Law Directive. Core aspects of the company law reform proposal summarised above could be put into use by businesses wishing to become more sustainable today. Changes in articles of association could clarify that the company has as its goal to create long-term sustainable value within the planetary boundaries, and that the board has as its duty to draw up a long-term, life-cycle-based, sustainable business plan to operationalise this purpose. With its inclusion of any global chains in a cradle-to-cradle perspective, such an approach would undoubtedly be seen as valuable by various stakeholders, such as environmental and human rights NGOs. With its potentially

46 An issue to be developed further is how this could be undertaken; most likely it can be covered by auditors with experience with sustainability assurance; see, for example, the Sustainability Accounting Standards Board, see www.sasb.org.

47 At least the former would require a change in the Public Procurement Directive, including documentation of a verified sustainable business plan in the list of documentation that can be required of all economic operators, see further below in Section 3. For a further discussion of the potential of the new public procurement regime in a sustainability perspective, see the other chapters of this volume, and see also the earlier contribution in an Art. 11 TFEU context: A. Wiesbrock, 'An obligation for sustainable procurement? Gauging the potential impact of Article 11 TFEU on public contracting in the EU', *Legal Issues of Economic Integration*, 2 (2013), p. 105.

stringent system of selecting and verifying all those KPIs that are relevant for the business of the company, in a life-cycle-based approach, and audited reporting against these KPIs, there is a much stronger basis for stakeholder trust in CSR declaration and in what is today known as non-financial or CSR reporting. The comparison is today's system, where environmental and social reporting is voluntary, the selection of issues to be reported on often appears to be random, and corporate social responsibility declarations as well as CSR reporting by business often appears more as corporate charity work or green- or blue-washing rather than true internalisation of environmental and social externalities.[48] In spite of an ever-increasing focus on reporting requirements as a way of promoting sustainable business, there is little reason to believe that the results have improved.[49] Putting the above proposal into action could change this.

While introducing it as a legislative requirement could make best practice mandatory, using the proposed regime on a voluntary basis could strengthen and make more comparable and relevant current best practice approaches. Sustainability-focused and responsible investors could be especially interested in investing in businesses that implement such an approach. These businesses could become market leaders for truly sustainable products or services and feed into the growing consumer demand for fair and responsible production of goods and services.[50]

A full life-cycle assessment, including supply-chain transparency and based on a thorough due diligence and broad risk-assessment, would substantially lower the risk of the business being sued or suffering reputational damage from scandals because of environmental harm or human rights violations. The long-term advantages for businesses engaging with such an approach are many, although there would be some initial costs of implementing a new system and undertaking any changes indicated through a life-cycle-based assessment of the basis for the value creation of

[48] On corporate charity work as opposed to true CSR, see B. Sjåfjell, 'Why law matters: corporate social irresponsibility and the futility of voluntary climate change mitigation', *European Company Law*, 8(2–3) (2011), 56–64.

[49] See the comparative analysis in C. Villiers and J. Mähönen, 'Accounting, auditing and reporting: supporting or obstructing the sustainable companies objective?', in B. Sjåfjell and B.J. Richardson, *Company law and sustainability*, pp. 175–225.

[50] This could, for example, lead to innovative business models such as renting a service of having a product instead of selling the product, and could contribute to mitigating the apparent incompatibility of the goals of the EU's Europe 2020 strategy of (infinite) growth and a 'smart, sustainable and inclusive economy', briefly discussed by Beate Sjåfjell and Anja Wiesbrock in Chapter 1 of this volume.

the company. There would also be potential substantial benefits already in the short term. The life-cycle assessment would make legal compliance easier (because all aspects of production are brought onto the table); it would increase efficiency, enable savings on, for example, energy and transport through greater efficiency, and allow for the identification and mitigation of environmental and social impacts.[51] Done properly, it would involve a full internalisation of environmental and social externalities, allowing the company to create value in a truly sustainable manner.

However, because of the short-term, narrow effect of shareholder primacy and the many economic drivers that support and strengthen this social norm, there are few businesses that will voluntarily engage in such a shift. This is where a strong economic driver such as public procurement could play an important role. Certainly public procurement would be an important enforcement driver if such a reform was adopted. However, the issue discussed in this section is whether public procurement could be front-runner and stimulate a voluntary shift over to such a sustainable business model. To what extent public procurement indeed could be a front-runner for the promotion of sustainable companies in line with the proposed company law reform here, depends very much on how the Public Procurement Directives are implemented in the Member States, and how the local procurement authorities use the scope given them by EU procurement law and national procurement law below the EU thresholds. As Anja Wiesbrock explains, the discretion left to Member States is a major weakness of the EU's sustainable public procurement reform.[52] However, considering the issue from the perspective of the potential the Directives give, we see that there are certain possibilities:

Member States are according to Article 18(2) of the Directive obligated to ensure compliance in the performance of public contracts with 'applicable obligations in the fields of environmental, social and labour law established by Union law, national law, collective agreements or by the international environmental, social and labour law provisions listed in Annex X'. Unfortunately, Article 18(2) combines placing the obligation on Member States, rather than directly on the contracting authorities, with a vague formulation of the duty: Member States are to take 'appropriate

[51] See claims of substantial savings through implementation of sustainable value chains, for example, 'A sustainable supply chain in the garment industry saves 4 major companies $15M annually' at Triple Pundit, see www.triplepundit.com/2015/04/a-sustainable-supply-chain-in-the-garment-industry-saves-4-major-companies-15m-annually/.

[52] See Anja Wiesbrock in Chapter 4 of this volume.

measures' to ensure this enforcement.[53] However, the duty is made more substantial in other parts of the Directive, notably as regards subcontracting, where the duty is placed directly on the contracting authorities.[54] As an integrated part of ensuring compliance according to Article 18(2), Member States should therefore apply a life-cycle-based approach, as the relevant obligations in the fields of social and labour law are those applicable at the place where the works are executed or the services provided[55] and include the working conditions of subcontractors.[56]

Although the internalisation of environmental and social externalities encompassed in the life-cycle-based sustainable business plan proposed above would go beyond legal compliance, it would have legal compliance as a minimum requirement, based on thorough due diligence. This could arguably provide an opening to require such a verified business plan in certain stages of the procurement process. The forms of evidence that may be required from economic operators in order to establish their eligibility to tender are listed exhaustively in the Directive.[57] This does not seem to give room for requiring documentation in the form of a verified sustainable business plan. However, it might perhaps be queried whether Member States could, as 'appropriate measures' to ensure legal compliance according to Article 18(2), include a requirement for such a plan.[58]

If not in the exclusion or selection phase, Member States could arguably include reference to such a verified sustainable business plan in the award criteria and contract performance clauses concerning legal compliance.

[53] See Anja Wiesbrock's discussion of this in Chapter 4 of this volume, Section 2.1.

[54] Art. 71, although the wording is vague here also: 'appropriate action' is to be taken by the competent authorities acting within the scope of their responsibility and remit, see Anja Wiesbrock in Chapter 4 of this volume, Section 2.2.

[55] Recitals 37 and 38 of the Directive; see also Recital 105 of the Directive and its emphasis on the significance of ensuring 'observance by subcontractors of applicable obligations in the fields of environmental, social and labour law' and of transparency in the supply chain.

[56] Art. 71 of the Directive.

[57] Arts. 60 and 62, the latter referring to certification according to the Eco-Management and Audit Scheme (EMAS) or other equivalent systems as regards compliance with environmental management systems and standards, albeit with an opening for 'other evidence of environmental management measures' in Art. 62(2), but only where supplying documentation for compliance with EMAS or equivalent standards is not possible.

[58] While the effectiveness of requiring EMAS documentation or equivalent to ensure legal compliance with all environmental regulation also in the supply chain may be discussed, environmental standards definitely do not include compliance with social law and fundamental labour rights.

The requirements could stipulate that a verified sustainable business plan and audited reporting in accordance with such a business plan would, in the absence of indications to the contrary, be accepted as documentation of legal compliance.[59] Conversely, Article 18(2), this new, mandatory provision in the Directive, should have as consequence that Member States' assessment of whether the potential contracting partners comply with the relevant provisions has teeth: non-compliance with relevant environmental and social provisions should lead to exclusion from the award procedure.[60] Such an approach with emphasis on the sustainable business plan would certainly have the potential of stimulating the use of such a plan on a voluntary basis.

The long-term aspect of the sustainable business plan collides with the often short-term nature of public procurement, addressed in Anna Becker's criticism of public procurement as regulation.[61] However, especially in innovation procurement, the focus of the procurement tender could dovetail with the long-term sustainable business plan, setting out clearly how the business intends to create value within the planetary boundaries, which very well may entail innovative and novel approaches and focus on research and development. The public procurement reform is meant to stimulate innovation for a resource-efficient, low-carbon global economy. Sustainable business plans have the potential of being a highly relevant mechanism for businesses wishing to position themselves to compete for innovation tenders.

The Directive promotes but does not prescribe a life-cycle costing approach, which includes all costs over the life cycle of a works, supplies or services contract. This quite novel approach should be fully employed by Member States, making a life-cycle-based approach mandatory, so that contracts are not awarded to those who have the lowest price based on externalisation of environmental and social externalities. As set out in the Preamble, the development of common methodologies on the EU level for the calculation of life-cycle costs for specific categories of supplies or services is promoted, and it is set out that where such common

[59] The LtSM requirement, see Abby Semple in Chapter 3 of this volume, entails that this should concern compliance with laws applicable to the contract at hand and not general compliance.

[60] Recital 39 of the Directive, and Art. 57(4)(a) where after contracting authorities are allowed or may be required, depending on the choice of the Member State, to exclude economic operators where the contracting authority 'can demonstrate by any appropriate means a violation of applicable obligations referred to in Article 18(2)'.

[61] See Anna Beckers in Chapter 10 of this volume.

methodologies are developed, their use should be made compulsory.[62] This could serve also as a basis for the development of standard approaches to a sustainable business plan. Although the focus for now is on environmental life-cycle costing, the Preamble encourages examination of the possibility for common methodology on social life-cycle costing.[63] Member States could encourage a full internalisation of both environmental and social externalities by including such a requirement in their public procurement laws, and stimulate the use of the sustainable business plan as a way of demonstrating compliance with such a requirement.

A limitation in the life-cycle cost requirement as way of stimulating sustainable companies is its restriction to those aspects that can be given a monetary value.[64] However, the limitations of the life-cycle costing requirement and its restriction to that which can be given a monetary value does not in itself hinder inclusion of broader environmental and social concerns in the Member States' procurement law and in other phases of the procurement process, as long as they are set out clearly and objectively. Indeed, it is important to distinguish these possibilities both from the mandatory requirements in Article 18(2) concerning legal compliance and from the important approach of life-cycle costing, with its inherent restrictions. Broader environmental and social concerns can be included in the technical specifications, in the criteria for the award decision and in the contract specifications.[65] These are all potentially relevant as stimulation of voluntary adoption of the sustainable business plan and its broader significance in encouraging business to have sustainable value-creation within the planetary boundaries as their long-term goal.

Operationalising the inclusion of broader environmental and social requirements could most likely not take the shape of mandating that

[62] Recital 96 and Arts. 67 and 68.

[63] Recital 96, with the addition that existing methodologies such as the Guidelines for Social Life Cycle Assessment of Products adopted within the framework of the United Nations Environment Programme should be taken into account.

[64] Recital 96. See further Dacian C. Dragos and Bogdana Neamtu's discussion of the life-cycle costing approach in Chapter 6 of this volume.

[65] See Art. 42 on technical specifications (see Chapter 3 of this volume by Abby Semple on the link to the subject matter limitation), Art. 43 concerning the requirement of specific labels in the technical specifications, the award criteria or the contract performance conditions (see the chapter by Roberto Caranta on eco-labels), Art. 67 on contract award criteria, favouring a price-quality ratio approach, including social and environmental criteria and Art. 70 on social considerations as conditions for performance of the contract, see Anja Wiesbrock's chapter for a further discussion of the potential that lies in Member States' implementation.

all economic operators wishing to take part in a tender would need to have an audited long-term sustainable business plan in place (as opposed to if this were to be adopted as a company law requirement). However, Member States' broader environmental and social requirements in their public procurement law could arguably be formulated with such an inclusive, life-cycle-based, cradle-to-cradle approach, that it would be justifiable, time-saving and efficient to give preference to businesses that had an audited long-term, sustainable business plan in place. Care would nevertheless have to be taken in the formulation of such requirements, so that they do not violate the Directive's link to subject matter requirement.[66]

All in all, we see that there is clearly a potential for public procurement to act as a front-runner and driver. However, it is not possible to implement all necessary company law changes through public procurement requirements – and the extent to which the potential is used depends fully on the way the Public Procurement Directives are implemented in the Member States and what contracting authorities do in practice.

4. What can sustainable public procurement learn from the sustainable companies project?

The topic of this section is whether European public procurement law with its sustainability objectives can learn anything from the research-based insights into the possibilities and barriers for sustainable companies from the Sustainable Companies Project. The link between these two areas, and the potential for lessons to be learned, lies in that the economic operators that public procurement seeks to encourage to become more sustainable include the business form on which the Sustainable Companies Project has focused.

First, an insight from the Sustainable Companies Project is the attitude of business to external law.[67] While public procurement undoubtedly is

[66] See Abby Semple's discussion of this in Chapter 3 of this volume in light of the Preamble's guideline disallowing requirements 'relating to a general corporate policy', 'which cannot be considered as a factor characterising the specific process of production or provision of the purchased works, supplies or services', and further: 'Contracting authorities should hence not be allowed to require tenderers to have a certain corporate social or environmental responsibility policy in place' (Recital 97).

[67] See B.J. Richardson and B. Sjåfjell, 'Capitalism, the sustainability crisis and the limitations of current business governance', in B. Sjåfjell and B.J. Richardson (eds), *Company law and sustainability*.

an important economic driver, the legal requirements of public procurement law are still an external force to companies. Many businesses may be tempted to circumvent public procurement requirements if they are perceived as too burdensome or foreign to the businesses' own policies. The short-term, narrow focus stimulated by shareholder primacy tends to lead to environmental and social concerns being treated as externalities, and external legal requirements regarded as something to be complied with or sought to be seen complied with in as cost-beneficial way as possible.[68] Public procurement requirements are unlikely to be treated differently. Requirements intended to integrate environmental and social concerns should require stringent and verifiable response from the economic operators. A critical approach should be taken to documentation by businesses, and especially to documentation in the form of declarations. To ensure proper compliance while also simplifying the public procurement law and practice, best practice should be sought made as generally applicable as possible, with well-founded requirements for verification of relevant key performance indicators directly related to the business of the company.[69]

Second, and based on insights from natural science, aiming for 'smart, sustainable and inclusive growth' is unlikely to be good enough to achieve sustainability.[70] Even if we read 'growth' as 'development', or conversely, believe that it is possible to totally decouple economic growth from the use of natural resources,[71] a mere attempt at balancing the three dimensions of sustainability: economic, social and environmental, will not suffice. Smarter, greener and more resource-efficient is not necessarily sustainable. The balancing of economic, social and environmental concerns and the search for low-carbon, resource-efficient solutions must take place within the ecological, finite limits of this one planet that we live on.[72] Article 11 TFEU requires that environmental concerns are integrated in all policies and activities of the EU with the aim of sustainability.[73] This

[68] See, for example, B. Sjåfjell, 'Internalizing externalities in EU law: why neither corporate governance nor corporate social responsibility provides the answers', *George Washington International Law Review*, 40(4) (2010), 977–1024.

[69] See further B. Sjåfjell, Corporate governance for sustainability.

[70] Recital 2 of the Directive.

[71] Communication from the Commission, *Europe 2020, a strategy for smart, sustainable and inclusive growth*, COM (2010) 2020 final, p. 6, briefly discussed by Beate Sjåfjell and Anja Wiesbrock in Chapter 1, Section 2, of this volume.

[72] See, for example, C. Voigt, 'Article 11 TFEU in the light of the principle of sustainable development in international law', in B. Sjåfjell and A. Wiesbrock, *The greening of European business under EU law*, pp. 31–50.

[73] See Beate Sjåfjell and Anja Wiesbrock in Chapter 1 of this volume.

entails that the concept of planetary boundaries concept should be integrated into public procurement law as well, ideally through a full reform of the Public Procurement Directives ensuring an integration of requirements as those proposed for company law, modified to fit the public procurement process.[74] As a minimum this should be done by including a reference to the planetary boundaries as general principle in the preambles, to raise consciousness about the difference between greener – as in incremental improvements of environmental performance – and sustainable. Such a reference should likewise include mention of the UN's sustainable development goals,[75] to remind us that the ultimate goal is a safe and just operating space for humanity.[76]

Planetary boundaries and sustainable development goals could – and should – serve as a guideline for Member States in their implementation of the Directives and their choices in how to use the discretion the Directives bestow on them. As a matter of EU law, Member States are to interpret and implement secondary law in light of the EU Treaties, their overarching objectives and notably Article 11 TFEU.[77] International commitments or environmental or social goals in national constitutions may similarly provide legislative goals and guidelines for the Member States' policy choices. It is certainly advisable that the implementation of the EU Directives in the Member States includes mandatory requirements that are as simple and clear as possible. This has the potential of reducing legal uncertainty and cutting costs through simplification, standardisation and increased transparency, while promoting sustainability.[78] However, as a third point, and as posited by Anja Wiesbrock in her chapter,[79] permitting Member States to include environmental and social concerns is not enough – certain minimum requirements of environmental and social integration should

[74] See the summary of the proposal in Section 2.2 above (based on the full proposal in B. Sjåfjell, 'Corporate governance for sustainability') and the discussion of the possibilities and limits for integrating these ideas in the current public procurement regime in Section 3 above.

[75] In the EU's position paper, explicit mention is made several times of the role of public procurement, see Commission Communication, *A global partnership for poverty eradication and sustainable development after 2015*, COM (2015) 44 final, see https://ec.europa.eu/europeaid/communication-global-partnership-poverty-eradication-and-sustainable-development-after-2015˙en.

[76] K. Raworth, *A safe and just space for humanity: can we live within the doughnut.*

[77] See B. Sjåfjell, 'The legal significance of Article 11 TFEU for EU institutions and Member States', in B. Sjåfjell and A. Wiesbrock, *The greening of European business under EU law*, pp. 51–72.

[78] Ibid. [79] See Anja Wiesbrock in Chapter 4 of this volume.

have been made mandatory on the EU level. That would have contributed to a level playing field and created a floor beneath which Member States could not go.[80] This is an insight which is supported by the results from the Sustainable Companies Project as regards the scope that company law gives companies – other short-term focused drivers that do not support long-term sustainability claim this room and restrict in practice the room of action that companies have.[81] The same may be said to apply to Member States and their highly varying attitude to how the discretion should be used.[82]

5. What can innovative procurement approaches teach company law?

In Section 4, some ideas on what procurement law could learn from the insights derived from comparative company law research were indicated. This section asks conversely: can innovative approaches in the new Public Procurement Directives inspire a further development of company law or business law in general? Drawing on the discussion above on the possibilities for using public procurement as a driver for sustainable companies,[83] we see that there are several interesting lessons to be learned for business law.

The mandatory approach suggested by Article 18(2) of the Directive legal compliance with environmental and social law including labour law commitments derived from collective agreements, should inspire business law. It is well known that the compliance rate with notably environmental law is low.[84] Environmental and social reporting requirements, meant

80 Preferably, of course, on the international level, but within the framework of international law, mandatory minimum rules promoting sustainability on the EU level are to be preferred to leaving a number of significant issues to the varying implementation in Member States; see further Anja Wiesbrock in Chapter 4 of this volume.

81 B. Sjåfjell and B.J. Richardson, *Company law and sustainability*.

82 See Anja Wiesbrock's discussion of this in Chapter 4 of this volume.

83 In Section 3 above.

84 See, for example, the EU Commission Staff Working Paper on the Implementation and Enforcement of Community Environmental Law: Even though we see an increasing amount of EU incentives on regulating CSR matters as environment and human rights, the implementation and enforcement of these laws is lagging. According to a 2004 survey of the European Commission, just under one-third of all complaints and cases alleging non-compliance with EU law that were investigated by the Commission concerned non-compliance with environmental laws. In 2005, the environment sector accounted for about one-fourth of the total number of open cases concerning non-compliance with Community law under investigation by the Commission references. Indeed, there is a greater lack of implementation and enforcement of EU environmental requirements than

to stimulate the internalisation of these externalities in the decision-making in businesses, are not taken seriously, in spite of these reporting requirements typically being included in accounting law with the same potential sanctions as those that apply to financial reporting.[85] The new Public Procurement Directives encourage that non-compliance with these areas of law should lead to the exclusion of economic operators.[86] If such an approach were taken in business law, this could greatly increase compliance. Possibilities include delisting of non-compliant companies from registered market places to striking non-compliant business from the business registrar (after warnings and in serious cases).[87]

As a follow-up of the above point: the Directive's provisions on rejection of abnormally low prices may be an inspiration for business law. Rejection in public procurement is mandatory where the abnormally low price is caused by non-compliance with environmental and social law.[88] In business law, it could be envisaged that abnormally low prices to customers in general could lead to a requirement for an explanation, and with business law sanctions if a convincing explanation were not given. As the problems typically may lie not in abnormally low prices to the end-consumer but rather too high a profit for the business because of

of any other area of EU regulation, see Commission Staff Working Paper, Sixth and Seventh Annual Survey on the Implementation and Enforcement of Community Environmental Law (August 2005 and September 2006), see http://ec.europa.eu/environment/law/pdf/6th/en.pdf and http://ec.europa.eu/environment/legal/law/pdf/7th_en.pdf.

85 See, for example, the case of Norway, B. Sjåfjell, 'Sustainable companies: barriers and possibilities in Norwegian company law', *International and Comparative Corporate Law Journal*, 11 (2015), pp. 1–58, and on a comparative basis, C. Villiers and J. Mähönen, 'Accounting, auditing and reporting: supporting or obstructing the sustainable companies objective?'.

86 Art. 57(4)(a) whereby contracting authorities are allowed or may be required, depending on the choice of the Member State, to exclude economic operators where the contracting authority 'can demonstrate by any appropriate means a violation of applicable obligations referred to in Article 18(2)'. Further, it is also possible to exclude economic operators 'guilty of grave professional misconduct, which renders its integrity questionable', Art. 57(4)(c). There may perhaps be some room for using this as a basis for exclusion of businesses where the legal situation is difficult to clarify, for example where a lack of due diligence in the supply chain may be linked to human rights violations or environmental damage, but where the legal liability is unclear. Art. 57 provisions are subject to the ability of economic operators to 'self-clean' and a maximum exclusionary period of three years.

87 The latter is for example the sanction for non-compliance with the gender diversity requirement for boards of Norwegian public limited liability companies; B. Sjåfjell, 'Gender diversity in the board room and its impacts: is the example of Norway a way forward?', *Deakin Law Review* (forthcoming), *University of Oslo Faculty of Law Research Paper*, No. 2014–48; see http://ssrn.com/abstract=2536777.

88 Art. 69(3) of the Directive, referring to Art. 18(2) of the Directive.

exploitation of workers of subcontractors or circumvention of environmental regulations, a further development could be this: Abnormally low payment to subcontractors would require documentation that workers are paid living wages and environmental regulations are complied with. Issues to be discussed, if such ideas were to take hold, would be who could require such explanations and who would make the decision on whether the explanations are satisfactory.

Taking the Directive's approach to ensuring legal compliance in a life-cycle-based context, by including workers in the supply chain (subcontractors) and emphasising life-cycle costing, contains the potential of dramatically reducing the pulverisation of responsibility that we see today in corporate groups and through the use of non-transparent supply chains. To really be effective, this would probably require a combined environmental and social life-cycle-based assessment tool for business, not restricted to that which is easily quantifiable.[89]

A lesson that one may wish that business law could learn from public procurement law, is the explicit policy recognition of the importance of sustainability objectives. How is such a recognition possible in public procurement law while still to a great extent being heresy in company law? A part of the answer of course lies in differences between the areas of law – the one regulating public expenditure where there is a tradition, after all, for pursuing public policy goals as well, and the other regulating the legal entities that to a great extent tend to be perceived as private actors only. However, the contribution of the Court of Justice of the European Union in the development of public procurement law should not be underestimated. Perhaps we need a *Concordia Bus Finland* for business law?[90] That would require for example that a Member State adopted a sustainability-focused company law provision, such as requiring a sustainable business plan of all companies or sustainability reporting as a listing requirement on its stock exchange, which was then challenged as a restriction of free movement.

Certainly public procurement law can show business law in general that combining the pursuit of strategic policy objectives with an economic efficiency approach is possible and indeed advisable.

[89] That is one of the aims in the new international research project being planned: Sustainable Market Actors for Responsible Trade, building on and developing further the insights of the Sustainable Companies Project, see www.jus.uio.no/companies under Projects.

[90] Case C-513/99 *Concordia Bus Finland* ECLI:EU:C:2002:495; see the importance of this case for public procurement law by Beate Sjåfjell and Anja Wiesbrock in Chapter 1, Section 2, of this volume.

6. Interaction between company law and public procurement law

This chapter has discussed the interface between company law and public procurement law. We have seen that thinking outside the box of business law through the lens of public procurement law shows how new solutions to old problems could be envisaged, and conversely, that public procurement law can learn from the insights of company law research.

To achieve sustainability, company law reform is arguably necessary. Public procurement can be an important enforcement mechanism in a new sustainable companies regime. As a driver, public procurement is important already today (and could be used better to shift us away from 'business as usual' and onto a sustainable path), but it is hardly sufficient on its own. It does, however, give public procurement authorities the opportunity to be a moral beacon and show how environmental and social externalities can be internalised. In that context, public procurement can learn something important from the company law research that we have drawn on in this chapter: permitting sustainable choices is probably insufficient; mandatory requirements are necessary. The strong social norm of shareholder primacy with its short-term, narrow focus requires a critical approach to self-declarations from economic operators. Most importantly, greener and better is not necessarily good enough: sustainability requires acting within the planetary boundaries.

This chapter argues that company law (or business law in general) and public procurement law both are significant pieces of the jigsaw puzzle of sustainability. Unfortunately, as regards business law, path-dependent legislators have barely started to recognise that the system may be flawed, and that the legal infrastructure for companies may in itself be problematic.[91] This fundamental assumption still stands strong in spite of all the criticism of this simplistic idea: that profit for shareholders entails increase in social welfare because shareholders have a residual interest that is only satisfied when all other involved parties have been dealt with fairly and properly.

[91] An indication of a dawning recognition is the statement by Internal Market and Services Commission Michel Barnier in connection with the presentation of the EU Commission's reform package of 9 April 2014: 'The last years have shown time and time again how short-termism damages European companies and the economy. Sound corporate governance can help to change that'. European Commission Press Release, 9 April 2014, 1. However, as discussed elsewhere, this recognition is not followed up with an understanding of the entrenchment of drivers for short-termism in the still-dominating mainstream corporate governance approach, see, for example, B. Sjåfjell, 'Corporate governance for sustainability'.

The idea that company law can concentrate on enabling the establishment of companies and protecting shareholders and creditors, is supported by the very compartmentalisation that horizontal integration rules such as Article 11 TFEU aim to mitigate.[92] The compartmentalisation of law and policy suggests that each sector can safely concentrate on its own sector objective, and that company law can leave to environmental law to ensure ecological sustainability. This is contrary to EU Treaty law and indeed to the very essence of sustainable development. In its essence sustainable development, as an overarching EU Treaty objective, therefore requires a holistic law and policy approach. Public procurement law has begun to recognise this, in its promotion of public procurement as a policy strategy instrument. While sustainable public procurement still has its issues, as the other contributions of this book serve to illustrate further, it is at least moving in the right direction. Business law has much to learn from public procurement law, and now needs to follow on to be a part of a holistic, sustainability-focused reform.

[92] See Beate Sjåfjell and Anja Wiesbrock in Chapter 1, Section 2, of this volume.

10

Using contracts to further sustainability?

A contract law perspective on sustainable public procurement

ANNA BECKERS

1. The contractual dimension of sustainable public procurement

The focus of this collection is on sustainable public procurement. From a legal perspective, this draws immediate attention to public procurement laws, in particular, the way in which this area of law facilitates or hinders public authorities in pursuing the policy objective of sustainable development through their procurement practices. However, that does not mean that one can ignore the other interlinked areas. Notwithstanding its public character, public procurement is characterised by the fact that the state acts as a private actor seeking supply on the market. As a result, alongside being bound by public laws, public procurement is subject to the general rules and principles of contract law. The starting point of this contribution is this contractual character of public procurement and how contract design and contract law, as the applicable legal framework, influence sustainable[1] public procurement practices. To that end, the contribution will focus specifically on the evidence and arguments provided by private law scholars on the use of contracts as regulatory instruments and as instruments to strengthen the enforcement of existing laws.[2] The specific question addressed is whether, and to what extent

[1] The term *sustainable* procurement practice is used here to describe procurement practices in which governments expect businesses as their contract partners to adhere to the Triple-P bottom line, that is, consider people (social), planet (environmental) and profit (economic) in their operations. On this understanding as the bottom line for sustainable business, see fundamentally J. Elkington, *Cannibals with forks* (Capstone Publishers, 1997).

[2] See in particular D. McBarnet and M. Kurkchiyan, 'Corporate social responsibility through contractual control? Global supply chains and other regulation', in D. McBarnet, A. Vioiculescu and T. Campbell (eds), *The new corporate accountability corporate social*

the further development of sustainable public procurement laws can benefit from experiences within the private sphere. Regarding this point, the contribution is intrinsically related to the discussion among public procurement scholars about whether public procurement, in order to be an effective instrument to further sustainability, needs to be aligned with private procurement practices.[3] This chapter argues that there are several aspects in which experiences with sustainable private procurement can indeed be beneficial for public procurement. Given the specific role of the state that is bound by public laws when acting as a market actor, however, careful consideration on what experiences can be useful is necessary.

The chapter starts by defining the core concepts that are used, namely the understanding of (public procurement) contracts as instruments to regulate and enforce existing laws (Section 2). It proceeds by discussing the way in which this form of regulation and enforcement differs from traditional regulation by public laws in its scope, content, duration and enforcement. As will be shown, in comparison to traditional governmental regulation, the use of contracts as instruments to regulate and enforce is more limited (Section 3). The core part (Section 4) is then devoted to discussing whether and to what extent attempts in the private sphere to improve regulation and enforcement by contract to further sustainability could be helpful in the discussion on sustainable public procurement. The two main aspects focused on are the specific contract design employed by private actors and the proposals in the scholarly debate for changes in contract law with a view to the capturing of this new regulatory function of contracts.

responsibility and the law (Cambridge University Press, 2007), pp. 59–92; M.P. Vandenbergh, 'The new Wal-Mart effect: the role of private contracting in global governance', *UCLA Law Review*, 54 (2007), 913–70; L.C. Backer, 'Multinational corporations as objects and sources of transnational regulation', *ILSA Journal of International & Comparative Law*, 14 (2008), 499–523; L. Vytopil, 'Contractual control and labour-related CSR norms in the supply chain: Dutch best practices', *Utrecht Law Review*, 8 (2012), 155–69; F. Cafaggi, 'The regulatory functions of transnational commercial contracts: new architectures', *Fordham International Law Journal*, 36 (2013), 1557–618; K. Peterkova Mitkidis, 'Sustainability clauses in international supply chain contracts: regulation, enforceability and effects of ethical requirements', *Nordic Journal of Commercial Law*, (2014), 1–30; P. Verbruggen, 'Regulatory governance by contract: the rise of regulatory standards in commercial contracts', *Recht der Werkelijkheid*, 35 (2014), 79–100.

[3] See for a pointed description of this reasoning C. McCrudden, 'Corporate social responsibility and public procurement', in D. McBarnet, A. Voiculescu and D. Campbell (eds), *The new corporate accountability corporate social responsibility and the law* (Cambridge University Press, 2007), 93–118, at 95–7.

2. Denoting sustainable public procurement as 'regulation by contract'

To start with, it is useful to outline what is meant when denoting contracts, including sustainable public procurement practices, as a genuine form of regulation and enforcement. Such an understanding appears not to be guiding, at least in the EU policy debate on sustainable public procurement practices. The European Commission describes sustainable public procurement rather as a policy instrument that relies on market dynamics rather than the law. This is clear from several EU policy documents, such as the Europe 2020 Strategy[4] and the renewed strategy of the Commission on Corporate Social Responsibility.[5] In the scholarly debate, sustainable public procurement is furthermore described as a matter of 'leading by example' meaning that the government aims to provide an orientation for the private sector on what is expected in terms of sustainable procurement.[6] Hence, sustainable public procurement is commonly treated as a mechanism that relies on the 'soft' power of market incentives and social pressure rather than the law.[7]

A closer look reveals, however, that sustainable procurement is not solely based on the power of social norms and market incentives. Once a procurement contract is concluded, genuine legal obligations are created that can be enforced on the basis of contract law.[8] In the specific case of

[4] European Commission, *Europe 2020: a strategy for smart, sustainable and inclusive growth*, COM (2010) 2020 final, 3 March 2010, p. 14, 'To enhance a framework for the use of market-based instruments', such as 'encouraging wider use of green public procurement'.

[5] European Commission, *A renewed EU strategy 2011–14 for corporate social responsibility*, COM (2011) 681 final, pp. 10–11, in which public procurement is perceived as part of 'enhancing the market reward for CSR'.

[6] See, for example, McCrudden, 'CSR and public procurement', p. 98; R. Steurer, 'The role of governments in corporate social responsibility: characterising public policies on CSR in Europe', *Policy Sciences*, 43 (2010), 49–72, at 64–5.

[7] See, for example, J. Howe, 'The regulatory impact of using public procurement to promote better labour standards in corporate supply chains', in K. MacDonald and S. Marshall (eds), *Fair trade, corporate accountability and beyond: experiments in globalising justice* (Ashgate, 2013), pp. 329–48, at 329 who describes sustainable procurement (with a view to labour standards) as a 'soft' law mechanism. See also the different understanding of Abby Semple in this volume, p. 72, who emphasises that sustainable public procurement 'should . . . not be equated to a form of market regulation' and consequently be seen as 'a lever than as a hammer'.

[8] See pointedly on socially and environmentally responsible public procurement as a legally binding contract subject to private law: D. McBarnet, 'Corporate social responsibility beyond law, through law, for law: the new corporate accountability', in D. McBarnet, A. Vioiculescu and T. Campbell (eds), *The new corporate accountability corporate social*

sustainable public procurement, this amounts to legal obligations for the supplying company to act in accordance with the requirements specified in the contract including specific obligations related to sustainable performance. These enforceable obligations can have as their content, on the one hand, compliance with existing laws, which renders the contract an enforcement tool.[9] On the other hand, the contract can contain provisions requiring compliance beyond existing laws or being used instead of legislation, which makes the contract an instrument by which the state undertakes genuine regulation.[10] In either way, procurement contracts become instruments by which the state continues to act as a regulator or public enforcer of the law, the only difference to traditional regulation being the use of a legal tool that is also available to private actors: the contract. The legally binding contract then obtains a double meaning: It remains the legal basis for a bilateral and mutual exchange of goods, performance of a service or work on the market. On top of that, it becomes a means to regulate the contractual partner with a view to a specific policy objective, in this case making businesses act sustainable.

Although the regulatory and enforcement dimension is not an entirely new phenomenon of public procurement practices,[11] it seems to have become increasingly relevant under the premises of globalisation, where traditional top-down regulation remains limited due to its narrow territorial scope and the lack of an international consensus on the appropriate form of regulation in relation to social and environmental matters.[12] The fact that nowadays private actors have also begun in their global supply chains to use contracts to regulate and to enforce existing laws may have contributed to the increasing attention.[13] Indeed, compared to top-down regulation, there are certain advantages of using the contract as a

responsibility and the law (Cambridge University Press, 2007), 9–58, at 43: 'National, local and indeed supranational governments are not only using conventional regulatory law to foster CSR, but are also using their market power, and *private law*, by including CSR obligations in their own procurement contracts' (Emphasis added).

9 See on this dimension also the contribution of Beate Sjåfjell in this volume.

10 See on the contract as a regulatory tool available to governments, R. Baldwin, M. Cave and M. Lodge, *Understanding regulation: theory, strategy, and practice* (Oxford University Press, 2012), pp. 116–7. See also on public procurement as a 'regulatory technique', Howe, 'The regulatory impact', pp. 330–2.

11 See fundamentally C. McCrudden, 'Using public procurement to achieve social outcomes', *Natural Resources Forum*, 28 (2004), 257–67 who provides historical evidence for the past use of public procurement contracting as 'social regulation'.

12 See, for example, with a particular view to the regulation of labour standards, Howe, 'The regulatory impact', p. 322.

13 See the evidence provided in footnote 2.

regulatory and enforcement instrument. One core advantage lies in its capacity to be responsive to the private sphere rather than attempting to intervene by general, mandatory laws. The use of the contract as the central organising mechanism in the private sphere allows the reaching of private actors directly, hereby avoiding several adverse effects of direct intervention under the condition of a functionally differentiated society.[14] Regulation and enforcement by contract is furthermore less constrained by territorial borders and thus capable of influencing the situation on a global scale, including in developing countries.[15] This is why it can be become an important tool in the new global regulatory order, as a pivotal component in an era of 'regulatory capitalism' where 'the state is embedded in the social and economic order'[16] rather than detached from it. Finally, it has to be emphasised that regulation and enforcement on the basis of contracts to make companies act sustainable can, as the editors underline, also be seen as one part in the jigsaw puzzle to further sustainable development that is supported by other (legislative) measures.[17]

3. The limits of regulation and enforcement by contract

Notwithstanding these advantages, the use of contracts as regulatory and enforcement tools faces certain limits in comparison to traditional top-down regulation when it comes to the scope, content, duration and the means of enforcement. This has its origin in the specific character of the contract and the rules of contract law as the applicable framework and it is valid regardless of whether it is a public or private actor who attempts to regulate and enforce by contract.

3.1. The regulatory scope

If public or private authorities choose to regulate or to enforce existing laws by means of including a provision to that end in a contract,

[14] On the advantages of this responsive form of regulation, see (despite important theoretical differences in detail) the socio-legal inquiries of, for example, G. Teubner, 'After legal instrumentalisation? Strategic models of post-regulatory law', in G. Teubner (ed.), *Dilemmas of law in the welfare state* (de Gruyter, 1986), pp. 299–325; I. Ayres and J. Braithwaite, *Responsive regulation: transcending the deregulation debate* (Oxford Socio-Legal Studies, Oxford University Press, 1992); N. Gunningham and J. Rees, 'Industry self-regulation: an institutional perspective', *Law & Policy*, 19 (1997), 363–414, at 402–5.

[15] For the potential of procurement as a regulatory tool in relation to developing countries, see Howe, 'The regulatory impact', in particular, p. 330.

[16] D. Levi-Faur and J. Jordana, 'The making of a new regulatory order', *The Annals of the American Academy of Political and Social Science*, 598 (2005), 12–32, at 14.

[17] See the concluding chapter by Anja Wiesbrock and Beate Sjåfjell in this volume p. 231.

this activity is governed by contract law. This is important to emphasise because contract law is based on the fundamental principle of the privity or relativity of contracts, meaning that obligations created by contract are valid only between the parties to the contract and without legal effect on outsiders.[18] This already renders contracts as regulatory tools very different from top-down regulation and public law enforcement, as the latter embraces legal obligations of a general character. With a view to sustainable procurement contracting, two core restrictions are noteworthy.

First, regulation by public procurement contract remains a tool that has limits in taking a holistic approach and regulating entire supply chains with a view to making them become more sustainable. A contractual obligation can in principle not be extended to parties that are not a party to the procurement contract.

Second, regulation and enforcement by contract excludes in principle those that ultimately benefit from the regulation. These can be employees insofar as social and labour regulation is concerned and local communities that are affected by pollution for which a regulatory clause in the contract provides for an obligation of emission reduction. As opposed to public laws through which such beneficiaries can acquire a right to enforce the regulation and obtain damages, their position in regulation and enforcement by contract is different. Regulation remains effectively done on their behalf; the contract treats them as 'third parties' that do not acquire rights to influence the obligation made for their benefit.[19] The main exception in which a right of third parties is recognised is when the written contract contains a provision conferring the third party the right to enforce the contract.[20] This contract design is, however, at least in the private sphere not common for clauses that deal with workplace standards and environmental protection.[21] This lack of explicitly

[18] In this regard, it has to be emphasised that the privity of contracts is conceptualised differently in different national contract laws. A particular strict form characterises English law, a less strict adherence to the privity of contracts characterises, for instance, Continental jurisdictions as German law. For an overview on the privity of contract with a view to different jurisdictions, see Cafaggi, 'The regulatory functions', 1594–5.

[19] See on this observation in relation to private contracting, Backer, 'Multinational corporations as objects and sources', 522. See also Peterkova Mitkidis, 'Sustainability clauses', 16–8.

[20] This is valid even for English contract law, which is otherwise known for its strict application of the principle of privity. See, s. 1(1)(a) and s. 1(1)(b) in conjunction with (3) Contracts (Rights of Third Parties) Act 1999.

[21] See Cafaggi, 'The regulatory functions', 1592–3; Verbruggen, 'Regulatory governance by contract', 90.

specified third-party rights in the contract could possibly be cured with the help of contract law, in particular the rules on contract interpretation and supplementation. Much depends then on the law applicable to the contract under scrutiny. The application of a legal system adhering to a contextual approach to the interpretation of contracts would make it considerably easier to interpret such regulatory clauses as creating third-party rights than systems with a textual approach. Yet, even contextual systems reach their limits in relation to sustainability clauses when the beneficiaries of such clauses are a large group or, as is the case in relation to clauses on environmental protection, the general public.[22] As a result, apart from contracts containing very specific wording, those benefiting from the regulation remain excluded in the regulation and enforcement by contract.

3.2. *The regulatory content*

Moreover, once public or private authorities employ contracts for regulatory purposes, the content of this form of regulation may change as a result of the function of the contract. As has been mentioned above, the use of contracts as regulatory tools adds another function to the exchange of goods or services, namely to make one or both parties to the contract comply with environmental and labour standards. The two dimensions – exchange of goods and services and the regulatory purpose – are, however, not always so easy to delineate. In principle, there are two different ways to include regulatory provisions or provisions as to the enforcement of laws in the contract. The contracting parties can either relate the regulatory provision to the exchange of goods and services by means of specifying it as part of the characteristics of the goods. Alternatively, it is also possible to detach the regulatory objective from the exchange of goods and services by including a general obligation in the contract to comply with certain social and environmental standards during the performance period.[23] Contracts exhibiting the latter design do, in fact, not differ significantly from public law regulation in their content, as they also require general compliance with social and environmental standards. Yet, in the former

[22] On this difficulty, see in detail A. Beckers, *Enforcing corporate social responsibility codes: on global self-regulation and national private law* (Hart Publishing, 2015), pp. 129–41 (on the basis of German and English contract law). See also Cafaggi, 'The regulatory functions', 1592–3 (with references to U.S. contract law).

[23] For these two options in relation to private procurement, see Cafaggi, 'The regulatory functions', 1596–7 (product vs. process standards) and public procurement, Howe, 'The regulatory impact', pp. 334–5.

contract design, the content of regulation is considerably more restricted. This is due to the fact that the obligations specified in the contract are restricted to the manufacturing and delivery of goods hereby requiring the contracting partner to treat them as an integral element in the production of the contracted goods. As will be discussed more intensively below, a core difference can be observed between public and private procurement. Private actors seem to opt for detaching contract exchange and regulation and thus give regulation a broader scope, but the requirement in the recent Public Procurement Directive to link sustainability requirements to the subject matter of the contract limits the capability of governments to take a similar approach.

3.3. *Durance of the regulatory activity*

A third feature of using the contract as a regulatory and enforcement tool is related to its durance, meaning the time period in which this particular form of regulation is valid. Being a contractual obligation, the regulation comes into existence the moment when the contract is concluded and it ends when the contract is put to an end, that is, when it is completely performed, terminated by one of the contracting parties, or when it expires as agreed upon beforehand. Although contract law scholars have emphasised that there exist contract relations with considerable length,[24] some even factually 'life time contracts',[25] contracts on the exchange of goods or performance of services remain mostly of a short-term and impersonal character. The fixed time span certainly has advantages, as it makes contracts a fluid and flexible form of regulation. It allows the contracting parties to change their sustainable procurement strategies over time, for example, with a view to new scientific insights on environmental aspects and changes in societal perceptions or policies on social matters. Regulation and enforcement by contract does not require a formal legislative procedure and the intense political controversy involved; it can simply be initiated in the course of purchasing goods and can be amended for future purchases if needed. It can also be initiated at all governmental levels from the federal to the municipal level and is available to private actors. These advantages notwithstanding, the reverse side of this flexibility is the uncertainty of this type of regulation for the regulated entities.

[24] Cf. fundamentally I.R. Macneil, *The new social contract: an inquiry into modern contractual relations* (Yale University Press, 1980).

[25] L. Nogler and U. Reifner (eds), *Life-time contracts: social long-term contracts in labour, tenancy and consumer credit law* (Eleven Publishing, 2014).

Companies supplying to public authorities are only bound by an obligation in a contract to operate in a socially and environmentally responsible manner for a specific time span. This means that a party bound by a sustainability clause in a contract does not have the same certainty that the obligations remain in place, as it can under a legislative measure. It is thus possible that companies opt for not initiating long-term changes solely on the basis of being bound by it for the period of performing the contract as this may turn out not to be very efficient.[26] Hence, the use of a contract with an inevitably fixed duration risks creating a quite unstable and uncertain regulatory environment. This may make it not very effective in facilitating sustainable behaviour on the side of businesses on a long-term basis.

3.4. *Enforcement in cases of non-compliance*

A final aspect in which regulation by contract differs from legislative measures relates to the characteristics of enforcement. For public procurement contracts, specific remedies are laid down in public procurement rules[27] and in EU Treaty Law. These are available to remedy breaches on the side of the public authority for breaches of public procurement laws. Insofar as enforcement of the contract provision against the supplying company is sought, the remedies available to governments as the contracting party (and third parties) are specified in the contract and the default rules of contract law.[28]

[26] An example could be the apprenticeships constellation discussed by Abby Semple in her contribution to this volume, Chapter 3, p. 68.

[27] See, in particular the Directive 89/665/EC on coordination of laws and administrative provisions relating to the application of review procedures to the award of supply and public service contracts, OJ 1989 (L395/33), Directive 92/13/EEC coordinating the laws, regulations and administrative provisions relating to the application of Community rules on the procurement procedures of entities operating in the water, energy, transport and telecommunications sectors, OJ 1992 (L76/14), amended by the Procurement Remedies Directive 2007/66/EC amending Council Directives 89/665/EEC and 92/13/EEC with regard to improving the effectiveness of review procedures concerning the award of public contracts, OJ 2007 (L335/31) as implemented in national laws. On the national implementation measures of the Procurement Remedies Directive, see S. Treumer and F. Lichère (eds), *Enforcement of the EU public procurement rules* (DJØF Publishing, 2011).

[28] See, in the same direction, Howe, 'The regulatory impact', p. 343. In order to avoid confusion, it is emphasised that the following section is mainly concerned with the enforcement of public procurement *contracts* and the sustainability clauses incorporated therein and thus discusses remedies for breach of *contract*. The remedies to enforce public procurement laws are only discussed as a side topic.

As a result, the choice of a public authority to pursue a regulatory objective by contract is also a choice for a specific enforcement regime for its regulatory activity. Contract remedies and those available to remedy the breach of public procurement laws take over the function that inspections and fines in administrative law and damage compensation under tort law have in relation to breaches of public laws.[29] This has practical consequences, as particularly remedies for breach of contracts function differently to remedies for breaches of laws. While the latter aim at restoring compliance in the interest of the public and compensating those having suffered from the breach, contract remedies are oriented towards the interest of the contracting parties in having the contract performed correctly.[30] As a result, remedies under contract law in the event of a breach are specific performance, and termination of the agreement in addition to any remedy specified in the contract that all serve the interest of the innocent party to the contract. Conversely, they do not fit for breaches of obligations that serve the interest of the public or a third party. This applies arguably also to the specific remedies under EU public procurement law. The remedies under the Procurement Remedies Directive have in the first place the objective to allow reviewing the decision to award a contract including the termination of an already concluded contract in the interest of a detrimentally affected third party.[31] They thus seek, in the interest of a detrimentally affected bidder, to end rather than reinforce the regulatory activity pursued through a contract. An exception is the remedy available to claim damages for breaches of regulatory provisions under both contract law and the Procurement Remedies Directive, which could possibly be a viable remedy. This will be considered more extensively below.

4. Improving regulation and enforcement by contract – experiences from the private sphere

Having discussed the restrictions of using contracts as instruments to regulate and to enforce existing laws, we may now turn to the reform

[29] See M.P. Vandenbergh, 'Private environmental governance', *Cornell Law Review*, 99 (2013), 129–99, at 196: 'Enforcement occurs not through administrative inspections and sanctions but through shaming, boycotts and contract disputes'.

[30] See on this shift from administrative to contract enforcement and the different character of regulatory and contract remedies, Cafaggi, 'The regulatory functions', 1611–16.

[31] See, in detail, S. Treumer, 'Enforcement of the EU public procurement rules: the state of law and current issues', in S. Treumer and F. Lichère (eds), *Enforcement of the EU public procurement rules* (DJØF Publishing, 2011), pp. 13–52, at 28–33.

necessary to overcome these restrictions. In particular, what does the evidence on the sustainable contracting practices of private actors suggest in terms of the contract design for sustainable procurement practices? And what can the scholarly debate amongst private law scholars on the reform of contract law offer that might be necessary to accommodate the new function of procurement contracts more appropriately? There are several experiences from the private sphere that are valuable for sustainable public procurement. However, given the specific double role of the state as a market participant that remains bound by public laws (in particular Treaty obligations and WTO laws on Government Procurement), it is clear that experiences from the private sphere have to be carefully adapted to the specific role of public contractors. The adoption of practices in the private sphere that put contracting authorities at risk of employing procurement practices of a discriminatory and intransparent character is certainly to be avoided.

4.1. Expanding the regulatory scope

How can, first, the scope of regulation and enforcement by contract be changed to take a more holistic approach towards regulating supply chains and strengthen the position of beneficiaries?

Regarding the contractual regulation of supply chains, private actors have responded to this call in three ways. First, in order to maintain oversight of the supply chains, companies begin to require transparency from their suppliers on the subcontractor and the subcontracted work. Subcontracting may even be subject to permission of the main contractor.[32] In addition, private contractors attempt to regulate their supply chains by imposing so-called perpetual clauses on their first tier suppliers.[33] Perpetual clauses are clauses in contracts that provide for an obligation of the supplying company to incorporate the regulatory provision in any contract with a subcontractor, which can be equipped with penalty clauses. Finally, one can also find private contracts in which clauses are included

[32] See, as an example, the supplier code of conduct by Marks & Spencer, which explicitly states at p. 9 that 'Subcontracting to other suppliers, sites or units is not permitted without pre-authorised permission from M&S'. For supplier code of conduct, see www.corporate.marksandspencer.com/plan-a/policies-and-consultations/policies/clothing-and-homeware/ethical-trading.

[33] See for evidence Vytopil, 'Contractual control', 166–8; Verbruggen, 'Regulatory governance by contract', 89. See also earlier evidence from McBarnet and Kurkchiyan, 'CSR through contractual control?', pp. 84–5.

that provide for liability of the supplying company towards the buyer for breaches of regulatory provisions.[34]

When it comes to public procurement contracting, the regulation of supply chains is arguably less developed, which suggests that the broader approach taken by private actors might be used as inspiration on what could further be done. The most developed aspect in relation to subcontracting is the requirement on transparency. Since the 2004 Public Procurement Directive,[35] contracting authorities are allowed or, at the discretion of the Member States obliged, to ask the tenderer to specify the share of the contract that he seeks to outsource.[36] The recently adopted Directive on Public Procurement[37] contains a similar provision,[38] but it goes further as to the transparency on the identity of the subcontractor. Contracting authorities are now obliged to require their contracting partner to provide information on the subcontractor and to notify them of any changes.[39] Despite this stricter approach, the margin of discretion given to Member States can – as argued for by Anja Wiesbrock in this collection – still hinder the effectiveness of the Directive in regulating supply chains.[40] Transparency akin to how it is used in the contracting practice between private actors, such as requiring contracting authorities to obtain full transparency on the contracted work, possibly even including a clause that obliges the supplier to obtain permission prior to the subcontracting of work, could be a step towards extending regulation from the contracting partner to the supply chain.

In relation to the liability of subcontractors, the Directive provides also a first step towards a stricter framework. It contains an obligation for Member States to ensure observance of EU environmental, social

[34] A prominent example of such a provision is the contract between the University of Adidas Wisconsin and Adidas, which was recently under scrutiny at a District Court. In the contract, it was laid down that Adidas is allowed to subcontract for the production of contracted goods, but in that case remains 'fully responsible for ensuring that the Licenced Articles are manufactured in accordance with the Licence Agreement' and 'must ensure that all manufacturers' comply with the code. See for evidence, statement of claim, para 13, see www.business-humanrights.org/en/adidas-lawsuit-re-university-of-wisconsin#c18941.

[35] Directive 2004/18/EC on the coordination of procedures for the award of public works contracts, public supply contracts and public service contracts, OJ 2004 (L134/114).

[36] Ibid., Art. 25.

[37] Directive 2014/24/EU on Public Procurement, OJ 2004 (L94/65) (in the following Public Procurement Directive). This contribution focuses on the EU Public Sector Directive, leaving aside the special procurement rules for Utilities and Concessions.

[38] Art. 71(2) Public Procurement Directive.

[39] Art. 71(5) Public Procurement Directive.

[40] See on this in detail the contribution of Anja Wiesbrock to this volume.

and labour law through 'appropriate action',[41] which includes ensuring that a system of joint and separate liability existing in national law is applied in conformity with the legal obligations.[42] A system of joint and several liability refers to the possibility of the contracting authorities to hold liable, jointly and separately, the contractor and subcontractor for their failures. However, here again the discretionary approach and the reference to already existing frameworks may hinder setting up an effective regulatory framework for supply chains.

Finally, one additional option to increase influence over supply chains and their environmental and social performance could be to incorporate similar perpetual clauses and subcontracting liability provisions in contracts with the direct supplier. A legal basis to impose obligations on contracting authorities to regulate supply chains is not provided for by the Public Procurement Directive, but the concept of a holistic approach towards regulating supply chains can be found in a nascent form. In relation to requiring the identification of the subcontractor, the Directive allows Member States to opt for an expansion of this requirement for entities further down the chain.[43] One could consider building on these initial steps for improving supply chain responsibility.

As far as the position of beneficiaries as third parties is concerned, the contracting practice in the private sphere seems not to offer significant guidance. Private contractors seem to be widely reluctant to frame the regulatory provisions in contracts as third-party rights.[44] However, this gap could arguably be closed with the help of contract law, in particular the rules on contract interpretation and contract formation. Technically, two options are conceivable to treat beneficiaries, workers or communities, as beneficiaries capable of influencing contract performance. One can either interpret the regulatory contract provision as having the purpose to benefit third parties, or treat the contractual agreement as being an enforceable unilateral promise or unilateral offer to contract.[45] The latter

[41] Art. 71(1) in conjunction with Art. 18(2) Public Procurement Directive.

[42] Art. 71(6) Public Procurement Directive.

[43] See, Art. 71(5)(b) Public Procurement Directive which allows Member States to extend the obligations related to the identity of the subcontractor to 'subcontractors of the main contractor's subcontractors or further down the chain'.

[44] See above, text accompanying footnote 21.

[45] See for these two options, for example, K.E. Kenny, 'Code or conduct: whether Wal-Mart's code of conduct creates a contractual obligation between Wal-Mart and the employees of its foreign suppliers', *Northwestern Journal of International Law and Business*, 27 (2007), 453–74, at 459–67; H. Revak, 'Corporate codes of conduct: binding contract or ideal publicity', *Hastings Law Journal*, 63 (2012), 1645–70, at 1654–62; Peterkova Mitkidis,

approach requires changes in contract law as it aims at recognising not only bilateral contracts, but also unilateral promises as the legal basis for an enforceable obligation.[46] The former suggestion, in contrast, can be realised on the basis of an approach to contract interpretation by which courts take the purpose of a specific provision as the core criterion for determining the content.

For public procurement contracting, such purported changes in contract law are in principle also of value, but they might not even be necessary. Contracting authorities could realise recognition of third-party rights for beneficiaries by means of using a specific contract design that explicitly views them as having an influence as third-party beneficiaries. The Procurement Remedies Directive[47] could possibly be helpful in facilitating this strategy. Pursuant to Article 1 of the Directive, Member States are obliged to ensure that review procedures are available to those being harmed or at risk of being harmed by an alleged infringement of public procurement laws. Given that the Public Procurement Directive determines compliance with environmental, social and labour law an integral part of the public procurement process, one could argue that government authorities could be taken to court by those at risk of being harmed by an infringement of exactly these laws if they fail to negotiate a provision in the contract that equips them with such rights or if they ignore breaches in the performance of the contract to the third parties' detriment. Moreover, since the Procurement Remedies Directive includes the award of damages,[48] beneficiaries could rely on the right to claim damages from the contracting authority for ignoring their rights. This of course remains an indirect measure allowing the third party to initiate a claim against the contracting authority rather than the supplying company that directly breaches the regulatory provision in the contract. For a third party beneficiary claim to be brought against the supplying company who is in breach, it remains necessary either for the contracting authority to choose a contract design that phrases regulatory provisions

'Sustainability clauses', 17f.; Beckers, *Enforcing corporate social responsibility codes*, pp. 81–107, 126–44. See also from case law *Jane Doe* v. *Wal-Mart Stores*, United States Court of Appeal for the 9th Circuit, 572 F.3d 677.

46 The doctrines that can be relied upon for this change are (depending on the specifics of the national contracts law) the unilateral contract concluded by an offer to the public, promissory estoppel, venire contra factum proprium and good faith or the enforcement of a unilateral promise.

47 See Procurement Remedies Directive, as referred to in footnote 27.

48 Art. 2 Procurement Remedies Directive.

as constituting a third-party right or to rely on the aforementioned suggested changes in the rules on contract formation and interpretation to read such rights in contracts that contain regulatory provisions.

4.2. *Expanding the regulatory content: from subject matter to self-standing regulation?*

The content of regulation by contract depends to a large extent on the negotiated contract and how it is interpreted according to the rules on contract interpretation and supplementation. To that end, a major difference can be observed between contracts that link regulation and the exchange of goods or performance of services and those that separate these two objectives. The wider regulatory content is to be found in the latter constellation, which is also how private actors mainly incorporate the regulatory purpose in the contract.[49] An example for such a general sustainability clause is, for instance, a condition imposed by a buyer on the supplier to have in place a policy in relation to climate change, to actively measure and report carbon and greenhouse emissions and to set targets to cut emissions, which is detached from the obligation to deliver a product with certain specifications.[50] In fact, detaching requirements related to sustainability, and obligations related to the actual economic exchange not only results in wider regulatory content, but also makes sense for private actors for different practical reasons. First, detaching obligations to adhere to a corporate policy from the subject matter of the contract has practical effects in relation to the performance of the contract. The burden of proof for the buyer is simplified when seeking to claim a breach of contract for non-compliance with a sustainability clause. If the contractual obligation to comply with a certain sustainability policy is not intrinsically related to the exchange, the innocent contracting party will only have to prove that the contractually agreed upon sustainability policy has not been upheld. It is, however, not necessary to prove that also the delivered good, service or work has been produced in violation of the standards let alone providing arguments that the required policy is actually an inherent characteristic of the product.[51]

49 Cafaggi, 'The regulatory functions', 1596–7.

50 See the BT Group sustainability clause as analysed by K. Peterkova Mitkidis, 'Using private contracts for climate change mitigation', *Groningen Journal of International Law*, 2 (2014), 52–77, at 65.

51 For the difficulties of relating sustainability clauses to the product characteristics under sales law, C. Glinski, 'Corporate codes of conduct: moral or legal obligation?', in

Second, defining the sustainability clause as a general policy matter captures more appropriately the actual character of this clause. The intention behind incorporating such a clause in the contract is namely not the interest of conducting a discrete exchange on a specific social or environmental product, but rather to codify a long-term obligation for the other contracting party to change the strategic orientation of businesses from cost-efficient to sustainable. This understanding of sustainability clauses has the further advantage of facilitating a specific interpretation of such obligations under contract law. Being detached from the subject matter, the content of these obligations can be interpreted in the light of existing policies rather than the default rules for sales contracts.[52]

For public procurement contracts, this strategy is difficult to realise, however. The Public Procurement Directive prescribes the incorporation of a sustainability policy in the public procurement contract within the technical specifications, award criteria and contract performance clauses to be linked to the 'subject matter of the contract'.[53] In fact, the intention is to explicitly proscribe contracting authorities to include criteria and conditions relating to a general corporate social and environmental policy.[54] The requirement has its origin in the decision of the CJEU in *Concordia Bus Finland*,[55] in which the Court argued that the requirement follows from the fact that the overall tender 'necessarily relates to the subject matter of the contract'.[56] Its prescription in the 2004 and the 2014 Directives is based on the consideration that the subject matter of the contract acts as a safeguard to 'ensure that the purchase itself remains central to the process in which taxpayers' money is used' and to avoid discrimination in the procurement process.[57]

D. McBarnet, A. Voiculescu and T. Campbell (eds), *The new corporate accountability corporate social responsibility and the law* (Cambridge University Press, 2007), 119–47, at 124–6; C. Glinski, *Die rechtliche Bedeutung der privaten Regulierung globaler Produktionsstandards* (Nomos, 2011), pp. 181–93.

52 See for this suggestion with further references to the debate, Beckers, *Enforcing corporate social responsibility codes*, pp. 144–5, 375–6.

53 See Art. 42(1), Art. 43(1)(a), Art. 45(1), Art. 58(1), Art. 67(2), Art. 70 Public Procurement Directive.

54 See recital (97), (104) Public Procurement Directive.

55 Court of Justice of the European Union, Case C-513/99 *Concordia Bus Finland* v. *Helsingin kaupunki and HKL-Bussiliikenne* [2002] ECLI:EU:C:2002:495.

56 Ibid., para 59.

57 See European Commission, *Green Paper on the modernisation of EU public procurement policy: towards a more efficient European Procurement Market*, COM (2011) 15 final, p. 39.

Arguably, the purpose of strengthening sustainable public procurement is, however, based on the idea of letting the purchase move slightly into the background in the procurement process in exchange for strengthening the capacity of contracting authorities to adopt a sustainability policy in their purchasing practices. Moreover, allowing the general corporate performance to be a self-standing element in the procurement process can have the result that companies internalise the regulatory purposes behind the sustainability requirements and change their long-term behaviour.[58] Against this background, it does make sense to relax the criterion of the 'subject matter of the contract' in further updates of the Directives and, to the extent possible, already in the implementation of the recent Directive. This could be desirable in order to make public authorities truly capable of using contracts as regulatory tools.[59] The main concerns with relaxing the subject matter of the contract, that is, verification by the contracting authorities and the risk of window-dressing by corporate actors through vague policy clauses[60] could arguably be mitigated through careful contract design and changes in contract law.

Concerning the lack of verification, public authorities could benefit from similar experiences in the private sphere. In fact, the problem of verifying process standards and general corporate performance is one of the core challenges of regulatory contracting between companies. The private sector has responded by relying on third-party monitoring by external auditors, partly even trade unions or NGOs.[61] Companies also make use of certification bodies that focus on process standards by which the certifier obtains information through frequent audits and passes on the information to the buyer who then is in the position to remedy non-compliance.[62] Contracting authorities could benefit here from this infrastructure by relying on monitoring formats that have proven to be effective in the contract performance phase.[63] They could also require

[58] See for this argument, Howe, 'The regulatory impact', p. 340.

[59] This follows also how public procurement is envisaged from the corporate social responsibility perspective, namely as a tool that should encourage and require companies to engage in self-regulation, see, for example, S.D. Murphy, 'Taking multinational corporate codes of conduct to the next level', *Columbia Journal of Transnational Law*, 43 (2005), 389–433, at 429–30; J. Wouters and L. Chanet, 'Corporate human rights responsibility: a European perspective', *Northwestern Journal of International Law and Business*, 6 (2008), 262–303, at 293–4.

[60] See for these two critical points the contribution of Abby Semple, Chapter 3, pp. 71–2.

[61] See McBarnet and Kurkchiyan, 'CSR through contractual control?', pp. 77–8.

[62] Cafaggi, 'The regulatory functions', 1604.

[63] Howe, 'The regulatory impact', pp. 341–3 who also provides evidence for such an approach from the public procurement practices.

process-related labels in the tender phase, the use of which is now less strictly regulated under the new Directive.[64]

The risk of having vague policy clauses incorporated into a public procurement contract and being exposed to the criticism of window dressing is also a significant problem that requires further scrutiny. In fact, the private sphere provides for several negative examples in which contractual obligations are phrased in such a vague way that no obligation can be derived from it with the consequence that the clause remains unenforceable.[65] However, the rules in contract law may again mitigate this concern. As is emphasised by contract law scholars, courts called upon to interpret clauses that only contain vague obligations must take note of the rules in contract law that contracts need to be interpreted before being rendered unenforceable for their vagueness.[66] Consequently, the possibility of phrasing the clause in a specific manner and the techniques in contract law to interpret vague content could mitigate the risk of vagueness potentially occurring when relaxing the subject matter of the contract.

However, one inherent risk remains which can admittedly not be so easily overcome. Relaxing the requirement of the subject matter would give contracting authorities more discretion in neglecting the exchange dimension behind contracts. In order to understand this concern, it is again important to emphasise a core difference between public and private procurement. Private actors are perceived as being inherently interested in the efficiency of a transaction. Companies have a need to be profitable; regulatory clauses are, in their contractual relations, rather an additional component in reaction to new social expectations. Contracting authorities, as public actors interested and obliged to realise public policy objectives, are presumably more prone to consider furthering policies when concluding contracts. Hence, relaxing the requirement of the

[64] Art. 43 Public Procurement Directive.

[65] See on the problem of vague policy clauses, Peterkova Mitkidis, 'Sustainability clauses', 15–6; Verbruggen, 'Regulatory governance by contract', 94–5. But see for evidence on very specific clauses in relation to labour standards Vytopil, 'Contractual control', 166.

[66] See Glinski, 'Corporate codes of conduct', pp. 122–3; E. Kocher, 'Private standards for the North – effective norms for the South', in A. Peters, L. Koechlin, T. Förster and G. Fenner Zinkernagel (eds), *Non-state actors as standard setters* (Cambridge University Press, 2009), 409–30, at 424; Beckers, *Enforcing corporate social responsibility codes*, p. 266, text, and accompanying footnote 181. See the various options of courts to interpret a vague content of the contract by relying on context factors, fairness considerations, and economic consequences, N. Kornet, *Contract interpretation and gap filling: comparative and theoretical perspectives* (Intersentia, 2006).

'subject matter of the contract' is inherently also about risking public authorities beginning to treat the policy objective, rather than the purchase, as the central purpose behind a procurement contract. Given the inherent tension between efficiency and social responsibility in consumption,[67] this risk appears unavoidable. Arguably, the claim for stronger consideration of sustainability criteria in public procurement suggests for good reasons that the policy objective should gain more weight at the expense of efficiency. Nonetheless, such a shift will remain a matter of intense controversy, as it moves the 'best value for money' rationale to the background and begins to treat public procurement contracts as regulation in the public interest rather than private consumption.[68]

4.3. *Expanding duration: from discrete exchanges to long-term collaboration?*

The significantly shorter time span in which regulation takes place may, as argued above, eventually be counterproductive in that the long-term adherence to social and environmental policies is disincentivised. In the private sphere, this is one core criticism of regulatory contracts, which has resulted, at least partly, in a change of the practice of private contractors. Empirical research on raising labour standards in supply chains has namely identified that one core condition for long-term improvement of social and environmental standards within contractual relations, is the long-term collaborative partnership between the contracting parties. The collaboration needs to be based on the mutual understanding that the contractual relation is a long-term commitment in which both parties contribute to the success.[69] Interestingly, private actors increasingly treat sustainability clauses as a form of long-term regulation. They extend the length of the regulatory activity by collaborating with their suppliers to improve sustainable performance beyond the concrete product

[67] See for this argument from the economic perspective: R.A. Posner, *Economic analysis of law*, 8th edn (Wolters Kluwer, 2011), p. 573 and the sociological perspective: J. Beckert, 'The moral embeddedness of markets', *Max-Planck-Institut für Gesellschaftsforschung Discussion Paper*, 06 (2005), 1–20, at 15–6.

[68] This controversy is also revealed in this collection. Compare, as a contrast to the approach taken in this contribution, the approach taken by Abby Semple in Chapter 3 of this volume, pp. 72–3.

[69] S. Frenkel and D. Scott, 'Compliance, collaboration, and codes of labor practice', *California Management Review*, 45 (2002), 29–49. See also pointedly with further references McBarnet and Kurkchiyan, 'CSR through contractual control?', p. 73: 'There is a clear business case for the partnership approach'.

order. Companies provide education, training and resources in exchange for a commitment of the supplier to remain loyal, reliable and accept control by the buyer.[70]

Such long-term commitments can take several forms. Some companies formalise the commitment by including it in the general terms and conditions or in umbrella agreements;[71] in some cases, they are kept as informal promises.[72] A prominent example for a formalised long-term commitment is the agreement between companies and trade unions in the aftermath of the factory collapse in Bangladesh. After this collapse, it was emphasised that an important component for the long-term improvement of working conditions in this country is the commitment by Western companies to contribute to sourcing from this country and take a more active role.[73] The 'Accord on Fire and Building Safety in Bangladesh', an agreement between corporations and trade unions, contains a legally binding commitment of the signatory companies to continue sourcing from their suppliers in Bangladesh for a longer period of time, provided that these comply with their contractual obligations.[74]

The formalised options of making long-term commitments are available for public contracts as well and should arguably be used. The most important one is probably the use of framework agreements through which contracting authorities can agree on general terms and conditions that govern all contracts awarded during a specific period.[75] On top of

[70] See J. Phillips and S.-J. Lim, 'Their brothers' keeper: global buyers and the legal duty to protect suppliers' employees', *Rutgers Law Review*, 61 (2009), 333–79, at 341–347; McBarnet and Kurkchiyan, 'CSR through contractual control?', pp. 73–4; Peterkova Mitkidis, 'Using private contracts', 70.

[71] See Vytopil, 'Contractual control', 162–3; Peterkova Mitkidis, 'Sustainability clauses', 13–4.

[72] McBarnet and Kurkchiyan, 'CSR through contractual control?', pp. 68–70; Phillips and Lim, 'Their brothers' keeper', 371–2; Peterkova Mitkidis, 'Sustainability clauses', 14–5.

[73] See prominently Statement by the National Contact Points for the OECD Guidelines on Multinational Enterprises, Paris, 25 June 2013, see www.mneguidelines.oecd.org/NCPStatementBangladesh25June2013.pdf.

[74] See Accord on Fire and Building Safety in Bangladesh', see www.bangladeshaccord.org, Section 23: 'Signatory companies to this agreement are committed to maintaining long-term sourcing relationships with Bangladesh, as is demonstrated by their commitment to this five-year programme. Signatory companies shall continue business at order volumes comparable to or greater than those that existed in the year preceding the inception of this Agreement with Tier 1 and Tier 2 factories at least through the first two years of the term of this Agreement, provided that (a) such business is commercially viable for each company and (b) the factory continues to substantially meet the company's terms and comply with the company's requirements of its supplier factories under this agreement'.

[75] Art. 33 Public Procurement Directive, see also in detail the contribution of Marta Andrecka to this volume.

that, long-term certainty can be provided through national strategy documents or provisions in national public procurement laws that specify what sustainability criteria contracting authorities are generally expected to include in the procurement tenders. This can provide supplying companies with a certain degree of certainty. In contrast, the use of informal commitments and the establishment of long-term relations with specific suppliers to improve their sustainability performance seem problematic. This is due to the fact that the contracting practices of public authorities remains subject to public laws, in particular the legal principle of non-discrimination as provided for by EU law and WTO rules. Establishing informal long-term relations with preference for certain suppliers to enhance their corporate performance may create a barrier for competitors to enter the procurement market and can result in awarding contracts in a discriminatory manner. In fact, the informal long-term commitments by private contractors are likely to have exactly this consequence. In the contracting literature, it is emphasised that there is a focus on long-term relations and informal social sanctions rather than the formalised discrete exchange[76] and private contracting seems prone to being concluded with preference to social relations ('the F-connection' of friends, family and firms[77]). In some sectors, this has led to contract formation and enforcement taking place in 'clubs'[78] in which access for outsiders is restricted.

In relation to sustainability requirements, this effectively leads to a paradoxical situation which *Vogel* has pointedly observed: 'Firms can demand adherence to labour and environmental standards by their global suppliers as a condition for doing business with them, whereas WTO rules restrict the ability of governments to make such standards a condition for market access'.[79] But what follows from that? Should governments be given more freedom in their procurement practices to engage in similar long-term relations with potentially effective informal social sanctions?

[76] See the seminal study of S. Macaulay, 'Non-contractual relations in business: a preliminary study', *American Sociological Review*, 28 (1963), 55–67.

[77] Y. Ben-Porath, 'The F-connection: families, friends and firms and the organization of exchange', *Population and Development Review*, 6 (1980), 1–30.

[78] See the seminal study on trading clubs in the diamond industry that provide for a complete extra-legal contract system from drafting to enforcement: L. Bernstein, 'Opting out of the legal system: extracontractual relations in the diamond industry', *The Journal of Legal Studies*, 21 (1992), 115–57.

[79] D. Vogel, 'The private regulation of global corporate conduct', *Business and Society*, 49 (2010), 68–87, at 75.

In fact, I would suggest the opposite, in line with what other critical voices in the debate have said, that is, that the strong relational character of private regulatory contracting faces legitimacy concerns.[80] Rather than aligning public contracting with private contracting and allowing their regulation by contract to be legitimised by the freedom of contract, it is arguably, for good reasons, suggested to consider binding private actors to public law principles when they appear on the market as regulators or enforcers of public laws. A concrete suggestion is to monitor the private procurement practices strictly as to their compliance with competition laws and WTO laws.[81] It seems here that it is rather private procurement that could learn from the public sphere rather than vice versa.

4.4. *Changing the strategies of enforcement: from contract remedies back to regulatory remedies?*

Finally, an important feature of regulation by contract is the different enforcement architecture, that is, the applicable remedies in case of non-compliance on the side of the contracting party that is obliged to comply with a regulatory provision. The use of a specific contract design and changes in contract law to broaden the enforcement options is considered particularly important with a view to the character and direction of the remedies.

Interestingly, the contracting practice between private contractors exhibits a tendency to subject the regulatory provisions in contracts to a separate remedial scheme that is detached from the remedies applicable to the exchange. This allows companies to separate the act of exchanging a specific good or performing a service, from compliance with regulatory provisions, and treat the former as successful while considering the latter to be in breach and in need of being remedied. In fact, companies have developed sophisticated remedial schemes for breaches of sustainability clauses that differ considerably from the 'ordinary' remedies for breach of contract. Ironically, these schemes resemble administrative enforcement under public law.[82] In enforcement relating to the breach of regulatory

[80] On the legitimacy deficit of private regulation through contract in detail Peterkova Mitkidis, 'Using private contracts', 72; Verbruggen, 'Regulatory governance by contract', 91–2.

[81] See, for example, Peterkova Mitkidis, 'Using private Contracts', 72; Verbruggen, 'Regulatory governance by contract', 92 and accompanying footnote 70.

[82] Backer, 'Multinational corporations as objects and sources', 518.

clauses, a three-step procedure is commonly applied: preventive monitoring, relational enforcement through, for instance, corrective action plans and termination as last resort.[83] Judicial enforcement in courts plays a rather marginal role,[84] but seems to be still important as a threat that can enhance the effectiveness of relational sanctions.[85] In addition, here contract law can have a gap-filling role. It can namely provide for a specific default regime for breaches of regulatory provisions that differs from the 'ordinary' remedies for breach of contract.[86]

In principle, this remedial scheme could also be handily available to public contractors for enforcement relating to non-compliance with regulatory provisions in contracts. In particular, the threat of terminating a contract and considering a supplier in breach of a regulatory provision, making them ineligible for future tenders, can be an effective remedy to safeguard the supplying companies' compliance with regulatory provisions.[87] Of crucial importance is also the option in the Directive for Member States to impose a requirement on contracting authorities to exclude from participation in the tender companies that have violated environmental, social or labour law and that showed significant deficits in the performance of prior contracts (which includes compliance with sustainability requirements).[88] For an effective remedial scheme to be in place it is arguably necessary that these provisions are stringently implemented in the Member States.

A difficulty for public contractors relying on such a separate enforcement regime might turn out to be the already-criticised requirement to link sustainability criteria to the specific need of the public authorities. If this requirement is upheld, the remedies available for breach of a regulatory provision must remain those applicable for a breach of the main performance obligation, that is, specific performance, termination and damages incurred for delivery of a 'contaminated' product. These do, however, not seem to be fit for purpose for regulatory provisions. Specific performance and damage compensation are oriented on the

[83] McBarnet and Kurkchiyan, 'CSR through contractual control?', pp. 74–81; Backer, 'Multinational corporations as objects and sources', 512; Peterkova Mitkidis, 'Sustainability clauses', 20–22.

[84] McBarnet and Kurkchiyan, 'CSR through contractual control?', p. 79; Vandenbergh, 'Private environmental governance', 137–8.

[85] See Peterkova Mitkidis, 'Sustainability clauses', 21–2 with further references.

[86] See Beckers, *Enforcing corporate social responsibility codes*, pp. 351–6, 377–9, 380–82.

[87] See, in this direction, Howe, 'The regulatory impact', p. 343.

[88] See Art. 57 (4)(a) in conjunction with Art. 18(2) Public Procurement Directive.

interest of curing a defective exchange[89] and not the breach of social and environmental laws or regulatory provisions. Moreover, the contract remedy of terminating a contract is viewed with some scepticism for good reasons, as it ends the regulatory activity and can thus even result in a worse situation for those benefiting from the regulatory clause.[90] Hence, also in relation to the remedies available for breaches of regulatory provisions it makes sense to relax the requirement for contracting authorities to relate sustainability criteria to the subject matter of the contract. It could open possibilities for contracting authorities to develop more freely a remedial scheme that fits the regulatory provision.

5. Contracts: how much exchange? How much regulation?

This contribution explores the recent discussion on sustainable public procurement from the perspective of contracting practice and contract law. For that purpose, an approach is adopted that defines sustainable public procurement as a regulatory and as an enforcement activity pursued with the instrument of the contract. In contrast to the contribution by Abby Semple in this volume ('consumption is not regulation'[91]), the transformation of contracts from an exchange of goods and services to becoming a basis for regulation and enforcement is generally advocated as promising. However, in order to become an effective regulatory instrument, the scope, content, duration and enforcement of regulatory provisions in contracts require attention by the public authorities in terms of the contract design. Moreover, specific changes in public procurement laws seem necessary in order to incentivise the use of this contract design by public authorities as well as changes in contract law that are directed at accommodating this new regulatory function of contracts.

89 See the difficulties of applying sales law remedies to breaches of sustainability clauses: Peterkova Mitkidis, 'Sustainability clauses', 23; Beckers, *Enforcing corporate social responsibility codes*, pp. 121–5, and with a view to consumer contract laws: Glinski, *Die rechtliche Bedeutung*, pp. 191–2.

90 The ambivalent character of terminating a contract for breach of poor social or environmental performance is emphasised by McBarnet and Kurkchiyan, 'CSR through contractual control?', p. 82; Peterkova Mitkidis, 'Sustainability clauses', 22.

91 See Abby Semple, Chapter 3 in this volume, p. 72.

11

Public procurement's potential for sustainability

ANJA WIESBROCK AND BEATE SJÅFJELL

1. The potential for sustainability

As major purchasers of goods and services from the private sector, public entities have significant market power allowing them to influence corporate behaviour by attaching environmental and/or social criteria to public contracts. Being a significant expense of the public sector, public procurement accounts for an important part of EU economic activity both in terms of total expenditure and as a percentage of overall gross domestic product (GDP).[1] The power of public procurement as a market instrument makes it an attractive tool for the promotion of non-economic goals such as environmental protection and social inclusion. By modifying their purchasing behaviour and favouring environmentally friendly and socially responsible products and services, public purchasing bodies can make a significant contribution to the overarching EU objective of fostering sustainable development.

It is beyond doubt that green public procurement strategies can have a major impact on the environment. For instance, it has been estimated that CO_2 emission could be reduced by 60 million tons if all public entities in the EU were to require the supply of green electricity.[2] Yet, the potential implications of integrating environmental and social criteria into procurement processes go beyond such direct numerical effects. By

[1] The total expenditure of the government public sector and utility service providers on public works, goods and services in the EU 27 has increased steadily in particular over the last three years to a total of slightly more than EUR 2400 billion in 2010, amounting to 19.7 per cent of EU GDP. Also the volume of procurement advertised at EU level has increased with the value of calls for tender published in the Official Journal constituting 18.6 per cent of the total expenditure on public works, goods and services and 3.7 per cent of GDP in the EU-27 in 2010. See European Commission, *Public procurement indicators 2010*, 4 November 2011.

[2] R. Pierrard, 'Results of the European calculation', in C. Erdmenger (ed.), *Buying into the environment: experiences, opportunities and potential for eco-procurement in Europe* (Greenleaf, 2003), Chapter 9.

favouring the supply of socially and environmentally friendly goods, works and services, public authorities can send a powerful signal to the market. Such sustainable procurement is likely to have a long-term effect in influencing the behaviour of private market participants in terms of stimulating the production and use of sustainable goods and services and allowing for the development of an adequate infrastructure. By purchasing sustainable products, contracting authorities indirectly respond to the interests and demands of the citizens and end-consumers as well as shaping the broader market for the goods or services concerned and encouraging a shift to sustainable production methods and market standards.

Hence, as highlighted by Beate Sjåfjell in her chapter, public procurement has great potential to serve as a front-runner and driver for the necessary transformation of business.[3] However, she also points to the inherent limitations of public procurement law in view of the overarching EU objective of sustainable development. The design of the Public Procurement Directives limits the possibilities to integrate environmental and social concerns, including, notably, the link to the subject matter (LtSM) requirement that Abby Semple discusses.[4] Further, as Anna Beckers also emphasises in her chapter, in spite of its potential to influence corporate strategies, public procurement law effectively only regulates a small portion of the market and does not impose any obligations upon companies that do not deliver goods, works or services to public bodies.[5] It is thus crucial to underline the importance of combining rules on sustainable public procurement with corresponding efforts in other areas of law, such as company law. Public procurement law is a significant piece but nevertheless only one piece of the jigsaw puzzle of sustainability, and it would have a greater impact and be more effective if it were a part of a broader, holistic reform for sustainability.

2. Balancing on economic premises?

As part of such a holistic approach, it is of fundamental importance to provide for a proper balancing of the three dimension of sustainable development, instead of treating environmental and social elements as derogations from the fundamental economic objectives of value for

[3] See Beate Sjåfjell in Chapter 9 of this volume.

[4] See Abby Semple in Chapter 3 of this volume.

[5] See Anna Beckers in Chapter 10 of this volume.

money and free competition. Arguably, the transformation of the EU legal framework since the initiation of EU public procurement law and the heightened focus on sustainability in the Lisbon Treaty warrant the adoption of a truly integrated approach in the area of public procurement.

As is well known, the process of European integration has, from the outset, been essentially market-driven. The founding Treaties bestowed on the Communities the exclusive competence to create and operate an internal market, whilst the pursuit of social policies and the responsibility for guaranteeing and maintaining social standards were reserved to the Member States.[6] The fundamental freedoms of the internal market came to constitute the cornerstones of the EU internal market that must be protected against restrictions and protectionism resulting from national law. In practice, social policy measures at the Union level tended to emerge to a great extent as accompanying measures for mitigating the effects of unrestrained competition, for instance in respect of transfer of enterprises[7] or equal treatment of men and women.[8,9] Due to the economic focus of the internal market framework, environmental and social protection measures were initially treated primarily as possible derogations to one of the fundamental freedoms.

However, over the last decades, the EU legal framework has undergone a fundamental transformation, with the CJEU as an important driver.[10]

[6] This was mainly due to the 'functional' market-oriented approach of early efforts of European co-operation, which focused on reaching integration through the establishment of a common market and the progressive approximation of the economic policies of the Member States. Hence, the economic and social dimensions of European integration have been 'decoupled' in the European integration process. See further D. Schiek, 'Re-embedding economic and social constitutionalism: normative perspectives for the EU', in D. Schiek, U. Liebert and H. Schneider (eds), *European economic and social constitutionalism after the treaty of Lisbon* (Cambridge University Press, 2011), pp. 17–47.

[7] See Council Directive 2001/23/EC of 21 March 2001 on the approximation of the laws of the Member States relating to the safeguarding of employees' rights in the event of transfer of undertakings, businesses or parts of undertakings or businesses, OJ 2001 (L82/16), 22 March 2001.

[8] The principle of equal pay for equal work for women and men is enshrined in what is now Art. 157 TFEU.

[9] M. Rigaux and J. Buelens, 'Can a stronger anchoring of European labour law and social security law to community law guarantee a sustainable European social model?', in F. Pennings, Y. Konijn and A. Veldman (eds), *Social responsibility in labour relations. European and comparative perspectives* (Kluwer Law International, 2008), pp. 25–46.

[10] With for example its recognition of environmental protection as a fundamental goal of the EU even before this was included in the Treaties, see B. Sjåfjell, *Towards a sustainable European company law: an analysis of the overarching objectives of EU law, with the takeover directive as a test case* (Kluwer Law International, 2009), s. 10.5, and about the similar role of the Court in the field of human rights, s. 10.8.

The EU Treaties, the Charter on Fundamental Rights and the comprehensive body of secondary legislation on environmental and social matters provide a rather different picture. The heightened emphasis placed on fundamental rights protection and environmental protection in the Lisbon Treaty has major implications on the balancing exercise between social and environmental objectives and market freedoms. Whereas previously the European Union (the European Community) was based on the principle of a free market economy, largely disregarding any non-economic objectives in the pursuit of free competition, Article 3(3) TFEU embraces the concept of a highly competitive *social* market economy, aiming, *inter alia*, at full employment and social progress.[11] Moreover, the provision now explicitly embraces a broad commitment to work towards sustainable development, aiming at a balance between economic, social and environmental objectives.[12] The Union institutions have defined sustainable development as the overarching long-term goal of the EU in which economic growth, social cohesion and environmental protection go hand in hand and are mutually supporting.[13] Hence, even though the objective of preventing any distortion of competition continues to be important, the new provisions of the Lisbon Treaty suggest a broader conception of an internal market that also serves non-economic objectives.

Moreover, the entry into force of the Lisbon Treaty has brought about a proliferation of integration principles, requiring the integration of a wide range of EU policy objectives, including environmental protection and social goals, such as employment, social protection and the fight

[11] See also A. Rösenkotter and T. Wuersig, *The impact of the Lisbon treaty in the field of public procurement*, European Parliament Study (January 2010).

[12] Even though the objective of sustainability was part of the EU legal framework already before the latest Treaty revision, the Lisbon Treaty for the first time embraces sustainable development as a concept in its own right rather than an 'adjective modifying economic activities'. F. Aldson, 'EU law and sustainability in focus: will the Lisbon treaty lead to "The sustainable development of Europe"?', *Environmental Law and Management*, 23 (2011), 284–99, at 294. For an argument that sustainable development was an overarching objective also before the Lisbon Treaty, albeit not expressed explicitly, see B. Sjåfjell, *Towards a sustainable European company law*, s. 10.7.

[13] European Commission, *Mainstreaming sustainable development into EU policies: 2009. Review of the European Union strategy for sustainable development*, COM (2009) 400 final, 24 July 2009, p. 2; Council of the European Union, Presidency Conclusions Doc 16616/1/07/REV I, 14 December 2007; see also the 6th Environmental Action Programme, which defines sustainable development as a prudent use of natural resources and the protection of the global ecosystem together with economic prosperity and a balanced social development, Decision No. 1600/2002/EC, Recital 6.

against social exclusion.[14] Hence, myriad sectoral policy objectives must be pursued, or at least taken into account, when decisions are being taken in the area of EU internal market law.

Yet, as highlighted by Suzanne Kingston in her chapter, in spite of a long-standing focus on environmental integration and regardless of the new Treaty provisions, the EU legislature fails to live up to the EU's integrationist narrative and tends to focus on economic aspects, in particular in times of crisis.[15] The EU's emphasis on market-oriented integration at the expense of social rights and social dialogue has been accentuated by the measures taken in the wake of the debt crisis, where the EU has taken on the role as a catalyser for deregulation and lax employment protection standards.[16]

In the area of EU public procurement law, the imbalance between economic, social and environmental aspects is particularly pronounced due to the categorisation of public procurement as part of the EU's provisions on the free movement of goods and the free provision of services. By approaching public procurement from an internal market perspective centred on the free competition principle, other policy objectives are in practice degraded to 'secondary' objectives that have to be justified and defended. Environmental and social policy objectives could just as well (and should) be placed on equal footing with internal market objectives in a public procurement context. Indeed, when the EU aims at building a smart, sustainable and inclusive economy (Europe 2020 strategy) or becoming the most competitive and dynamic knowledge-based economy in the world based on sustainable economic growth with more and better jobs and greater social cohesion (Lisbon strategy), it is essential to integrate such horizontal objectives next to economic/competition objectives into the EU's public procurement policy. Hence, in the light of EU's focus on sustainability, its overarching Treaty objectives and the

[14] In addition to the environmental integration principle (Art. 11 TFEU) and the principle of social policy integration (Art. 9 TFEU), the Lisbon Treaty introduced a principle of gender equality integration (Art. 8 TFEU), a principle of non-discrimination integration (Art. 10 TFEU), a principle of consumer protection integration (Art. 12 TFEU) and a principle of animal welfare integration (Art. 13 TFEU). Furthermore, a general principle of integration policy objectives is contained in Art. 7 TFEU, requiring that the Union must ensure consistency between its policies and activities, taking all relevant policy requirements listed under the TFEU into account in the adoption of any legislative measure.

[15] See Suzanne Kingston in Chapter 2 of this volume.

[16] C. Barnard, 'The financial crisis and the Euro Plus Pact: a labour lawyer's perspective', *Industrial Law Journal*, 41(1), (2012), 98–114.

obligation of taking an integrated approach, horizontal objectives in procurement should not be regarded as 'secondary' to the functional economic objective of securing value for money. Instead, a dynamic, teleological and contextual interpretation leads to the conclusion that environmental and social concerns must be considered to hold equal status to the economically inspired functional objectives of public procurement. The new Directives show traces of such an understanding amongst the EU institutions, but they do not go far enough and do not result in an equilibrium between economic and environmental and social objectives, precisely because economic and social objectives are treated as derogations that have to be justified.

The requirement of an integrated approach towards public procurement that allows for a balancing of economic, social and environmental considerations has a number of concrete implications. Arguably, the Treaty provisions on environmental and social policy integration do not allow for a situation where non-economic considerations are entirely disregarded in the procurement process. This means that national authorities should be precluded from procuring without taking sustainability considerations into account, just as they are not allowed to disregard economic considerations. As argued by Anja Wiesbrock in her chapter, this implies that contracting authorities should no longer be permitted to use lowest price as the sole award criterion, just as contracts cannot be awarded on the basis of environmental or social considerations alone.[17] Moreover, Abby Semple highlights in her chapter that there are strong reasons for loosening or even abandoning the LtSM requirement, which has emerged as a major limiting principle for sustainability considerations in public procurement. As Abby Semple points out, other mechanisms, such as the application of the principles of proportionality and effectiveness, may be more appropriate to assess the legitimacy of sustainability measures in public procurement.[18]

3. The economic good sense of social and green public procurement

It is furthermore crucial to recognise that the economic, environmental and social objectives in public procurement are not necessarily contradictory, but may in fact be pursued simultaneously. For a long time,

[17] See Anja Wiesbrock in Chapter 4 of this volume.
[18] See Abby Semple in Chapter 3 of this volume.

there was perceived to be an inherent tension between the promotion and enforcement of high environmental and social standards and the objective to seek value for money by determining the most economically competitive tender. In recent years, it is increasingly recognised that the incorporation of environmental and social criteria in procurement processes is not necessarily contradictory to the pursuit of the primary objectives of securing value for money as well as competitive tendering throughout the EU. In its proposal to revise the procurement regime, the European Commission has pointed out that the two objectives of increasing the efficiency of public spending to ensure the best value for money and the use of public procurement to support non-economic goals are indeed complementary.[19] Indeed, as emphasised by the Commission, a common European approach to sustainable procurement may prevent distortions of the single market by alleviating the burden placed on undertakings operating in several Member States to comply with a diversity of national criteria.[20] There are a number of mechanisms in the new Directives through which environmental, social and internal market objectives can be pursued simultaneously and which should be implemented and used widely by the contracting authorities.

One mechanism included in the Directive that allows for the promotion of environmental protection objectives whilst avoiding conflict with economic aims is the possibility to take life-cycle costs into account when calculating the costs of a product, as discussed by Dacian Dragos and Bogdana Neamtu in their chapter.[21] Under a life-cycle costing approach, contracting authorities are required to take into account potential long-term costs arising from the disregard of social and environmental considerations, even if such costs are harder to quantify. As confirmed by the United Nations Office for Project Services,[22] life-cycle considerations fall within the principle of the best value for money, as taking into account the whole life cycle of a product helps ensuring that the most advantageous offer is identified, revealing costs of resource use that otherwise may not receive proper attention. When life-cycle costs are taken into

[19] European Commission, *Proposal for a Directive on public procurement*, COM (2011) 896, 20 December 2011, p. 2.

[20] European Commission Communication, *Public procurement for a better environment*, COM (2008) 400 final, 16 July 2008, p. 3.

[21] See Dacian C. Dragos and Bogdana Neamtu in Chapter 6 of this volume.

[22] UNOPS, *A guide to environmental labels – for procurement practitioners of the United Nations system* (2009), see www.ungm.org/Areas/Public/Downloads/Env_Labels_Guide.pdf, p. 7.

consideration, environmentally friendly products are often the least expensive option. This can be the case, for instance, if costs related to hazardous waste disposal and waste management are taken into consideration when selecting non-hazardous goods or when considering the costs saved by the reduced energy consumption of goods with energy saving features. A study carried out in 2009 in seven Member States most active in green procurement[23] showed that when taking life-cycle costing and the total amount spent on all green goods into account, green procurement contributed to a slight overall decrease in cost.[24] Hence, the use of life-cycle costing provides a way of promoting environmental concerns without compromising the objectives of securing value for money. In order to guarantee competitive tendering and to avoid the favouring of specific undertakings, the Directive contains a requirement that the data requested for life-cycle costing can be provided with reasonable effort by normally diligent economic operators and that life-cycle costing methodologies must be established for repeated or continuous application, rather than being developed and applied to one specific contract.[25]

Similarly, the possibility contained in the Directive to make use of labels that are mostly based on life-cycle costing provides an example of how contracting authorities are given the opportunity to procure environmentally friendly, organic and fair-trade products, without undermining the principle of non-discrimination between potential tenderers. As highlighted by Roberto Caranta in his chapter, whilst the Directive permits contracting authorities to refer to specific labels when choosing the most economically advantageous tender, it also contains safeguards preventing a limitation or distortion of competition by requiring contracting authorities to accept other labels based on equivalent requirements and possibly

[23] National authorities in countries such as Sweden, Denmark, the UK and the Netherlands increasingly commit themselves to greener public procurement, see C. Erdmenger, V. Eri, V. Führ, B. Lackner, A. Schmid and N. van der Grijp, *The world buys green: international survey on national green procurement practices* (The International Council for Local Environmental Initiatives, 2001).

[24] Price Waterhouse Coopers, *Collection of statistical information on green public procurement in the EU*, (2009), see http://ec.europa.eu/environment/gpp/pdf/statistical_information.pdf.

[25] However, as Dragos and Neamtu point out: 'not everything that can be counted counts and not everything that counts can be counted'. There may be challenges both in choosing the relevant to include of all potential costs and as regards the difficult of assigning a monetary value to the internalisation of environmental and social externalities; see Dacian C. Dragos and Bogdana Neamtu in Chapter 6 of this volume.

other appropriate means of proof.[26] However, as Roberto Caranta points out, there is certainly room for improvement here, in particular in terms of establishing common, science-based methodologies for the calculation of life-cycle costs for specific categories of supplies or services at the EU level. This applies in particular to the social aspects of life-cycle costing, which can be difficult to objectivise and quantify. Clear EU guidelines on life-cycle costing methodologies and labels or certificates based on them would certainly contribute to both sustainability and internal market objectives by facilitating the uptake of sustainable public procurement, whilst at the same time making sure that this does not translate into distortions of competition in the internal market.

Another example of how economic and sustainability objectives can be pursued simultaneously is the mutually beneficial relationship between fostering the participation of small and medium-sized enterprises (SMEs) and including sustainability criteria in public procurement. Amongst the aims of the new public procurement package was to improve the involvement of SMEs in the public procurement market. As Sarah Schoenmaekers argues in her chapter, quite contrary to the prevalent perception of stringent sustainability requirements constituting a barrier to SMEs, small and medium-sized businesses can in fact benefit economically from a greater focus on sustainability in public procurement.[27] If SMEs internalise sustainability concerns, they will be better adapted to markets that require higher environmental standards. Indeed, due to their specialisation and know-how, sustainable public procurement practices will allow SMEs to unlock their growth and innovation potential. At the same time, subjecting SMEs to sustainability criteria can have a great impact on key environmental objectives. Due to their specialism and potential for innovation, SMEs can develop sustainable products and their shorter approval routes allow for more flexibility and customised solutions.

Indeed, fully integrating the life-cycle approach with the inclusion of supply chains that the Public Procurement Directive promotes, based on a thorough due diligence and broad risk-assessment, would substantially lower risks and potentially save costs for businesses of all sizes. The risk of being sued or suffering reputational damage from scandals because of environmental harm or human rights violations will be drastically reduced. A life-cycle-based approach would make legal compliance easier

[26] See Roberto Caranta in Chapter 5 of this volume.
[27] See Sarah Schoenmaekers in Chapter 8 of this volume.

(because all aspects of production are brought onto the table), it would increase efficiency, enable savings on, for example, energy and transport through greater efficiency, and allow for the identification and mitigation of environmental and social impacts. An anecdotal example of such savings is provided by the US environmental group, Natural Resources Group and its Clean by Design Program. The results of this programme, targeting the Chinese apparel industry that serve as suppliers for many US and European companies, apparently resulted in significant improvements for the 33 mills that participated:

> 61000 tons of coal not burned; 400 tons of chemicals not processed; 3 million tons of water saved; 36 million kilowatt hours of electricity conserved and on the financial side, US$14.7 million dollars saved over the year, with a five-year projection totaling US$56.4 million.[28]

Notably, tomorrow's market leaders in the business world will undoubtedly be those that have managed to find ways to contribute to dealing with the societal challenges that we face. Businesses that internalise those costs which today, in a short-term, narrow profit-maximisation focus are environmental and social externalities, will be the businesses that will present us with tomorrow's solutions, the low-carbon, long-lasting, environmentally friendly and ethically sound products and life-cycle-based services.

Hence, a consistent value-for-money approach implies that the lowest price will not necessarily be preferred. Many other values may be considered in addition to price, including the environmental and social impact of a purchasing decision. If the predominant consideration when awarding public contracting is to achieve the best value for money, sustainability considerations that are of importance to the contracting authority ought to play a central role in procurement decisions.

4. Implementation and enforcement will decide the direction

Even though the new Directive provides for considerable opportunities to foster sustainability considerations in public procurement, its effectiveness depends largely on national implementing measures and a proper interpretation and enforcement by national and European courts. As

[28] 'A sustainable supply chain in the garment industry saves 4 major companies $15M annually' at Triple Pundit, see www.triplepundit.com/2015/04/a-sustainable-supply-chain-in-the-garment-industry-saves-4-major-companies-15m-annually/. See more about the Clean by Design Programme: www.nrdc.org/international/cleanbydesign/.

argued by Anja Wiesbrock in her chapter, even though the Directive provides notable opportunities for the promotion of social objectives through public procurement procedures, its potential effect is prejudiced by the discretionary nature of most sustainability provisions. She illustrates how the large margin of discretion granted to Member States and contracting authorities threatens to undermine the effectiveness of the Directive's social clauses, in particular the so-called 'mandatory social clause', the use of the best price–quality ratio in the award of contracts and the provisions on subcontracting.

Other contributions in this book equally reveal problems related to the discretionary nature of most sustainability provisions in the Directive, in particular the rules on subcontracting. As pointed out by Marta Andrecka in her chapter, making use of the information and control requirements on subcontracting contained in the Directive will be especially important for securing respect for environmental and social conditions in the context of framework agreements.[29] In the context of framework agreements, the topic of Marta Andrecka's chapter, the issue of control may be particularly complex, for example, in cases involving a framework agreement with many suppliers and an elaborate basket of products or services. In this situation, it may be especially difficult to follow the suppliers' supply chains. Hence, it is extremely important that Member States and contracting authorities that have concluded framework agreements make use of the possibility provided for in the Directive to increase transparency and control along the supply chain.

In addition, an important responsibility in correctly interpreting and effectively enforcing the sustainability provisions contained in the Directive lies with the national and European courts. As Suzanne Kingston has argued in her chapter, the CJEU is the most integrationist of the EU institutions. Recent case law including in the area of public procurement law provide evidence of the EU's willingness to fulfil its role as the guardian of the Treaties, protecting the constitutional imperative of environmental protection. Since the rules of the new Directive are quite complex, it is likely that the CJEU will be required to interpret several of its provisions and to evaluate the adequacy of national schemes.

The most important tool in the hands of the CJEU and national courts to exercise a balancing exercise is the application of the proportionality test. As highlighted by Abby Semple in her chapter, the proportionality assessment plays an important role in interpreting the LtSM requirement.

[29] See Marta Andrecka in Chapter 7 of this volume.

In fact, applying a loose LtSM test, as she suggests, would bring it closer to the general proportionality test applied by the Court in many areas of EU law.

The public procurement case law of the CJEU has shown us that the environmental integration principle implies that objectives related to the protection of the environment and the promotion of sustainable development must be balanced with the fundamental principle of obtaining best value for money.[30] Arguably, a true balancing exercise requires thus not only to consider whether the environmental protection measure is least restrictive of competition, but also whether the measure chosen to promote the internal market is suitable and necessary and the least restrictive means available.[31] If it is assumed that there is no hierarchical relationship between environmental, social and economic objectives as prescribed by the overarching Treaty goal of sustainable development, this implies that not only the restriction of environmental measures on the fundamental freedoms may not go beyond what is appropriate, necessary and reasonable to realise the social or environmental objective. Indeed, this entails that restriction on environmental protection or fundamental social rights by a fundamental freedom may not go beyond what is appropriate, necessary and reasonable to realise that fundamental freedom.[32]

In her chapter on public procurement seen through the lens of contract law, Anna Beckers highlights the potential and problematic aspects of the enforcement of sustainability provisions in public procurement contracts. In her contribution, Beckers also reminds us about the limitations of 'regulation through procurement'. Seen together with Beate Sjåfjell's contribution on the interface of company law and public procurement law, the point is emphasised that sustainable public procurement, an important economic driver and potential moral beacon that it is, is just one piece in the necessary jigsaw puzzle of sustainability that we so

30 Case C-513/99 *Concordia Bus Finland* [2002] ECLI:EU:C:2002:495, paras 57ff.

31 A. Wiesbrock, 'An obligation for sustainable procurement? Gauging the potential impact of Art. 11 TFEU on public contracting in the EU', *Legal Issues of Economic Integration*, 40(2) (2013), 105–32.

32 See also C. Barnard, 'Free movement and labour rights: squaring the circle?' (12 August 2013), *University of Cambridge Faculty of Law Research Paper*, No. 23/2013, see http://ssrn.com/abstract=2313088, discussing, with the backdrop of the *Viking* and *Laval* cases, the much-criticised approach of the CJEU and its 'unwillingness to engage in a genuine balancing between the economic and social dimension of the EU'. Barnard here also discusses four possible ways of ensuring a better fit between the economic approach of promoting the internal market and protecting fundamental social rights, including a reform of the proportionality principle.

sorely need to get into place. A holistic reform based on policy coherence, where various sector policies in addition to their specific aims, have as an overarching objective to contribute to a safe and just operating space for humanity,[33] is what the ultimate aim of the EU Treaty: the promotion of peace, of the values of the EU and the well-being of its peoples, requires.[34]

As for the potential of sustainable public procurement, we have seen that the overall value of the Directive and its effectiveness depends to a large extent on the two variables of national implementing measures and national and European practice, both by the procurement authorities and in case law. If the Member States and contracting authorities make use of the various opportunities provided in the Directive, they have the possibility of implementing a comprehensive and effective sustainable procurement policy. The Directives thus provide for a positive example of how internal market law, if used effectively, can contribute to the strengthening of national environmental, social and labour law provisions. Even further, the Directives contain elements necessary to stimulate the internalisation of environmental and social externalities in the global supply chains of EU businesses. Public procurement is an area where the European Court of Justice as it has done before can take a progressive and forward-looking stance that provides for a successful integration of economic, environmental and social requirements. It gives the Court an opportunity to counteract criticism on its case law for giving precedence to economic freedoms over social rights and the inherent danger of destabilising national social welfare systems and undermining labour rights at the national level.[35]

The EU public procurement reform, for all its faults and limitations, presents an opportunity for Member States and procurement authorities, supported by forward looking case-law, to rise to the occasion and ensure that public procurement rules and practice contribute to global sustainability, to a balancing of social and economic development, ensuring the fundamentals of quality of life for all people, within the ecological boundaries of the planet we live on. What greater goal could there be?

[33] K. Raworth, *A safe and just space for humanity: can we live within the doughnut* (Oxfam International, 2012), see www.oxfam.org/sites/www.oxfam.org/files/dp-a-safe-and-just-space-for-humanity-130212-en.pdf.

[34] Art. 3(1) TEU. The values of the EU are set out in Art. 2 TEU: 'respect for human dignity, freedom, democracy, equality, the rule of law and respect for human rights, including the rights of persons belonging to minorities'.

[35] For example, see C. Barnard, 'Free movement and labour rights: squaring the circle'.

INDEX